Swords of Lightning

SPECIAL FORCES AND THE CHANGING FACE OF WARFARE

Swords of Lightning

SPECIAL FORCES AND THE CHANGING FACE OF WARFARE

Terry White

BRASSEY'S (UK)

LONDON · WASHINGTON · NEW YORK

First English edition 1992

UK editorial offices: Brassey's, 165 Great Dover Street, London SE1 4YA
orders: Marston Book Services, PO Box 87, Oxford OX2 0DT

USA editorial offices: Brassey's, 8000 Westpark Drive, First Floor,
McLean, VA 22102
orders: Macmillan Publishing Company, Front and Brown Streets,
Riverside, NJ 08075

Distributed in North America to booksellers and wholesalers by the
Macmillan Publishing Company, NY 10022

*The right of Terence White to be identified as author of this work has been
asserted by him in accordance with the Copyright, Designs and Patents Act 1988*

Library of Congress Cataloging in Publication Data
available

British Library Cataloguing in Publication Data
A catalogue record for this book is
available from the British Library

ISBN 0–08–040976–8 Hardcover

Printed in Great Britain by BPCC Wheatons Ltd., Exeter

*To John, Ted
and Ron R.I.P.*

Contents

Acknowledgements   ix

Introduction: Origins and Roles of the Special Forces   1

**Part One: Techniques for the Impossible: Selection and Training
for Special Operations**   17
1. Selection   19
2. Continuation Training   39
3. Training for Any Role Anywhere   63
4. Covert Insertion and Extraction   81
5. The Hidden Heroes of Special Operations   94

Part Two: The Military Roles of the Special Forces   103
6. Helping Your Friends to Help Themselves – Training
    Anti-Insurgents, Partisans and Mercenaries   105
7. Hearts and Minds: Indo-China   131
8. The Long Range Reconnaissance Patrol   152
9. Combat Rescue   172
10. Raids, Sabotage and Assassination   196

Part Three: The Changing Face of Warfare   219
11. War by Proxy – Deniable operations   221
12. Counter-Terrorism   232
13. The Quick Reaction Force   250

Postscript   263

List of Acronyms   269
Bibliography   274
Index   279

Acknowledgements

I would like to thank all serving and former members of the services who provided insights, anecdotes and analysis for various areas of this book. Most chose not to be named and I have respected their wishes.

The writing of this book demanded much in the way of research and I am indebted to Mark Lloyd for his contributions on the Soviet Union, maritime operations, intelligence-support and psychological operations, and to Guy Taylor for his advice and the excellent map that appears in Chapter 7. The 'hidden heroes' of research are of course the librarians. A continuous flow of books and journals was enthusiastically provided by the library staff of the Royal United Services Institute for Defence Studies, the Army Medical College, Millbank, and my local library in Oxfordshire.

Other contributions were no less valuable and I would like to thank all the military attachés, police liaison officers and public affairs officers who were more than generous with their time and resources. Special thanks to Captain S.H. Bassindale of the Canadian Special Service Force; Colonel John W. Dye III, US Army Public Affairs Officer, USSOCOM, MacDill Air Force Base; Captain R.M. Weston of the Australian Army's Directorate of Infantry and Colonels C.A.M. Roberts and T.J. Nolan, Headquarters Special Forces, Australian Department of Defence, Canberra.

I am also indebted to Mr Willis of the Department of Photographs, The Imperial War Museum, London; Teddy Neville of TRH Pictures; PMA Pictures; and friends and public affairs officers who provided the illustrations for this book. Guy Baskin and his film crew were accorded the highest accolade in being invited to film Australian SASR selection. My thanks to Guy whose unstinting generosity made a valuable contribution to this book.

My thanks also to the editorial staff at Brassey's who worked hard to make this book possible, and my reader who meticulously corrected the manuscript and realigned my thinking in several crucial areas. All opinions and any remaining errors are mine alone.

Finally, I would like to express my appreciation to my wife, Kathy, and my agent, Juri Gabriel, both of whom were a constant source of advice and encouragement.

Introduction

Origins and Roles of the Special Forces

Special Operational Forces: Small, carefully selected military, paramilitary and civilian units with unusual (occasionally unique) skills, which are superlatively trained for specific rather than general purposes, and are designed to undertake unorthodox tasks that ordinary units could accomplish only with far greater difficulty and far less effectiveness, if at all.
                  Green Berets, SEALS & Spetsnaz: US & Soviet Special
                                    Military Operations *by* J.M. Collins.

The Special Forces are personnel who receive specialised training to execute tasks behind the enemy's lines in support of conventional military operations or a counter-insurgency campaign. Additionally, they may be asked to undertake covert special operations in support of foreign policy aims.

The first natural grouping is the **Reconnaissance/Guerrilla Commando**. As the name implies, these troops spend indefinite periods deep in the enemy's territory, collecting intelligence, raiding or conducting a prolonged campaign of guerrilla warfare. Deep behind enemy lines, they are difficult to supply and, *in extremis*, must live off the land and use captured weapons and ammunition to continue the fight. It is generally accepted that these units will find their own way home, fight until relieved or, where this proves difficult, enter a 'combat-survival mode', – living off the land in concealed positions until the military/political situation changes. The ideal emphasis on the use of units such as the SAS, Green Berets and the 'professional-elements' of Soviet Spetsnaz is **strategic**. Their operations should either support the battle indirectly or affect the overall conduct of the war.

The second group has been called 'semi-special forces' by the late Brigadier Richard Simpkin in his masterly book *Race to the Swift*, but I think **Assault**

The Reconnaissance/Guerrilla Commando is trained to operate deep behind the enemy's lines for extended periods. In the event of a foreign incursion into Australia's empty north, these SAS soldiers would perform reconnaissance, surveillance and harassing operations against the aggressor. (*Special Forces HQ; Australian DOD*)

Commando is a more descriptive term. These are the paratroops, rangers, marines, army commandos and the 'non-professional' elements of Russian Spetsnaz. They differ from the recce-commando in their reliance upon re-supply or relief by the vanguard of advancing forces. Historically they have been employed as raiders or as special assault forces for seizing strong-points, key bridges, towns or roads prior to an invasion or battle-field offensive. While they may be used in the guerrilla role or to conduct special operations, their missions have usually had a tactical emphasis.

The third member of the Special Forces community is the covert action departments or teams of the *foreign (overseas) intelligence service*. In the years before the Second World War, most intelligence agencies confined themselves to gathering and sifting information. Their primary role was to warn their political masters of foreign developments. Although the modern genre of spy novel would have us believe otherwise, there was little point in recruiting a 'good mind' from Oxbridge and then putting a gun in his hand. Thus the British Secret Intelligence Service (MI6, now DI6), trained its men as intelligence analysts or as case-officers, the latter being responsible for controlling agent networks. Agents recruited by intelligence were not required to undertake paramilitary activities, their primary task being to build up cover for spying. Few intelligence services had the capacity for direct action, one exception being Russia's Unified State Political Administration (OGPU, later KGB) which employed assassination as a means of removing political opponents and foreign intelligence officers.

Western intelligence services expanded into paramilitary operations during the Second World War. The primary task of the British Special Operations Executive (SOE) and the Operational Groups of the American Office of Strategic Services (OSS) was to conduct sabotage operations against the political/economic infrastructure in the occupied countries. They were tasked with organising partisan forces, whose activities would reach a synchronised crescendo immediately before the arrival of the conventional forces. Like many of the military commando units, both these organisations were disbanded at the end of the war, but not before they had introduced a new term into the military lexicon: 'Special Forces.'

There is a fourth member of the Special Forces: the *partisan* or *guerrilla*. In the traditional sense partisans and guerrillas are 'popular' armed groups arising from a conquered people to continue to fight the occupying forces (eg. paramilitary elements of the Resistance). However, they may also be a specially created force of nationals motivated by ideology or mercenaries with little or no popular support who are created, and certainly aided and funded, from outside.

THE ROLES OF THE SPECIAL FORCES

Special operational tasks fall into a number of well defined areas.

Training partisans and guerrillas:

Guerrilla warfare has existed throughout history. The Spanish 'guerrilla' and Russian 'partisan' confronted the French army during the Napoleonic Wars but for the most part their activities were not co-ordinated with those of the conventional forces. In 1812, the United States was sucked into war with Britain, partly as a result of the Royal Navy's habit of boarding and press-ganging the crews of American merchant ships trading with Europe. In the

Partisans gathering up a parachute supply drop in France, 1944. The Allied paramilitary organisations trained and armed the Resistance of the occupied countries during World War Two. More recently, the guerrilla has played a central role in the 'low intensity conflicts', both as an enemy and an ally of Western military forces. (*Imperial War Museum*)

southern United States, Andrew Jackson's attempts to clear Indian lands for plantation brought the Americans into conflict with the southern Indian tribes. Britain capitalised upon this state of affairs by landing Major 'Fighting' Nicholls and a party of three officers and 70 Royal Marines in eastern Louisiana where they raised a guerrilla force from the Creek and Choctaw Indians. Their raiding activities were intended to draw American forces from the main conflict in the north.

During the First World War, the Arab Revolt was supported by a British officer, Colonel T.E. Lawrence, who led his forces into Damascus on the flank of the British Army. However, it was not until the Second World War that wholehearted attempts were made to harness the Resistance in occupied countries to the overall war effort.

Indeed, the Second World War changed the nature of warfare. Much of the old political order was swept away, setting the scene for further political changes, some as the result of major Communist guerrilla initiatives. Military thinkers, distracted by the impact of nuclear weapons and accelerating battlefield technologies, were suddenly forced to confront guerrilla warfare, which generated a new Special Forces role: counter-revolutionary warfare. The Special Forces and their erstwhile, guerrilla partners now found themselves on opposing sides. These were conflicts that laid the foundations for a new military lexicon: revolutionary warfare, proxies, surrogates, internal defence, internal development, rural development, anti-terror and counter-terror.

Reconnaissance and surveillance patrols:

Intelligence gathering remains the primary function of many specialist military units. Perhaps the first real military special forces unit was Roger's Rangers – formed by the British as an irregular militia in the American colonies during the French and Indian Wars (1754–63). The conventional military tactics of the day adapted poorly to the American wilderness and the Rangers were used to gather information on the chain of French forts which effectively pinned the English settlements to the coastal strip of north eastern America. It was the Rangers' intelligence-gathering and pathfinding abilities that led the British forces to form their own Ranger units. These militia also conducted raids and ambushes and their overall role was not dissimilar to the 'Recce-Ambush' activities of the modern special forces in Borneo and Vietnam.

During the protracted Maori Wars in New Zealand (1843–72) there was another re-run of the Roger's Rangers story. In 1843, the warlike Maoris went to war with the New Zealand Company to resist colonisation of the North Island. Here, too, the tactics of the Imperial British Army were unsuited to the fierce enemy and mountainous terrain, so military settlers and local volunteers formed the Bush and Forest Rangers, used both for deep patrolling and scouting. Writing in 1879, Thomas Gudgeon reminds us that they lived '. . . frugally in the rebel held forests for many days without even the glimmer of a campfire to betray their presence but well armed with carbine, revolver and bowie knife'. They were supported by a highly mobile military special force, the Movable Column. Their intelligence-gathering usually resulted in the storming of the Maoris' fortified camps by the regular troops, while the surrounding bush was cleared by the Rangers who then set up a blocking force on the other side of the fort.

During the Second World War, dedicated deep reconnaissance units appeared. The primary role of the Long-Range Desert Group (LRDG) was gathering information on enemy road movements and surveying the desert to update Allied maps. Another reconnaissance unit was Phantom or, more officially, the GHQ Liaison Regiment. Phantom was created in 1939 to gather intelligence in the far forward areas and transmit the information straight back to Command HQ. Patrols consisted of intelligence-trained linguists and radio operators with orders to report events as they occurred, from 10 to 500 miles distance. Phantom personnel, frequently attached to commando forces, served in Greece, the Middle East, Italy, Sicily, Austria, France, Belgium, Holland and Germany. In Normany, after the D-Day landings the morning Army Corps conferences were said to be almost wholly dependent upon Phantom's intelligence, gathered on either side of the front line.

The men of the 1st Commando Regiment (Army Reserve) are Australia's 'steel fist from the sea'. Historically the Assault Commando has provided raiding forces or airborne or sea-borne commandos that seize strong-points, key bridges, towns or roads prior to an invasion or battle-field offensive. (*Special Forces HQ; Australian DOD*)

In the Far East, the American Rangers and Marine Raiders and Australia's Independent Companies and M Special Unit conducted reconnaissance activities, often using dedicated sub-units such as the Alamo Scouts or forward observation teams. Maritime reconnaissance in both theatres fell to units such as the British Combined Operations Assault Pilotage Parties and Special Boat Section and the American Sea Reconnaissance Unit.

The Second World War also saw the birth of Long Range Surveillance Units (LRSUs) which, unlike Long-Range Reconnaissance Patrols (LRRPs), maintained observation of enemy bases and supply routes from permanent, static observation posts. The Royal Australian Navy recruited civil servants, planters and missionaries in the Pacific Islands north of Australia as *Coastwatchers*. These civilian stay-behind forces, later reinforced with intelligence officers, were given naval rank and were asked to report on Japanese air and naval traffic. In North Africa, the LRDG often employed static *roadwatches*, noting the type and volume of German traffic servicing their front-line in the Western Desert.

During the post-war 'low-intensity' conflicts, intelligence gathering became an essential component of the overall counter-insurgency campaign. Under the nuclear umbrella, peacetime reconnaissance was left to intelligence gathering technology or the clandestine agents of the intelligence services. However, particularly difficult or dangerous recce operations were sometimes allotted to commandos. Israeli Military Intelligence – Aman – used commandos to monitor Syrian Army telephones on the Golan Heights. Britain is reputed to have used the SAS to monitor Soviet missile launches, probably from observation posts (OPs) inside the Soviet Union.

Special Forces' responsibilities also include the recovery of agents and aircrew from behind enemy lines; raids and sabotage against strategic targets; covert operations as an instrument of foreign policy and, counter-terrorism ('the newest form of warfare') which can include the rescue of hostages.

COMMAND AND CONTROL

The Special Forces are necessity's children, created to support military operations, but increasingly directed by governments. Israeli commandos have provided the cutting edge of many of Mossad's (the Institute for Intelligence and Special Operations) and Aman's operations, and French commandos have carried out operations for their foreign intelligence service: the *Service de Documentation Extérieure et de Contre-Espionnage* (SDECE). The KGB is reputed to maintain its own Spetsnaz units, while other 'units of special designation' are tasked by Soviet military intelligence (GRU). Both the CIA and DI6 (SIS) employ their own field officers, usually ex-soldiers, but have also used the services of their respective Special Forces. The Secret Intelligence Service uses the SAS for overseas operations and the American Special Forces ('Green Berets') have supported CIA operations in South East Asia and the Americas.

The guerrilla or partisan fights alone or in conjunction with his own or other Allied forces. When foreign governments offer military training and weapons, the insurgents can find themselves fighting as proxies or surrogates for that country's intelligence service. These inter-relationships may be seen if the development of the Special Forces of the two super-powers, the United States and the Soviet Union, is studied.

The Second World War saw the creation of paramilitary units such as SOE and the OSS. These organisations were tasked with collecting intelligence, organising resistance and conducting sabotage operations in the occupied countries. (*Imperial War Museum*)

US SPECIAL FORCES

The OSS was America's first real intelligence agency, created during the Second World War, tasked with intelligence-gathering and, operationally, the organisation of underground and partisan forces in Europe and the Far East. Though not always popular with theatre commanders, these activities undoubtedly had a psychological impact on the enemy. When it was disbanded in 1946, projections suggested a return to a more 'civilised role' for Intelligence – all cloak and no dagger. Even the spy, or human-intelligence (HUMINT) source, would become subsidiary to photographic or electro-optical imagery intelligence (IMINT), with reconnaissance platforms (aircraft and satellites) providing the 'deep-intelligence' on nations such as the Soviet Union. Additional intelligence would be provided by utilising the entire electromagnetic spectrum (ELINT); – notably communications (COMINT) and signals intelligence (SIGINT).

The National Security Act (1947), which created the CIA, called upon it to perform 'other such functions and duties related to intelligence affecting the national security as the National Security Council may from time to time direct' – a blank cheque. Nobody had told the Communist bloc that the days of spies, guerrillas and KGB paramilitary operations were over and the CIA would feel impelled to respond in kind. Ex-OSS officers represented a major source for recruitment and such OSS veterans as Allen Welsh Dulles, Richard Helms, William Colby and William Joseph Casey were to steer the Agency during critical periods of its development.

Although the commitment to unconventional warfare was restored, the capability for large-scale paramilitary covert operations was still missing. So the CIA attempted to control events across the world by recruiting 'hired-help'. The Agency manipulated the internal politics of Iran (1953), funded a secret guerrilla army in Guatemala (1954) and used dissident military officers in the Dominican Republic (1960). The CIA also used mercenaries in the Congo (1960) and in the disastrous Bay of Pigs episode in Cuba (1961). They started supporting, and sometimes training, rebel forces for operations in Burma (1951), Indonesia (1957), Tibet (1959) and South-East Asia (1959).

Meanwhile, under the command of Brigadier General Robert McClure, and in the guise of the Special Operations Section think-tank, three other OSS veterans, Colonels Wendell Fertig, Ross Vockmann and Aaron Bank, had begun a programme to provide an unconventional warfare capability in the American Army. The 10th Special Forces Group (Green Berets) was formed on 1 May 1952, with Aaron Banks as its commanding officer; aptly their motto was 'Free the Oppressed'. Pure OSS, their purpose was 'the organis-ation of resistance movements and operation of their component networks, conduct of guerrilla warfare, field intelligence-gathering, espionage, sabotage, subversion and escape and evasion activities'.

However, in the face of the 'low-intensity conflicts' the Green Berets' prime task became teaching and organising countries to defend themselves from Communist insurgency. Where the CIA had initiated programmes, the Green Berets took over. The Special Forces began training regular South Vietnamese troops in 1957; by 1960, they had become involved in a CIA project that would be called the Civil Irregular Defence Program. This embraced every-thing from psychological warfare and organising anti-Communist militia, to civil engineering projects and medical care.

Special Warfare became an academic discipline and the 'brightest and the best' among the Army's officers and NCOs came to learn the trade at the John F. Kennedy Special Warfare Centre and School at Fort Bragg. The 10th Special Forces Group (operations in Europe and Africa) has since been joined by others; each orientated towards a different part of the globe or held in reserve: 5th (South-East Asia & Pacific), 1st (North-East Asia), 3rd (Sub-Saharan Africa), 7th (Caribbean, South and Central America), 11th (US Army Reserve, Fort Meade, Maryland), 12th (US Army Reserve, Arlington Heights, Illinois), 19th (Army National Guard, Salt Lake City, Utah) and 20th (Army National Guard, Birmingham, Alabama).

The American Special Forces ('Green Berets') continue the traditions of their wartime predecessor: the OSS Operational Groups. (*PMA Pictures*)

To counter subversion in America's backyard, the US Army Caribbean School at Fort Gulick, Panama, became the United States Army School of the Americas and Spanish replaced English as the teaching language. The emphasis of the curricula changed from military technology to counter-revolutionary warfare. By the time Fort Gulick reverted to Panamanian control in

1984, 44,000 Latin American military personnel had passed through the counter-revolutionary warfare course. Throughout the Americas, the Green Berets helped create local Special Forces and trained them in counter-insurgency. Other countries were encouraged to set up SF-schools, like the Centre for the Instruction of Special Troops at Cochabamba, Bolivia.

In his Keynote Address to the 1983 Symposium on *The Role of Special Operations in US Strategy*, Secretary of the Army John Marsh recalled some of the early difficulties faced by the Special Forces,

> Over the years in the United States there has been resistance among leaders of conventional forces towards unconventional methods of coping with irregulars, partisans, or guerrillas. The soldier who tries to fight guerrillas with their own methods is often misunderstood by his conventional counterparts ... In addition, it has been difficult for American officers to establish an orderly career service pattern in unconventional units ... promotion boards were more likely to favour a commander of a conventional rifle company over the leader of a 12-man special operations force.

Under President Reagan's administration, special operational forces were integrated into their own self-contained commands. On 1 February 1982, the Air Force established its 1st Special Operations Group. The Army created its 1st Special Operations Command (SOCOM) eight months later.

On 16 April 1987 the United States Special Operations Command (USSOCOM) was activated as an umbrella organisation for all special warfare units. It has four essential components: US Army Special Operations Command (USASOC) is headquartered at Fort Bragg and consists primarily of the Special Forces Groups, 75th Ranger Regiment, Psychological Operations, a Special Operations Aviation Regiment, Civil Affairs Groups, signals and other support units; The Navy Special Warfare Command (NAVSOC) is located at Coronado, California, providing Naval Special Warfare Groups composed of SEAL Teams, Special Boat Units and SEAL Delivery Vehicle Teams. The Air Force Special Operations Command (AFSOC) at Hulbert Field, Florida, provides USSOCOM with air-support; and the fourth command, the Joint Special Operations Command (JSOC), is located at Pope Air Force Base, North Carolina, responsible for studying the special operations requirements and techniques of all services to ensure standardisation. In addition, each of the three service arms maintains Special Warfare schools to develop doctrine and provide training. An Assistant Secretary of Defence for Special Operations and Low Intensity Conflict (SOLIC) has been appointed to represent its interests. USSOCOM's insignia shows a spearhead on a black background, symbolising the initial force of attack under the cover of darkness. Appropriately enough, it was adapted from an earlier insignia, designed by Major General 'Wild Bill' Donovan for his OSS.

SOVIET SPECIAL FORCES

Since the Russian Revolution, the Soviets have used special units, subordinate to the Communist Party, to serve their domestic and foreign policy goals. During the early 1920s, the state began a programme to destroy the traditional social structure of the peasantry and to force them into collective farms and factories. Such a task was unsuitable for the 'politically unreliable' Red Army, which drew its conscripts from the peasants and workers. In Central Asia, troops from the secret police mounted operations against the Moslem Basmachi rebels who were resisting Soviet rule.

At the same time, Soviet theoreticians laid plans for clandestine units to support workers' insurrections in capitalist countries and thus accelerate the Marxist revolutionary process throughout the world. In the early 1930s, the future Marshal, Mikhail Tukhachevskiy, created elements of the Red Army capable of exporting the Soviet revolution. It was envisaged that Soviet intelligence would support and initiate insurrections in the target countries of Eastern Europe. Red Army special-purpose battalions would link up with the insurgents and provide the force and expertise necessary to capture and hold the seats of government. The revolutionary government would then request the assistance of their fellow 'socialist workers'. In response, long-range armour units would cross the frontier, with the massive corps of paratroopers jumping ahead of them to seize bridges, road junctions and military strongpoints – in essence, providing an airborne carpet for the 'non-stop' offensive by conventional forces. Tukhachevskiy was liquidated in the purges of 1937–38 but he died leaving a conceptual legacy to the modern Red Army on the design and use of Russian Special Forces.

The Spanish Civil War (1936–39) provided the opportunity for the USSR to test its more clandestine operatives. Soviet Military intelligence (GRU) was allotted the task of organising the operations of Republican commandos behind the Nationalist lines, while the NKVD (later KGB) conducted more sinister sabotage and guerrilla warfare operations. These included the theft of Spanish gold reserves (which were taken to the Soviet Union for safe-keeping and never returned), the assassination of Trotskyites, anarchists and other Leftists who were obstacles to a Communist government in the advent of a Republican victory, and keeping a close eye on their GRU counterparts. In the event, the Republicans lost to Franco's forces but Spain was to serve both as a cradle for Soviet thinking on covert warfare and as a 'combat-laboratory' for many of the units and their techniques.

Confronted with the almost irresistible thrust of the German Panzers and infantry in 1941, the bulk of the paratroops and special purpose battalions were expended as infantry and shock troops. The intelligence troops fared little better, being reformed into shock armies to slow the momentum of the Germans. Some intelligence staff and forces of special designation, such as combat-engineers, were tasked by the Central Staff of the Partisan Movement. Peasants and soldiers, trapped by the advancing invader and hunted down by the SS extermination units, had formed partisan groups. This time they were organised and their operations co-ordinated with the Soviet counter-offensives. The official Soviet history credits these forces with capturing and killing hundreds of thousands of German troops and collaborators. More importantly, they had a devastating effect on the lines of communication; they derailed more than 18,000 trains, destroying thousands of locomotives and tens of thousands of railway cars. This effectively hindered the Germans' rapid reinforcement. Other Spetsnaz units were formed to support operations in the Soviet Far East and the Murmansk-Kirkenes area.

Modern Soviet Special Forces are still drawn from both the military and the organs of State Security. The Red Army maintains 7–8 airborne divisions under the operational control of the General Staff. Soviet paratroops are deployed with anti-tank and air-defence weapons, artillery, signal and engineering support battalions. The troops are highly mobile and equipped with BMD amphibious combat vehicles. The divisions are trained in strategic, operational, tactical and special missions and may be deployed up to 300 miles behind enemy lines. Their operational targets can range from capital cities and economic and industrial centres, to the tactical capture of army headquarters, bridges and geographical choke-points.

The special purpose airborne troops, or Spetsnaz (*Spetsnaznache-niya Voz-dushno-Desantnykh Voysk*) are more specialised and operate in smaller groups. Some at least are under the command of Soviet Military Intelligence (GRU) and are assigned to potential tasks such as the destruction of enemy nuclear weapons, reconnaissance, espionage, diversionary raids, assassination and the creation of panic in the enemy's rear. The clearly identifiable units are the Independent Companies, attached to each Army, the Long-Range Reconnaissance Regiments and the Spetsnaz Brigades. While the majority are mainly conscripts or non-professional troops, within each Brigade there is one headquarters company consisting of regular soldiers. These highly-trained soldiers are given the most sensitive missions and are trusted to liaise with foreign agents. Many are athletes of national, and even Olympic, standard and both men and women are included in this group. One 'worst-case' estimate puts the total Spetsnaz strength at 21,600–28,000 officers and men.

The Soviet Navy has a Spetsnaz Brigade attached to each Fleet. Adapted to naval commando operations, the Brigades include combat-swimmers, a midget-submarine group, parachutists and support elements. In addition, the Naval Infantry is trained for amphibious assault and commando operations.

The Ministry of Internal Affairs (MVD) has over 260,000 Internal Security troops organised as Motorised Rifle Divisions. Serving basically as a praetorian guard to the Communist Party, these formations also include élite units with special operations capability, such as the Dzerzhinskiy Division. MVD troops allegedly took part in covert operations in Hungary in 1956, Czechoslovakia in 1968 and, more recently, have operated in Afghanistan.

The other arm of state security, the Committee of State Security (KGB),

Specialised and highly trained forces are the vanguard of the Soviet Union's immense military machine. (*TRH Pictures*)

maintains over 250,000 internal security troops and probably has effective control over the forces of the GRU and MVD. These troops are rumoured to have been committed to intelligence operations in Afghanistan, possibly attacking *mujahedin* bases in Pakistan and certainly countering their raids into the USSR at Tadzhikistan. KGB troops have played a role in exporting the revolution by serving as advisers in North Vietnam during the Vietnam War. They undoubtedly form part of security/military-aid teams sent to other countries in South East Asia, Africa, Central and South America and the Middle East.

The KGB also maintains a 'wet affairs' or 'executive action' department within the First Chief Directorate of the KGB. From the infamous 'mobile squads' of the 1930s to the department's present-day connections with international terrorists, the Directorate maintains a highly secret capability for assassination, kidnapping and sabotage. Until recently, the KGB maintained facilities for training insurgents and terrorists. It also participates in the teaching at Moscow's Patrice Lumumba Friendship University, whose foreign students, largely from the Third World have, at least until recently, been encouraged to pursue revolutionary tactics on their return home.

The immense size of Soviet special designation forces underscores the USSR's commitment to unconventional warfare, compared, say, with the American 82nd Airborne, which totals around 18,000 men. Despite East-West arms control agreements, the USSR continues to enlarge and upgrade its Special Forces. The Soviets have committed themselves to raise all the Soviet Airborne to 'non-professional' Spetsnaz standard – over 100,000 men trained in clandestine warfare. As Richard Simpkin commented in his book *Red Armour*: 'While massive enough, the frontal threat [of conventional forces] on which the West focuses its attention is only the tip of the iceberg.'

Part One

Techniques for the Impossible: Selection
and Training for Special Operations

1

Selection

*When they have finished here – oh yeah, they have certainly
changed. They form a bond with the people, and their whole thing
is on a different wavelength; their outlook on life is different. They
form a new family. Very few mix with their old mates back in civvy
street, 'cos they are now in a different world.*

Parachute Regiment Sergeant-Major.
The Making of a Para by Rory Bridson.

The qualities required of the Special Forces soldier have not changed signifi-
cantly since the days of Roger's Rangers. Major General David Lloyd Owen,
one of the wartime commanders of the Long Range Desert Group (LRDG),
provides a full description of the ideal applicant in his book, *The Desert My
Dwelling Place:*

> The primary role of gaining information of what was going on
> behind the enemy lines was one which required men of resource, of
> initiative, of intelligence and of infinite patience . . .Men who can
> suffer the tedium of boredom, the disappointment of failure and
> not be turned by success; men who can live together pleasantly
> without getting on each other's nerves as a result of the strain and
> tension . . . They are not toughs in the accepted sense of the word.
> But they were the very ordinary and decent type of man with a high
> sense of responsibility and duty; with a rather higher than average
> standard of intelligence and, therefore, a wider range of interests.

Selection for the LRDG was by interview and those who failed the acid test of
operational deployment were returned to unit. Today's selection courses

provide a more objective and cost-effective net but the various units have developed different solutions to the problem of selecting recruits. The philosophy of British courses is based on the premise that under great physical and mental hardship, a man's true nature will emerge. The selectors not only look for maturity, intelligence, self-reliance, endurance and motivation – 'the outward signs of inward grace' – but the combining of these qualities into an unprecedentedly high standard of personal professionalism. This is forcibly brought home by a senior NCO Royal Marine instructor at the Commando Training Centre in Lympstone, who recently conducted recruits on the 30-mile selection speed-march across Dartmoor. On the course were a number of trained foreign commandos, on an exchange visit to the Royal Marines, who had decided to try their luck on Marine selection. He recalls a conversation with one such officer:

> With the mist coming down, I started to check that individuals knew where they were going. I asked him to show me the bearing on his compass. He told me that he had left it back at the barracks, so I asked him how he thought he was going to find his way to the next RV? He replied that he would navigate map-to-ground and I asked him how he intended to do that in the mist? I walked away. A trained commando! I was disgusted.

BY AIR, BY SEA

Britain's Royal Marine Commando selection course evolved from the wartime commando course taught at the Commando Training School at Achnacarry. The Parachute Regiment's 'Pegasus Company' course was originally designed as a selection for non-regular cadre soldiers. Today, the two courses differ only in style. Recruit training conducted by the Parachute Regiment is fast and furious (16 weeks), while the Marine's teaching and selection course – the Common Recruit Syllabus – takes place over 30 weeks.

The first hurdle for the novice para is quite literally just that, it is called the Steeplechase and is a test of individual effort. The Regiment's version of the Grand National is a muddy 1.3km assault course that has to be completed twice in approximately 17 minutes. This is immediately followed by the Log-Race: teams of eight men complete 2.8km of sandhills and tank-training areas carrying a log the size of a telegraph pole. The 'race', itself, is not important but if a student lets go of his rope handle, and does not immediately get 'back on the log', he fails selection and additionally lets his mates down as they have to continue to carry a greater load. The next test is a straight height- and weight-matched fight in a ring for one minute, the Milling. Boxing, or the use of martial arts, is discouraged in this simple test of courage and aggression.

The second day starts with the Speed March, designed to test the individual

Recruits for Britain's Parachute Regiment complete the infamous 'Log Race' selection test. (*PMA Pictures*)

in the sort of fast assault that follows parachute deployment. This test of endurance, with each man carrying 22kg of equipment (Bergen and belt-order), is over 16 kilometres of roads and country tracks and must be completed in 1 hour 45 minutes. To complete the course in the time, at least half must be run at double-quick time. The novices then meet the Trainasium – a confidence course of scaffolding and planks seven metres high. Here the student will run along narrow catwalks, spring across confidence leaps and demonstrate his control of fear on 15-metre shuffle bars. These tests end with the Trainasium black-spot: a standing jump across a two and a half metre gap. Three attempts only are allowed on all the Trainasium tests. Nobody attempts to disguise the fact that a fall will result in serious injury. This is a test of reaction to orders and, in some subsequent exercises and all operations, obeying orders will involve a degree of danger.

The novices are now halfway through selection and the pressure is kept up as they attempt three circuits of an 18-obstacle assault course (1.2km) in approximately seven minutes. The Course then moves to the Welsh Mountains for the Endurance March of 28km, carrying 22kg and completed in four hours, and a shorter circuit: 15km over the infamously steep Pen-Y-Fan and Fan Fawr peaks in two hours. Selection finishes with another 10km Speed March and the Stretcher Race, a final team event where teams of 12 must run with an 80kg stretcher for 12km across the mountains.

The Marine Commando Course involves applicants carrying heavier loads over longer distances than the paras but it is integrated into a longer instructional period, to prepare marines for the many trades in the fully autonomous amphibious Corps. All tasks on the Commando course are completed carrying 19kgs. The first task for the novice marines or 'Nods' [a name derived from their habit of nodding at the instructor's commands] is an assault course that begins with aerial obstacles (Tarzan course) and leads to a more conventional course with an underwater tunnel, as befits a marine unit. This must be completed in 13 minutes. Recruits also participate in six- and nine-mile Speed Marches that must be completed at a rate of 10 minutes a mile. Other selection hurdles include an Endurance Course followed by a four-mile run (73 minutes) and finally a 30-mile endurance march, or 'Yomp', across the wilderness of Dartmoor, which has to be completed in eight hours. The 30-week selection course also allows time for combat survival training, swimming and, additionally, the recruits are expected to become highly proficient in the climbing and abseiling techniques that are essential for rapid cliff assaults.

The key-word on both courses is endurance and this is generated by a bloody-mindedness, leavened with more than a little humour. If the recruit is not an extrovert, he must become comfortable within the extroverted training cadre, sharing in the team spirit and élan of the recruits. Ultimately, he will be selected both as an individual and as a member of a team but he will be buffered from the hardships of training by the group as he struggles to reach the required standard. A Parachute Regiment soldier, one of the younger members of his course, explains:

> On the first couple of speed marches, I only reached the end by being carried by the front men. I hadn't experienced anything like that before and I was exhausted. On one occasion, I made them drop me before we reached the four-tonner. I was in a world of pain and I thought 'that's me failed'. I was surprised when one of the sergeants stopped and said 'good effort'. I thought it was all one or zero, either you passed every task or you were out. It came

Opposite: Selection for the Royal Marine Commandos includes tests in climbing and abseiling, techniques essential for rapid cliff assaults. (*PMA Pictures*)

as a huge surprise when I realised that they were looking for triers at this point in the training and this spurred me on.

Instructors issue their commands in a more laid back fashion than their counterparts in other units. A mixture of stinging contempt and humour is used to correct faults. Even the all-too-common punishments are not punitive but are designed to increase fitness and focus concentration. The common design here is to build confidence and initiative, rather than break men like unsaddled horses. The rationale is simple: these soldiers are given tasks that continually put them at risk of separation from the command structure. This is particularly true of parachute assaults at night as evidenced by the D-Day para-drops, where some parachutists found themselves fighting alongside not only different companies but, in some instances, completely different formations. This philosophy of fostering personal initiative bore fruit in the Falklands when junior NCOs, and even ordinary soldiers and marines, assumed command when the unit commander had been wounded or killed in action.

Selection is also the ticket to an élite, relatively classless society. Here, as noted by Field Marshal Montgomery's reference to the paras, 'every man is an emperor' and the aristocracy is bound by the simple acquisition of a coloured beret. All will have been moulded in the same cauldron – there can be no exceptions. A Marine Commando officer recalls the instructor's reaction to finding that they had a padre on selection,

> Now the padre didn't have to carry a rifle, so the NCOs went down to the workshop and had a shepherd's crook made up at the same weight and size as an SLR [standard infantry rifle]. It was fitted with a sling and this became his Arm [specialisation] equivalent weapon. Training for the 30-miler, the course stopped beside the dirtiest peat-bog I've ever seen and they asked the padre to show 'commitment' by walking across the surface. As he waded up to his waist in the putrid water, the instructors were shouting, 'Come on Sir, you're not even trying! There are Yo-Yo's [young officers] here who don't even go to church and could manage a few steps on the surface'. All of us, even the padre, were falling about laughing.

A very important consequence of the 'One Company' philosophy has been the avoidance of that traditional barrier between the 'Gentlemen and Players'. The Assault Commandos' more versatile chain of command was succinctly outlined in Nigel Foster's book *The Making of a Royal Marine Commando*,

> ... NCOs act as the middle management. Young officers are still learning their jobs so that much of the day-to-day running of a troop is the responsibility of the troop sergeant. No one feels

too upset about this, or put out. It doesn't affect discipline, and
ultimately results in a far better officer, if only for the type of roles
both the Marines and Paras undertake. But that is a very British,
a very commando or special forces attitude and it has not spread
uniformly throughout the British Army ...

Ultimately, this sharing of responsibility results in soldiers of all ranks
taking some responsibility for the overall standard of professionalism of the
unit. What was initiated in selection is thus carried throughout a man's career.

MORE SPECIALISED DUTIES

The Parachute Regiment and the Royal Marines both deploy more highly
specialised formations. The men of the Royal Marine Commandos Mountain
and Arctic Warfare Cadre are tasked with teaching mountain and arctic skills
to fellow marines, acting as guides and advisers and operating as a recce-
commando unit in the frozen wastes of NATO's northern flank. The course
begins with cliff-climbing on the coastal pinnacles of Lands End in Cornwall
before moving on for more climbing instruction in Wales and then to survival/
resistance-to-interrogation training in the Scottish Hebrides. A large section
of the teaching (UHF morse transmission, reconnaissance, sniping) is then
conducted at the Cadre's headquarters at Stonehouse Barracks, Plymouth.
During this period the recruits must plan and execute a raid on a coastal
signals installation.

The next phase of the course is winter warfare and survival in the bitterly
cold forests and mountains of Norway. After taking the military ski instructor's course at Rjukan and three months of intense arctic training, all the
recruit's new skills are tested on an 11-day exercise that mirrors the Cadre's
wartime role of providing tactical reconnaissance for 3 Commando Brigade.
This takes the form of a 200-mile, long-range reconnaissance patrol under
simulated wartime conditions. Skiing across the unrelenting snowscape, lying
up in snow-holes and carrying out detailed reconnaissance of military targets,
such as railways and enemy bases, the four-man patrols must collate the
information for later sabotage raids. Much of this information is passed to
'partisans' at night-time agent-RV's. In return, the agents (usually Norwegian
Special Forces) resupply them with food and replace faulty equipment such as
radio-transmitters. The language of agent-line is, naturally, Norwegian and
this places an extra stress on the contacts. As the patrols complete their tasks
they will be funnelled down a line of agent-contacts back across the lines to
safety.

After spending the winter in Norway, the students complete a 'Pathfinder
Course' in the Ben Nevis area of Scotland, followed by a static-line parachute
course at RAF Brize Norton. The final months of the course are spent in the
Lake District, in Cumbria, learning and teaching 'Alpine Technique' which is

Candidates for the Mountain and Arctic Warfare Cadre must prove themselves capable of performing as recce-commandos in the frozen wastes of NATO's northern flank. (*PMA Pictures*)

tested on Exercise ICE FLIP in Switzerland. The selection process on this course is by continual assessment and is based on both classroom and field work. Not surprisingly, the pass rate is often as low as 20 per cent.

The sister Arm to the Cadre is the better known Royal Marine Special Boat Service (SBS) which is now organised into a headquarters element and squadrons, and operates as part of UK Special Forces Group. Trained for long stays behind the lines, the Squadron specialises in 'inserting onto the target' using Klepper two-man canoes, small inflatables or diving equipment. The two-week pre-selection for the unit is arduous and, in common with other courses, is designed to persuade the poorly motivated man that this is just not his line of work. Pre-selection starts with the usual timed 20-mile endurance walk carrying a 50lb Bergen. Upon completion, the successful candidates spend the night in the open, alone and without any special survival equipment. The next morning they face a 30-mile endurance walk. These walks have the added refinement of unexpected river crossings, which require the men to swim across the river with their Bergens. Confidence in the water is tested again when the men are asked to swim with their equipment to a Landing Craft a quarter of a mile off the beach. For the survivors, much of the rest of pre-selection is spent testing their suitability for diving.

SBS training is not conducted in the azure, crystal clear waters of the holiday brochure, but in the muddy green waters of northern Europe, which remain dark and murky even when the surface layers are lit by strong sunlight. Restricted vision, and the absence of contact with either the surface or the bottom in this hostile environment, induces claustrophobia and disorientation in many totally normal people. In addition, the service expects its recruits to be able to cope with the cramped conditions of the 'lock-out' chamber as they leave or enter submerged submarines. It is thus of little surprise that many students find that they cannot adapt to this sort of 'zero visibility' diving, which requires an unusually confident and relaxed personality.

The selection/training course for the unit is divided into aptitude testing and trade training, and encompasses the general special force skills, with the additional refinements that hone the men for covert waterborne operations. These include beach survey and photography, endurance canoeing and swimming exercises, small boat training, parachute descents at sea, and coastal, astro and underwater navigation. The SBS also has a maritime counter-terrorist role and the men are taught how stealthily to board ships and oil-rigs to carry out hostage rescues.

The Parachute Regiment also fields a more specialised unit: the Pathfinders. The Pathfinders are tasked with 'lighting up the dropping-zones' and performing deep penetration raids and patrols. There is no permanent establishment within the unit and successful candidates serve with the unit for two years (officers) or three years (enlisted men), before rotating back into the Brigade. The Pathfinder platoon numbers only 30 men and the competition to join the unit is intense. The total selection course is compressed into three weeks and, in Parachute Regiment tradition, it is a blur of activity. From the first intense 90 minutes of manic physical activity, codenamed 'Magic Moments', the platoon is searching for the man who can offer something more than the usual professional skills. Navigation and endurance walks (approximately 100km in three days) culminate in the applicants 'tabbing' 50km across the Welsh mountains or the wilds of Dartmoor's North Moor, carrying an equipment load of 55lbs.

The survivors are now organised into four-man patrols, for a tactical phase that involves live firing and contact drills on Close Quarter Battle ranges. Later, 'fire and movement' is preceded by a formidable series of assault courses. In the third and final week, the students are tested on a four-day long-range reconnaissance patrol exercise, where they are tasked with close target reconnaissance of enemy positions. Few men win the coveted Pathfinder flash of a white arrow on a red and green background. Unlike other special units, the entire platoon is trained in High Altitude Low Opening (HALO) free-fall parachuting, which is their covert means of 'inserting' into battle.

The central feature of SAS selection is the series of long endurance walks, where the candidate must 'demonstrate the self-discipline, initiative and strength of character to keep going, when the going gets really tough'. (*PMA Pictures*)

SPECIAL OPERATIONS INC

The length and complexity of the selection and training process is related to the number of special operational tasks that a particular unit might be asked to undertake. The SAS has become renowned for a willingness to embrace all aspects of unconventional warfare. The philosophy and ordeals of British SAS selection are well documented but another interesting and 'open' SAS selection course is run by the Australian SAS Regiment (SASR). The Regiment, being based in Perth, Western Australia, is a long way from the majority of the country's population and the rest of the Australian Army. This poses problems in attracting recruits to the Regiment as the spectre of failure not only involves a dent to morale but another major move for the man and his dependants. While the British SAS searches for the candidate who has already developed the attainments of the SAS soldier, the Australian selectors look for men with the necessary mental and physical attributes who, with the right training, can develop the SAS skills.

The course is thus, in essence, a test of character and, on average, just under 50 per cent of the recruits pass. The majority of the failures either leave voluntarily or are retired due to injury or an inability to cope with the punishing schedule. Such has been the success of this philosophy that SASR selection has been adopted by the US Army's John F. Kennedy Special Warfare Center and School for their officer selection. Recently, in order to advertise its course and philosophy, the Regiment took the unusual step of allowing Guy Baskin and his production crew to film its selection process. The resulting film, *The Battle for the Golden Road*, provided a unique record of the selection and training of Australia's most secret soldiers.

Even before joining the three-week selection course, the aspiring candidate is advised to start exercising heart and lungs and to develop stamina. As in all facets of military training, this is most easily and efficiently achieved by running. An Australian SAS captain explained:

> I remember when I did the course. I prepared myself for anything but I was still really apprehensive. I had spent the past six months preparing for the course by taking long runs carrying bloody bricks in my pack, by day and by night, sweating over past basic training. But there were still parts of the course that caught me off-guard.

The Australian SAS Regiment's Reinforcement Wing places a lot of emphasis on the first few days of the course, with runs and assault courses which are designed to weed out the unfit and poorly motivated. A Wing Sergeant Major explains: 'What we try to achieve here is to identify the people who have come on the course for the wrong reasons or are not prepared to put in their best effort. Once we've identified those types of people, we can single them out later to keep more of an eye on them'.

Finally, after learning to keep their rifles clean and within arms length at all times, they are ready for the first selection test – the timed-run. Each would-be 'Ranger' carries a rifle, two magazines, two full water-bottles and a day's rations, weighing in total 10kgs. The course is over 14.5km and must be completed in 90 minutes. A staff instructor described the type of man that he is looking for at this stage: 'We're looking for the guy who puts in a hundred per cent effort all the time, whether he finishes two or three minutes ahead of time or two or three minutes behind time. We know in that case he's going to be trainable and he's going to be trustworthy in time of combat'. During this phase, the men are also tested on their willingness to walk alone at night in the bush and cope with confined spaces and heights. In training, the Rangers will be expected to swim with their rucksacks across rivers and may be required to undertake combat-swimmer missions. All must pass a swimming test but the poor swimmer finds that the selection staff are eager to provide additional coaching.

The endurance-march phase takes place in the arid Stirling Ranges in South Western Australia, which boast peaks of over 800 metres. Codenamed Happy Wanderer after the Regimental marching song, the course starts with a short 12-hour navigation walk over a single peak. However, this is mere preparation for the main event, a five-day endurance march that takes the men over five mountain-top check-points. Each recruit carries a 50kg rucksack which alters his centre of gravity and makes it even more difficult to climb the steep sides of the mountain. The rucksacks also have a habit of snaring themselves on the dense mountain scrub and each time they are lifted off they feel that little bit heavier. On some stretches of the march, it may be necessary to free the pack more than eight times in an hour. A member of the selection staff commented on the philosophy behind the exercise:

> Here the man with the self-discipline, initiative and strength of character to keep going, when the going gets really tough, will succeed. He has to navigate a route across five peaks in five days; alone. He must prove he can make rational decisions and maintain his morale without a companion to encourage him or act as a prop.

Selection is followed by an SAS Patrol Course which teaches individual patrolling skills, and then by the obligatory static-line parachute course. At this point the soldier is posted to the Regiment and enters the Reinforcement Training Cycle to learn basic demolitions, weapon handling and survival skills. A Regimental Signaller's Course follows, conducted by the staff of 152 Signals Squadron. At its conclusion, each soldier must demonstrate an ability to send and receive Morse Code at a speed of 10 words per minute. Students are now taught combat-medicine by attached staff from the Army School of Health. The medical course emphasises the treatment of injuries, particularly gun-shot wounds.

Following these courses the 'reinforcements' are given training in the basic skill of the Troop to which they will be posted. This includes small boat handling and underwater swimming (Water Operations Troops), free-fall parachuting (Free-Fall Troops) or an SAS-oriented drivers' course for those who have chosen a Vehicle Mounted Troop. The complete selection and

The 'three-times' Ranger volunteer faces a multi-terrain selection course. Ranger School takes the applicant to the very pinnacle of US infantry soldiering and prepares the Ranger battalions for a commando role in support of the Rapid Deployment Force and US Special Operations Command. (*PMA Pictures*)

training cycle takes approximately ten months. However, on being posted to a squadron, the new Ranger undergoes a period of 'Advanced Training' covering subjects such as shooting, fieldcraft, land and astro-navigation and small unit tactics. This is followed by more advanced training in the Troop specialist skills and the tasks applicable to all SAS operations.

THE AIRBORNE-RANGER ROUTE

The purpose of the units in the more integrated American system are well defined by their politico-military doctrine. The US Ranger's specialities are described as 'quick-strike and shock action over short periods, such as raids, ambushes, interdiction, and temporary seizure operations, deep inside hostile territory . . . They are not trainers, but fighters whose job is to kill people and destroy things'. In contrast, the Special Forces are seen as personnel who are 'proficient at raids, ambushes, and sabotage, but employing Green Berets for such purposes . . . wastes their special talent, which is to develop, organise, equip, train, and direct indigenous military and paramilitary forces in unconventional warfare and foreign internal defence'.

The career route of the US Army Special Forces Airborne Ranger starts at the 4th Airborne Training Battalion, United States Infantry Centre, Fort Benning, Georgia. All the men and women applying for 'jump training' have already undergone a self-selection process and are 'two-time' volunteers, having volunteered first to join the army and then the Airborne. All applicants must be medically fit and be able to pass the Army Physical Readiness Test. The parachute course is divided into three weekly phases: Ground Week, Tower Week and Jump Week. Any misconceptions that they are training to become simply infantrymen who deploy by parachute are quickly dispelled by the aggressive training, which is designed to develop the 'Airborne Spirit'. The training starts with morning PT and runs, but the students will find that running is the natural form of movement around the camp. On the battlefield, the airborne élan and speed of these troops enhances the shock-effect of their arrival by parachute.

For the 'triple volunteers' who wish to serve with a more specialist force, induction into the 75th Ranger Regiment is by way of the 4-week Ranger Indoctrination Programme. The course starts with two days of parachute descents using steerable 'chutes, and then quickly tests the applicants on basic infantry combat skills. Students are also assessed on their performance in helicopter insertion, which may involve a 200-foot abseil descent, raiding and ambush drills and climbing skills. In the third week the students are driven to exhaustion to test their reserves of stamina. Operating from a simulated forest patrol base, the course is continuously kept active, patrolling and ambushing while avoiding counter-ambush and the enemy force that is sweeping the forest looking for them. Throughout the exercise the command positions are rotated, allowing the selectors to evaluate the men's ability both to lead and to be led. Many of the applicants do not meet the high professional standards maintained by the Regiment and half to two thirds of the course may be returned to unit.

After nine months to a year with a Ranger Battalion, the soldiers are ready for the Ranger School at Fort Benning, although younger or weaker candidates are prepared for the challenge by the Pre-Ranger School Course. Paradoxically, most of the students on the course are drawn from other units. All experienced Airborne personnel are eligible for the School, which produces 'Ranger Qualified' personnel, and the Marine Corps and Air Force use the School as an advanced leadership programme for their NCOs and officers.

The harsh and challenging course lasts for 58 days and the applicant must be prepared to work 18 hours a day, seven days a week, throughout the programme. The students spend the first 19 days at Fort Benning, before moving to Dahlonega, Georgia, for a mountain training phase lasting 17 days. The final 'swamp phase' of the course is held at Elgin, Florida. Throughout Ranger School, the students are challenged by hunger, exhaustion, bad weather, formidable terrain and mounting emotional stress. Continuous day and night operations are conducted against a simulated enemy force and operational briefs force students to cross fast-flowing rivers and mountains to infiltrate the 'enemy's' forward areas. Once 'behind the lines', they use road-ambushes and raids to slow the momentum of the enemy's advance, and deep-reconnaissance to pinpoint strong-points, headquarters and the locations of special weapons such as missile-sites.

The qualified Ranger serves a 22-month tour with a Ranger Battalion on an arduous 48-week annual training cycle in a variety of climates. The Rangers serve as a 'mailed-fist' within USSOCOM and as an integral part of the US Rapid Deployment Force. They can also carry out tactical long range reconnaissance patrols and special operations for conventional formations. An experienced Ranger can apply for the Ranger Leadership course that qualifies him to command élite Army units and/or he may later decide to become a 'four-times volunteer' to serve with the 'Snake-Eaters'.

THE SNAKE-EATERS

'Do you know what they have to do in that unit? They eat snakes and other things. I'd rather die than do that!' This was an American civilian's comment on survival training in the US Army Special Forces: the Green Berets. It very accurately reflects the divide between the majority of the population and those few who are sufficiently motivated to learn the skills necessary for long stays behind enemy lines. In truth, any reasonably fit person can pass these courses but in the words of one American selector, 'you've got to want it enough'.

An aspiring Green Beret needs a number of basic qualifications to go to the John F. Kennedy Special Warfare Centre and School (SWCS) at Fort Bragg, North Carolina. He must be airborne-qualified, a high-school graduate and have passed the advanced physical readiness test, advanced individual military training and junior NCO's course (E4-E7), and be able to swim 50 metres in boots and uniform. He will also be vetted for a security clearance. On arrival at the School the aspiring Special Forces candidates face a gruelling three-week pre-selection test, known as Special Forces Assessment and Selection (SFAS), introduced as a cost-effectiveness procedure. Candidates who may well have dropped out of Special Forces selection after consuming valuable time and money, are now eliminated at the very beginning. Approximately half of an average class of 300 survive SFAS to win a place on the Special Forces Qualification Course ('Q Course').

The common-skills phase of the 'Q Course' lasts five weeks and covers patrolling, close combat, airborne insertion, survival and land navigation. The Land Navigation and General Subjects Committees teach survival, camouflage and concealment, rope-work, abseiling and navigation. Meanwhile, the art of patrolling within the 'A' Team is taught by the Patrolling Committee. The test of this training takes place over 12 consecutive nights, when the students are asked to navigate from point to point in the forest. This has proven to be a major blackspot in the Beret course, and indeed all other courses of this type, because, at this point, the soldier finds himself in the woods at night and on his own. Such is the powerful psychological barrier represented by this test, that other units, such as the Australian SASR, introduce a short solitary night walk early on in the course so that any individual who is unable to cope can be removed. In contrast to the British system of testing applicants in interrogation and escape after a prolonged period in a survival situation, the Americans test the students in all aspects of Survival, Evasion, Resistance to Interrogation and Escape (SERE) simultaneously. After a period of instruction by Green Berets who were themselves captured by the Viet-Cong, the course is released into the Uwharrie National Forest. At the end of the SERE course, students, armed only with a knife, are required to live off the land while avoiding their pursuers during three days of manhunts.

At the beginning of Week Six, the successful students are required to specialise in one of the 'A' Team basic skills: weapons, communications, combat medicine and engineering. All the classroom and practical work is brought together in the last five weeks of the course, when the students are parachuted into the forest and swamps of the Uwharrie National Forest as part of Exercise 'Robin Sage'. In this simulated 'hostile nation', the students have to rendezvous with 'friendly natives' drawn from families that live around the park who have provided assistance for the U.S. Army's war-games since the Vietnam era. The students have to demonstrate that they can teach the locals weapon handling and organise them into guerrilla units. Meanwhile, 82nd Airborne's hunter-killer teams search for the 'partisans' and their Green Beret instructors. In the final phase of the exercise, the prospective Green Berets lead their 'guerrilla units' on ambushes and raids against the 'aggressor force'. There is a further complication to this exercise. Some of the local 'mountain men' have natural sympathies for the 82nd Airborne and only good agent contact drills prevent the students from falling into the wrong hands, thus jeopardising their chances of selection for the Special Forces. Currently, the American Army Special Forces are phasing in a new selection course based on the Australian SASR course for their officer candidates. Should this prove successful, it is expected to be applied to the selection process for all candidates.

There are three other notable Special Forces units within the American

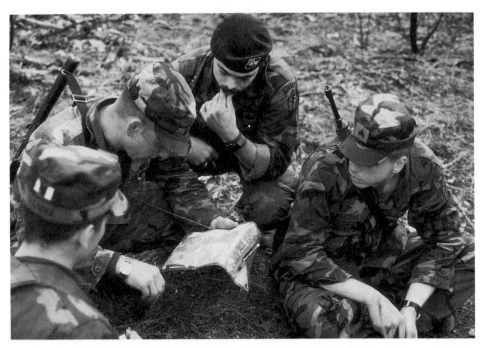

As part of the US Army Special Forces' 'Q' Course, instructors from the Land Navigation Committee teach the 'toughest land navigation course in North America'. (*PMA Pictures*)

Armed Services. Operational Detachment-Delta was formed to increase US Special Forces capability in counter-terrorism and hostage-rescue. Personnel are primarily drawn from the Army Special Forces and initial selection owes something to British SAS selection. The United States Navy's SEAL Teams provide maritime special operations capability. Selection for small boat and diving tasks is similar to the British SBS but the Americans encounter a greater range of submersible swimmer delivery vehicles and explosive ordnance disposal is an important part of their training and work. The US Marine Corps has its own special force in the form of the Reconnaissance Units or 'Recons' and these experienced Marines undergo a less specialised selection and training to the Navy's SEALs.

SELECTION SOVIET-STYLE

Selection for the Soviet Special Forces is by continuous assessment or, it may be argued, self-selection. The process begins many years before the start of obligatory military service. Most men and women selected for the Soviet clandestine services have parents in the Communist Party, with impeccable political backgrounds. As young children they are encouraged to join the Octobrists, transferring at the age of 10 years to the Pioneers. At this stage the process of pre-selection is already well advanced. Their impressionable minds are exposed to highly idealised stories of Red Army valour during the Great Patriotic War. They are encouraged to see the Soviet Union as an island surrounded by potential enemies and the need for eternal vigilance is impressed upon them, subconsciously sowing the seed of xenophobia. For these Soviet children, the Party, Armed Services and intelligence apparatus are the sword and shield of the Motherland.

They are introduced to basic military training at the *zarnitsa* (summer lightning) camps under the watchful eye of retired military officers. The process of continuous assessment has begun and they are watched to see how enthusiastically they embrace the rigours of military training with its emphasis on discipline and regulations. At these camps the children are introduced to drill, guard-duty, civil defence and first-aid (particularly crucial for the girls). Basic soldiering and tactics are introduced as a game, often with the added attraction of support from a local regiment.

From the age of 15 years, the young recruits' political and military education undergoes acceleration. They are expected to join the *Komsomol* (Young Communist League) with whom they will attend *orlyonok* (Little Eagle) camps to develop skills in map reading and weapon handling. Political education also continues as the children are apprised of the advantages of Party membership, for which they become eligible in their early 20s. Throughout their time in the *Komsomol* their progress is monitored by the KGB, GRU and by the Party itself, each of which vies with the others for potential recruitment.

Whilst in the *Komsomol*, the potential recruit joins DOSAFF (Voluntary Society for Co-operation with the Army, Air Force and Navy) with which he or she will undertake further *orlyonok* camps, together with a minimum of 140 hours of training spread over two years. As well as conventional military skills, radio procedure and maintenance, driving skills and mechanics, the recruit for the Special Purpose Forces may well gain his glider pilot's wings and learn to parachute and freefall. His excellent military potential will certainly place him far above his peers, and many of them will have become deeply disillusioned by the 'pacifist' tendencies now apparently permeating every strata of Soviet society. At the end of *Komsomol* training the sexes diverge. Officially there are no women in Spetsnaz and those women officers photographed by the West are undoubtedly part of the 'Professional' element, numbering around 3,000 and drawn from professional athletes. However, the *Komsomol* serves as an excellent springboard to all professional cadres in the Soviet Union, including the professional sports clubs.

Should his studies result in a deferral of his military conscription, the aspirant to Spetsnaz must become involved in *Gotov k trude i oborony* (GTO). This was once responsible for maintaining high standards of physical fitness among the young and preparing them for the rigours of military conscription, but today the GTO programme is proving less successful, with an increasing

Selection starts early for the Soviet Special Forces. While still in DOSAFF, the aspiring candidate learns to parachute and may well gain his glider pilot wings. (*TRH Pictures*)

number of draftees being rejected as physically or educationally below par. It does, however, still provide an excellent opportunity for representatives of the Ministry of Defence to vet potential recruits for its élite units.

The majority of the men considered for the 'non-professional element' of the Soviet Special Forces are conscripts. They are filtered through selection boards during the six-monthly drafts for national service. Basic training is harder for the airborne and Spetsnaz recruits than the conscripts sent to conventional units. This appears to be due partly to an entrenched system of bullying in the Soviet Army by the older recruits, or *stariki*, partly to the primitive living conditions in the Soviet barracks and partly by design. The harsh regime in the Soviet Army, where the comforts of life are markedly absent, provides a psychological bridge to life in the Spetsnaz units, where exercises are conducted as though they were the real thing and soldiers can spend up to a year in the field.

During a one-month training period, the recruits are taught basic fieldcraft, navigation, camouflage and weapons training and the natural leaders who emerge from this system are sent to training battalions to become sergeants. However, most qualified sergeants return to their units as privates and provide a reserve to replace existing NCO's who become casualties in combat or are removed for failing to maintain standards.

WHY IS SELECTION IMPORTANT?

For an American Special Forces sergeant, the rationale for selection bears an uncanny resemblance to the philosophy of his Australian SASR counterparts: 'If a man just sits down when he thinks he's tired, you can't do anything with him but the guy that's exhausted and keeps going is trainable'. For the selection committee, successful completion of the process provides the unit with a guarantee of commitment, self-discipline and motivation. In his book *Anything but a Soldier*, Captain John Hislop, a member of the wartime Phantom Signals Squadron, provides a cash-value interpretation of this guarantee:

> In straightforward warfare a man in the line who breaks down or proves wanting can be sent back. But if he does so on an operation behind enemy lines he is a menace to himself, to his companions and to the whole project and there are no means of getting him out of the way.

Selection also confronts the candidate with the realities of two key words that can be used to describe his future military career: commitment and risk. A Green Beret expresses his own view of the continuum of risk in the armed services:

> There are many guys in conventional units who don't want to jump out of an aeroplane with the paras or go to war in a landing craft with the marines. And there are guys in those units who don't want to do the things the Special Forces do. In the Special Forces, there are guys who don't want to do what some of the men in that unit do!

Reflecting on the role of some of the smaller, aggressive Green Beret units in Vietnam, such as the Roadrunner teams and the SLAM (Search-Locate-Annihilate-Mission) companies, one is forced to agree. If differences do exist between the men of the Special Forces and other people, perhaps it is in choosing this style of soldiering and accepting the risks that go with it.

2

Continuation Training

Train hard, fight easy.
SAS Training Wing

An American Green Beret's induction started with a simple question that implicitly underscored the dangers of his unit's work in Vietnam, 'Do you mind if we try to get you killed?' The trick, of course, is to defy the odds and stay alive. In the parlance of 22 SAS, this is called 'beating the clock', after their tradition of placing brass memorials on the regimental clock at Hereford. Training, equipment, unit philosophy and the 'little things' taught in continuation training will provide the novice with the very best opportunity of staying alive.

TRAINING FOR SPECIAL OPERATIONS: FROM THE JUNGLE TO 'VIRTUAL REALITY'

The Weapons Instructor brought out the rifle that had become almost a household word in the pages of hundreds of books and on the cinema screen. As he went through the stripping procedure on the Soviet AK-47 Kalashnikov assault rifle, he recited its specifications: weight, muzzle velocity, range, rate of fire and calibre. One thought crossed the students' minds: compared to the then current standard British infantry rifle, the SLR, the AK-47 seemed incredibly easy to field-strip and clean. The instructor looked at the students and motioned to the parts of the weapon, 'Anything strike you about the design of this weapon?', he asked. Eliciting no reply, he explained that the AK-47, produced in greater numbers than any other modern small arm, had become the most popular weapon for guerrillas and revolutionaries. Its chief design feature was simplicity as it was intended for use by poorly educated Soviet soldiers and often illiterate insurgents. The weapon functioned well in humid, dusty environments and would fire when dirty, thus being admirably suited to operations in the Third World. So began instruction on an SAS foreign weapons course.

Foreign-weapons training plays an important part in the training of any unit destined to operate in the enemy's rear areas for extended periods of time. Ammunition for personal weapons will be in short supply but the successful raid and ambush will yield a harvest of enemy weapons and ammunition. Some special force units prefer to use enemy weapons on operations. During fire-fights the alert enemy will detect the characteristic sound, or signature, that the weapon of another country produces when fired, and can thus locate the opposition.

A Green Beret Weapons Specialist with an 'A' Team will be expected to have expert knowledge of around 60 foreign weapons, to demonstrate an ability to service and repair them and to develop a proficiency as a weapons instructor. For the non-specialist, this list is reduced to his own country's infantry weapons and the major small arms of countries perceived as presenting a threat to national security.

In standard infantry practice, a weapon is considered to have been mastered when a soldier can demonstrate that he can field-strip, clean and fire the weapon by day and night, demonstrating the vital 'stoppage' drills that return the gun to service in the event of a misfire. However, the very nature of the tasks required of the lightly armed special units ensures that weapons training continues far beyond basic infantry drills. Their high proficiency in weapons skills has resulted from the continual need for special weapons, speed and accuracy. The weapons training that today's Special Forces recruit meets in basic training ranges from the lessons and mistakes experienced in earlier wars to imaginary wars generated by computers.

At the end of the Second World War, the British SAS (Malayan Scouts) was resurrected to fight a counter-insurgency campaign in Malaya. The Regiment quickly employed imaginative and realistic training techniques to prepare for their role. One such technique was to use air-rifles to hone stalking and sniping skills. Two opponents, armed with air-rifles and wearing protective fencing masks, crawled towards each other through the jungle. The victor was the soldier who was able to place the first accurate 'killing-shot'. However, the jungle war soon generated the need for 'special' weapons.

In the dark claustrophobic confines of the jungle, where visibility was sometimes measured in feet, weeks of unrelieved boredom could end with a sudden contact with the enemy. Survival in such sudden, close confrontations depended upon effecting surprise and opening fire with split-second deadly accuracy. Under these conditions, the lethal spray of pump-action shot-gun fire often proved to be more effective than a rifle. In his book *Who Dares Wins*, Tony Geraghty relates these brutal encounters:

One interesting form of weapons training was used by the newly formed SAS in Malaya. It involved two opponents stalking each other with air-rifles. (*Imperial War Museum*)

... he [Sergeant Bob Turnbull] pursued a notorious guerrilla leader called Ah Tuck, a man who always went armed with a Sten carbine ready cocked. When the two men finally encountered one another in the bush at a range of 25 yards, Ah Tuck died still holding his unfired weapon. According to one officer who served with him, Turnbull used a repeater shotgun with such speed and accuracy that it would 'fill a man with holes like a Gruyere cheese'.

Vital split-second speed for members of the patrol, armed with an earlier version of the Sterling sub-machine gun and encumbered with a heavy Bergen, was gained by jumping around to face the enemy, landing squarely on both feet and firing the sub-machine gun with the butt held firmly into the stomach. Such 'body-line' shooting had been pioneered in the SOE training schools by Sykes and Fairburn – two of Britain's early experts in close combat and guerrilla warfare. SOE instructors had rejected the traditional dualists stance for pistol shooting in favour of a low crouch with the pistol held in a two-handed grip, so that the weapon formed the apex of a triangle at waist-level, with the marksman's body as its base. The weapon was fired by instinct, instead of being carefully aimed. Using this system, the marksman fired two quick shots at the target as insurance – a technique later known as 'double-tapping'.

In later jungle encounters in Borneo, the SAS found themselves matched against regular Indonesian para-commandos. Here the Regiment discovered that the right-handed man, shooting his rifle with the butt in the right shoulder, was slower to react when covering an arc of fire to his right. The vital seconds lost in changing grip and bringing the rifle to the right shoulder could be regained by teaching the operators to fire from both the left and right

SOE, and later the SAS, rejected the traditional one-handed duellist's stance for pistol shooting. (*Private Collection*)

shoulders. An SAS Sergeant recalls the training: 'We spent most of the time between patrols on the range learning this technique; thousands of rounds were used in getting it right. It was a bitch, it didn't feel natural and the spent cartridge cases kept hitting you in the face.' It did, however, buy the men the vital extra seconds. The bitter, brief fire-fights were fought with automatic weapons, grenades and Claymore mines. The jungle proved no place for the tradition of 'double-tapping'. Unprofessional behaviour, such as the accidental discharge of a rifle, could be punished by being returned to unit or, as in one instance in Malaya, being ordered to carry a live grenade about for a week – minus the pin. Later the Regiment discovered that techniques developed in the jungle wars were excellent training for the other campaigns.

In recent years, particularly in America, the close quarter battle range, live firing exercise and the use of blank rounds on realistic exercise scenarios have been supplemented by laser and computer-driven battle training systems. Laser-based small-arms simulators fire laser pulses that simulate bullets and neutralise an 'enemy' wearing target sensors on his uniform and helmet. Tactical Engagement Simulation (TES) has effectively ended the confusion and disgruntlement that accompanied tactical training with blank ammunition. No longer do the 'dead' come back to life to confuse commanding officers and umpires as to 'who killed whom and when.' The laser can be activated by blank- or dry-firing, the former providing a realistic bang when the weapon is fired. When hit by a laser 'bullet', a soldier's sensor system gives out an audio 'kill' signal. The American Multiple Integrated Laser Engagement System (MILES) requires the 'dead' soldier to insert a key into the soundbox which is carried on a harness in order to stop the noise. The key is connected by wire to the laser transmitter on the rifle, making further participation in the exercise almost impossible. Other systems require the 'dead' soldier to lie on his back.

During exercises a Special Forces team may well have completed their primary and secondary tasks but did they all really make it back to the submarine pick-up? TES ensures that training is as realistic as possible, testing not only marksmanship but also all aspects of fieldcraft. Guy Willis, an ex-Parachute Regiment Officer, commented on the difference that laser engagement systems had made to exercises for his journal the *International Defence Review*:

> With laser simulators, soldiers have to move across country as they would in combat. Everyone knows how to do it, but they get lazy . . . If only blanks are being used, you tend to stand up and move upright because it's easier. In fact, my regiment found in the Falklands that the only safe way to move under fire, even at night, was on all fours. Using laser simulators, you rediscover this because otherwise, you start taking 'casualties'.

Other systems are more sophisticated, with the laser beam also carrying information identifying the weapon that fired the shot and allowing sensors on, say, a tank, to discriminate between an anti-tank weapon and an assault rifle. At the end of the exercise, the umpire's 'gun' collects information from all the individual sensors and this is down-loaded onto a computer database. With each of the players coded, post-exercise analysis reveals whether the victim was hit by direct or indirect fire, who killed him and with what weapon and how many shots the victim fired before being 'killed'. Colonel Ray Seymour, New Zealand Director of Infantry and the NZ Special Air Service, believes the Infantry Weapons Effect Simulation System (IWESS), produced by the New Zealand firm Oscmar Products, as 'a system for the 21st Century', has drastically changed training, improved shooting and enhanced the reality of exercises.

Laser engagement systems have obvious disadvantages; the marksman does not have to estimate range or allow for crosswinds and there is little weapon recoil. Most importantly, unlike a bullet, the laser beam lacks any penetration power. Live-firing on computer driven ranges overcomes these disadvantages and supplements the tactical training provided by systems such as IWESS. On the 'all singing and dancing' ranges being developed for the Special Forces, the approach of a team can be detected by infra-red sensors, allowing the computer to activate radio-controlled targets and battlefield illumination and noise. Three-dimensional life-like figures close on the patrol, performing life-like evasive movements. As the soldiers fire on their 'opponents', some systems further simulate reality by allowing the computer to drop the target only after multiple or 'lethal' hits. Systems currently under design will return fire with airguns, wax bullets, dye-filled capsules or the ubiquitous laser beam. As the team withdraw from the contact and prepare to continue the mission, other infra-red barriers activate further sets of targets to engage the patrol. Meanwhile, the all-seeing computer will generate a blow by blow account of the fire-fight for the Training Officer.

Computer technology is also being used in indoor shooting arcades. Here the soldier is coached while he 'dry-fires' weapons, equipped with a long-range light-pen or laser, at realistic computer generated graphics. Systems such as the Spartanics *Weaponeer* coach the soldier on such fundamentals as aiming position, breath control and trigger squeeze, based on movement of the barrel between the interval when the weapon first interacts with the target and the shot. Action replays show the target as seen through the front-sight. Light infantry support weapons and foreign firearms can be adapted to arcade simulation and extended battlefield scenarios add to the stress of the training. In the future, the lessons of the past will be taught not only on the close quarter battle range but in the imaginary worlds known as 'Virtual Reality'. This

Opposite: Laser-based small-arms simulators have effectively ended the confusion and disgruntlement that accompanied tactical training with blank ammunition. These British paratroops on an American exercise are using weapons equipped with MILES. (*TRH Pictures*)

software, currently under development by organisations such as the US Air Force, allows an operator wearing special goggles to interact with a world generated by a computer. A combination of the satellite imagery used to make three-dimensional maps, powerful computers, simulation technology and 'Virtual Reality', may enable the soldier of the future to train for a mission in an imaginary world that closely resembles his target. Currently under development for flight simulation, 'Virtual Reality' could be the battle training scenario of the future.

SKILLS FOR SPECIAL OPERATIONS:

Languages

Meeting agents, training indigenous personnel and listening to the enemy's radio traffic are just three tasks that require a reasonable knowledge of the local language. However, fluency can range from simple tourist lingo to an ability to read the written word and speak a language with the same inflections and intonation as a native. Where there are multiple dialects, language specialists or soldiers with a particular aptitude for languages may be recruited or attached to the unit. This was found necessary during the British campaign in Borneo, where there were over 20 tribal dialects.

Matters are simplified in the Green Berets where each Special Forces Group is orientated towards operations in a particular area of the world and will therefore be faced with a small number of languages. The ideal in the Berets is for each 'A' team to have a specialist in a particular language with all other members of the team having a working knowledge. In fact, until recently, the most common foreign language was Spanish, reflecting the ethnic backgrounds of the recruit intake. With the current level of language skills well below par, the American Army is just completing a five year programme to teach elementary foreign languages to three of the 12 men in an 'A' Team. The Americans are also considering introducing the British system where elementary language skills are professionally taught with modern laboratory systems. After the initial training, the man is paid for his skill but is expected to maintain and develop the language in his own time.

As far as the theoretical opposition is concerned, it is claimed that Spetsnaz units have only minimal language skills to enable them to deciper signals traffic and captured documents and to interrogate prisoners. Linguists may be attached to a unit to make up the deficiency on deep-strike operations; interestingly some of these are reported to be women.

Communications

Signals and, in particular, high-frequency morse transmission serve as an umbilical cord, attaching the operator to his home base. Without radio communications, the team cannot request re-supply, co-ordinate activities with conventional forces or arrange a time and place for their safe extraction. Equally, the immediate transmission of information on enemy positions and movements provides 'real-time' intelligence that enables raids, air-strikes and fire-missions to be planned and executed.

During the Second World War, radio operators carried their large, heavy transmitter/receivers into battle, packed into a suitcase or rucksack. In the city they could be operated off mains electricity but in the field batteries or a portable generator had to be found to provide the power. Later in the war, most transmitters were equipped with auxiliary batteries as one of the German

A wireless operator with the Chindits prepares to transmit from behind Japanese lines. Second World War radio sets were relatively large and their continuous wave signals were easily pin-pointed by the enemy. (*Imperial War Museum*)

counter-intelligence ploys was to locate transmitters by systematically cutting off the power to different parts of a city.

To make it difficult for an enemy monitoring the flow of traffic to estimate the number of radios in the field, the operator was provided with set, irregular transmission times and frequency changes. Messages were encoded using simple 'book-codes' where a paragraph on a certain page of a book, held by both the operator and his base, provided the cipher for encoding and decoding the messages. However, books can be lost or damaged or may fall into the wrong hands and a simpler expedient often lay in the memorisation of the lines of a poem. Later in the War, one-time code pads came into use, which effectively removed any patterns in the messages that could be used by the enemy as a basis for decoding.

German and Japanese counter-intelligence organisations also attempted to locate the radio and its operator by triangulating the continuous-wave signal with direction-finding (DF) equipment. One counter to this was the use of simple codes such as the merchant shipping international 'Q' Codes and 'crack signals', allowing the operator to come onto the air for long enough to signal 'I am well' or 'Moving location' or 'Call me at 1800 hrs'. Longer messages, reporting enemy activities, needed to be encoded and broken into the five-letter blocks that form the signallers' 'words'. These could take up to half an hour to send and the operator needed to move his set constantly about the countryside to defy the enemy's direction-finding equipment.

Today, the covert radio operator's art is made more difficult by the web of electronic 'ears' that cover the Globe. Enemy and friend alike collect signals (SIGINT) and other forms of electronic (ELINT) intelligence using a range of familiar devices that dot the countryside. The material is then passed back to the code-breakers and their supercomputers which look for patterns, for instance the recurrence of common letters such as vowels. As a consequence, the state-of-the-art radio transmitters, designed for Special Forces use, have evolved into small, light, compact sets. The message is typed into the transmitter 'en clair' and then encoded or scrambled before the signal is sent out in a short burst of morse at high-frequency to defy Direction Finding (DF) equipment.

Not surprisingly, DF technology has kept pace with the developments in transmitters. It was reported that the Argentine garrison on the Falklands had equipment that could DF burst transmissions in a matter of seconds. One American signals manual warns its students that within a mere 2–3 minutes of their radio-transmission being pinpointed by the enemy, artillery and air-strikes could be hitting their position.

One answer to the problem is to employ a totally different principle. 'Frequency-hoppers' like the VHF/HF System 4000, built by Plesseys from equipment developed for the Australian Army under Project Raven, makes pre-arranged frequency changes many times each second. This results in eavesdroppers, or DF equipment scanning a particular frequency, detecting only a small fraction of the message. Southcom has developed an ultra-light

HF frequency-hopping manpack radio, ideal for Special Forces. The transmitter 'hops' between nine set frequencies in the 2–30MHz range at a rate of 10 hops/second.

However, even transmitters employing the frequency-hopping principle are not the complete answer. Rohde & Schwarz have advertised the new Integrated Broadband Signal Interceptor and DF System PA 2000-Hopper Trap. This system provides, 'bearings of frequency-hopping networks with up to 1000 hops/sec ... A hopper radio set operating within a frequency band of 10MHz, for example and remaining at a frequency for 3ms [3 milli-seconds] will be detected in an average of 0.25 seconds'. Equally, their Broadband Doppler Direction Finder PA 055 is capable of determining the direction of a 10ms signal burst with the accuracy of 1° of the compass.

According to one soldier who has traded in his radio for a place in Britain's space programme, total security might mean that radio transmitters will have to be sacrificed:

> For the really secure operation in the short-term, the intelligence can only come one way, from the base to the man. The need for radio transmitters is inherent in the way we plan operations, we make them dependent on re-supply, dependent upon meeting somebody else, dependent on meeting a chopper or submarine to get out. The safest way is to let the man find his own way out. In the distant future, totally secure communication systems may be optical based, like the blue/green lasers now being designed for satellite-submarine communications.

Communications satellites are already providing the Special Forces with a more covert means of communications. More than 90 per cent of all US and NATO inter-continental communications are sent by satellites such as AFSATCOM in geostationary orbit 22,370 miles (36,000km) above the earth. While these satellites' primary function is command and control (relaying orders between national command centres and field units, naval vessels and strategic missile command posts), their use has obvious advantages for special operations as was demonstrated during the Gulf War. The transmission of highly directional signals skywards minimises the possibility that they will be intercepted by enemy ground stations. Equally, transmission from the satellite is directed at a very limited area on the ground around the SF-team – this is known as the satellite's 'foot-print'.

While the radios have changed, all civilian and military students are still taught the basic principles of voice and morse transmission, to produce operators with a high degree of competency on a wide range of equipment and under all conditions. Students learn to transmit and receive morse at speeds of about 8 words per minute. The professional signallers will 'send' at more than 15–30 words per minute. The great value of morse is that it provides a very power-efficient signal for transmission, allowing, for example, a signal to be

Today's Special Forces use small, light, compact radio transmitters. The message is typed into the transmitter in 'clear' and is then encoded or scrambled before the signal is sent out in a short burst of morse at high speed, to evade any Direction Finding (DF) equipment. (*PMA Pictures*)

bounced off the moon using half a kilowatt of power and providing a matrix for the secure encoding of messages.

Also taught is the theory of aerial construction and how to increase the operating range in difficult terrains such as desert, jungle and mountainous regions and in face of cold and ionospheric disturbances in the Arctic. Radio-nets are covered in some detail and the soldier learns how his messages travel through the signals-net to arrive back at Headquarters. In Vietnam, where the Americans enjoyed total air-superiority, aircraft on permanent station above the Cambodian-Laotian border relayed the signals from LRRP teams to MACVSOG. Long distance transmissions can be relayed by satellites or bounced off astronomical bodies. In the pre-satellite days, the unwanted 'ears' presented difficulties for long range transmissions but, while enemy ground stations may have been listening for signals being bounced-off the moon, there are the old tried and tested 'ham' techniques of bouncing signals off the ionised tails of meteorite showers.

Combat-Medicine

Behind the lines, combat medicine is one of the most important skills. The medic must serve as a doctor to his patrol and any guerrillas or partisans they are training and he also becomes a valuable asset in any programme directed at winning the 'hearts and minds' of the local civilian population. Few men will continue to fight in any war if they know that they will be left to die of wounds and, behind-the-lines, the inevitable battle casualties are compounded by infectious disease, poor diet and inadequate sanitation. Boredom, fear and the death of casualties through wounds and disease all contrive to lower morale.

During the Second World War, guerrillas fighting the Japanese in the Dutch East Indies were able to rescue some Allied prisoners. This appeared to be an extraordinary stroke of luck, when one of the prisoners was a civilian doctor. Their celebration soon turned to bitterness when it transpired that the doctor was an academic who knew little practical medicine. The son of one of the combatants relates the consequences:

> The men used to paint coloured spots on their skin and ask 'What's this Doc?' He would tentatively suggest some disease with a long name but was totally unable to suggest a treatment. They would wait to stand beside him in the bush shower so that he could watch their 'spots' wash off. My father always remained very bitter about this experience. After the war we came to Australia. My father was very pleased when I went to university but when I enrolled in medical school and told him that I wanted to be a doctor, he cut off all support.

Geoffrey Parker, a medical officer who operated with the French *Maquis* during the Second World War gave an account of his experiences to the *Journal of the Royal Army Medical Corps*, which bore out this view. 'The effect on the morale of these irregular fighters of the presence of a few men and women with even the elements of medical training is entirely out of proportion to the actual medical services they may be able to render to the sick and wounded.' Parker reminds the medical officer who finds himself on the other side of the lines, that

> . . . he must be prepared to fight in defence of his wounded and himself . . . He must be prepared not only to bear arms but he should be skilled in their use, so that he can give a good account of himself should the necessity arise . . . he will get no respect and support from the fighting man unless he shows himself ready to play his part in this respect if called upon to do so . . . and he and his patients will die together if they have the misfortune to be captured.

Many of Parker's experiences with the partisans involved treating the wounded, while being mercilessly pursued across forests and mountains by the German Army. Operating conditions were primitive and sterility was reduced to pots of boiling water. The stress of surgery was often compounded by the fear of capture and execution:

> Abdominal wounds, in this type of war, carry with them an almost 100 per cent death rate, owing to the impossibility of operating under anything like proper surgical conditions . . . I was fortunate to have only one case of this sort due to enemy action. This man we managed to sneak down into the nearest town at night, where we operated on him in the local hospital which the *Maquis* 'took over' under the noses of the Germans for the hour and a half required to get him to the hospital and to repair some small bowel perforations, do a colostomy and open the rectal wound. The man made a good recovery.

The US Army Manual ST 31–91B *Special Forces Medical Handbook*, provides an illuminating insight into the level of skill required of the Green Beret paramedic. Early sections deal with anatomy, physiology and communicable diseases and prepare the student for more involved chapters covering symptoms and treatment of a wide range of illness and conditions. Here the topics reflect the medic's dual role. War surgery, anaesthesia, intravenous fluids, preventive medicine, dangerous animal bites, dental surgery, cardiopulmonary resuscitation, primitive medicine, mental illness, blast- and temperature-injuries are the stock-in-trade of the guerrilla doctor. Other topics such as veterinary medicine, paediatrics, gynaecology, obstetrics, orthopaedics and laboratory procedures cover the other proficiencies of a man required to bring the skills of the general practitioner to people in the often remote operational areas.

This manual serves as a text-book for what has been hailed as the 'best SF medical course in the world'. The first 18 weeks are spent on basic medicine at Fort Sam Houston in Texas. Returning to Fort Bragg, the students learn the practical aspects of the job, with emphasis on battlefield surgery. As part of this 21-week phase, the aspiring medics take part in 'Petticuts' where they learn to treat and manage animal patients suffering from gunshot and fragmentation wounds. The last four weeks are spent on attachment at the casualty department of a military hospital. More advanced training can be obtained under a scheme of rotating army medical personnel through the civilian hospitals in the Washington area, which are attempting to cope with the enormous number of knife and gunshot wounds received in the region's 'Crack Wars'.

Once in the field, the medic requires initiative and creativity, and is expected to add to a pool of medical knowledge not found in the modern text-book. The Rhodesian SAS are credited with the idea of using tampons to pack bullet wounds. Small and easily inserted into the bullet hole when dry, the cotton-wool tubes have a large absorbent capacity and expand, when wet, to fill the wound cavity and exert pressure on the cavity walls to reduce further

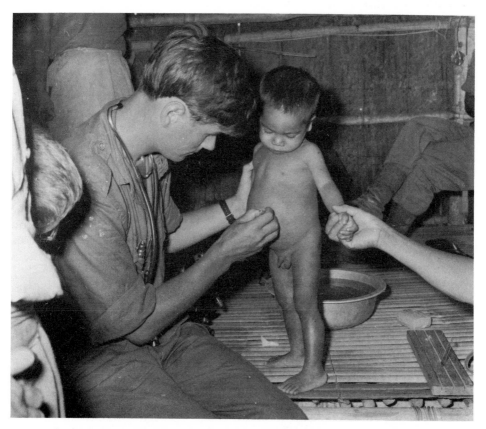

The Special Forces medic is expected to bring the skills of the general practitioner to people in the often remote operational areas. (*Imperial War Museum*)

bleeding. There are other stories of the Viet-Cong using tree sap, naturally pumped under considerable pressure to the tops of tall trees, as a plasma expander to replace blood loss in their severely wounded. Equally, the skills of the old fashioned country doctor, who was forced to practise without today's medical education and 'wonder drugs', are well suited to remote patrolling. Manuals advise that hot water and maggots will clean wounds and provide some substitute for antibiotics; tannin from tea leaves or tree bark can be used to treat dysentery; the hepatitis victim should be force-fed; and, in the absence of antibiotics, it is best to keep the patient with pneumonia on his feet.

SURVIVAL, EVASION, RESISTANCE TO INTERROGATION AND ESCAPE (SERE)

Christopher Syke's article on Operation LOYTON in the December 1961 edition of the SAS regimental magazine, *Mars and Minerva*, began: 'Every member of the SAS ought to know the name of Moussey'. Moussey was a small town in the Vosges mountains, in eastern France, and the operational area of Lieutenant Colonel Brian Frank's 2 SAS. The first elements parachuted into the area on 13 August 1944, with orders to co-operate with the Resistance in attacking German installations and lines of communication, to support the Allied invasion. The first drop was quickly followed by others until 91 SAS soldiers and six jeeps had been parachuted into the area. The operation was planned to last 10 days but six weeks later the SAS were still behind the German lines. General Patton's Army Group had been held at Nancy by a supply shortfall, allowing the Germans to stabilise the front-line. Short of supplies and pursued not only by the Wehrmacht but by counter-insurgency units of the Gestapo, Milice and SS, the unit withdrew to Moussey, where they were welcomed and provided with the much needed necessities of life. The town paid dearly for their support. On 18 August, the Germans swooped on the area and the town's 256 male inhabitants were either shot out of hand or transported to concentration or extermination camps where 144 of them died. Many other towns in the Vosges suffered a similar fate.

By September the fighting had become more confused. SAS patrols frequently returned to their base to find that the HQ had been moved to avoid encirclement and were forced to move to emergency RV's in the hope of re-contacting the main force. Other SAS men disappeared while fighting rearguard actions that allowed the rest of the unit to escape from German encirclement. With only two men killed in action, Frank's unit withdrew from the area on 9 October and moved west to contact the American Army. An exfiltration RV was left for 31 missing men, but to no avail; they had mostly been captured, tortured and executed.

SERE is about providing soldiers with the best opportunity of surviving operations that, like LOYTON, do not always run according to plan.

Survival

Survival training was starting to be taught during the Second World War. In his book, *Setting Europe Ablaze*, Sir Douglas Dodds-Parker recalls the training SOE operatives received before being dropped into occupied Europe,

> Survival training – living off the countryside – and unarmed combat were most taught at Arisaig, from a house belonging to a friend. Feeling ran high when a trainee put a grenade in the best salmon pool and, worse still, put in the game book '34 salmon'!

Today, survival training takes place under less genteel conditions. British Special Forces usually undergo 'in unit' resistance to interrogation training before attending a longer course run by the Joint Services Interrogation Unit. Training is held on the bleaker mountains and moorlands of the British Isles and usually starts with a survival phase, during which the soldiers are expected to live off the land for a period of 5–10 days. The extreme climate of these areas soon focuses the students' minds on the essentials of life: shelter, food and water. Clad in ill-fitting battle-dress and old army great-coats, the students are advised to build their shelters as small as possible to conserve their body-heat. Ideally, the small 'tactical' shelter can be constructed on a framework of branches, covered with sods of earth, with the floors lined with a deep layer of dry ferns or grass. All too often, the stark landscape provides little natural material, requiring the use of farm-yard garbage such as old corrugated tin which, with a little imagination, provides a passable alternative. For one Royal Marine, on the run from his pursuers, the ideal small, warm, tactical shelter proved to be an excavated badger sett. Another soldier found short-term sanctuary in the deeper recesses of a large bramble bush, the thorns deterring a too thorough search by the ever watchful instructors.

The students are advised to keep continually busy, improving conditions in their shelter and searching for food. By these means they escape the real enemies of the 'combat-survival' situation: boredom and a creeping lethagy that results from too little energy-producing food. Combined, they produce a depression that can overwhelm the man faced with constant hardship.

Prior to the course, the students have been trained in edible plant identification and in the recognition of common poisonous plants. One instructor has a simple method of dealing with the confusing array of Northern European wild plants: 'Unless you expect the students to become botanists, you have to teach them to recognise about 10 very common edible plants and to avoid all others.' Other instructors teach the students to rub the plants on their gums; if the plant is not bitter and if after an hour there is still no sensation of numbness or burning, it can be eaten, but initially only in small amounts. Soon the tops of young ferns, nettle and dandelion leaves and a range of nuts and fruits become part of the soldier's natural larder.

The students also receive instruction in the use of snares, fishing-lines and

Ideally, the small 'tactical' survival shelter can be constructed using a frame-work of branches covered with sods of earth. The floors are lined with a deep layer of dry ferns or grass. (*Private Collection*)

gill-nets. However, snares and lines can be inappropriate for the man on the move and the probability of a rabbit appearing in a snare can be low and alternative sources of food will have to be found. Contrary to popular opinion, wild fungi contain the same calorific value as common vegetables and considerably more protein. Smaller animals such as worms and snails are abundant and easier to catch than larger game but this represents a powerful cultural barrier to people used to eating a very restricted range of foods. As for water, this must invariably be boiled; an acute attack of 'Montezuma's Revenge' can result in a tolerable survival situation becoming desperate.

The Australian SASR place a lot of emphasis on identifying recruits who are reluctant to embark on culinary adventures. The Regiment must be prepared to meet future invaders in the desert and scrub of Australia's 'Top End'. The difficulty of re-supplying them means the Rangers will be forced to use the same natural foods as the indigenous aboriginals. A simple initial test involves presenting the recruits with unplucked chickens which have been killed and boiled. The men are expected to clean the birds before searching for the meatier morsels. Although this is not such a far cry from the usual Sunday lunch, there are a surprisingly large number of refusals.

Other units also expect their students to transcend the fixation for pre-packaged food. The American Green Berets' nickname, 'Snake-eaters', is earned on their survival course. The Berets have passed on their techniques and their students, the South Korean Rangers, not to be outdone, have added the refinement of killing their poisonous meal with a karate strike and eating it raw. More exotic dishes are to be found on the dinner table at the end of the British Exmoor course. Here the multi-course meal is a fair representation of the native fauna, consisting of hedgehog, rat, squirrel, wild plants and seaweed, cooked or *au natural*.

Occasionally survival training leaves a student with a craving for a particular dish and one RAF Forward Air Controller attached to the Parachute Regiment was moved to capture his meals on the hoof in the parks around Aldershot. Finally, he was brought in front of the CO and reminded that 'it is unseemly for an officer to be seen trapping squirrels in public'.

Survival training teaches self-reliance and, apart from providing an essential alternative to re-supply, it can enable a soldier to live for long periods in a 'combat-survival' mode while evading capture or waiting for his country's conventional forces to make an appearance. No longer should there be a desperate need to risk betrayal and capture by making the dangerous contact with local civilians; a contact, as demonstrated by Operation LOYTON, that can be as dangerous to them as it is to him.

Resistance to Interrogation

Survival training is frequently used as a softening-up process for resistance to interrogation. It generally ends with a short evasion course where, for the purposes of the exercise, even the most cunning and adept soldiers, who successfully avoid contact with the 'enemy' and reach the final RV, will find themselves captured. By now the men are cold and exhausted and are experiencing the slowing down of the body that results from insufficient food. A further softening-up process follows capture, when the 'enemy force', usually an infantry unit, manhandle the bound and blindfolded captives on and off vehicles. The interrogation training that follows must be limited in its aims as all the captives know that for reasons of time and expense these exercises are allotted a finite timespan. In Britain, resistance-to-interrogation training only takes place after a medical examination and little or no physical abuse or torture is applied. The emphasis is on psychological stress and physical discomfort to break down the soldier's resistance to questioning.

The power of the interrogator first had a galvanising effect on Western intelligence officers during the Korean War. Gone was the crude and often self-defeating technique of coercion through torture. The product of Communist re-education was a docile individual who not only co-operated with his captors but appeared in public to denounce America and extol the virtues of his new life under Communism. Worse followed repatriation, when some prisoners publicly announced that they had no wish to live in America and sought to return to their new comrades. Veterans appeared on the streets, handing out leaflets condemning the American way of life and urging the American people to withdraw from the conflict.

To Alan Dulles, the ex-OSS Director of the CIA, ordinary American kids had been transformed into enemy aliens by 'brain-washing': a systematic destruction and remoulding of their personality, beliefs and values. It is therefore no surprise that it was to Western psychiatry that the CIA looked for answers. The programme was encapsulated in an infamous project (MK-ULTRA), designed to learn the secrets of mind-control and turn these techniques back on the Communists. The project ranged from farcical experiments in which LSD was administered to unsuspecting victims (although this was stopped after the LSD-induced suicide of an operative), to horrendous attempts to remould the personalities of Canadian psychiatric patients and Vietnamese prisoners-of-war.

In reality, the philosopher's stone that enabled the Communist interrogators to redesign the human personality was a keen appreciation of the everyday social behavioural props that we all depend upon. For most of us, social interaction is important; isolation is abhorred. For American prisoners in Vietnam, the isolation started when they were told that they had been posted 'Missing in Action', 'You are ours', they were told, 'Nobody knows that you are here.' The process was calculated to breed despair, force co-operation and convince the prisoner that there was little point in continuing to hold out.

Conditioning can take place under conditions of solitary confinement, when the prisoner's conception of time and place begins to dissolve. Removal from reality can be taken further by hooding, or by the more advanced technique of total immersion in warm, black, neutral buoyant water designed to achieve total sensory deprivation. Alternatively, constant high level noise or discordant 'white noise' maintains and intensifies the fear that the prisoner is experiencing. In his book *Tiger Men*, Barry Petersen relates his experiences during a 12-day interrogation conducted at the Australian School of Military Intelligence (nicknamed the 'School of Torture' by the Australian media), for soldiers trained for special operations in Vietnam. 'I was losing all sense of time. There was no night or day, no measure of hours, nor any clear routine to give life an intelligible pattern. I was in a constant state of apprehension about unpleasant experiences that were always imminent.'

Isolation can take other forms and the prisoner's captors may seek to isolate him socially from his fellow prisoners. On a British exercise, the interrogators provided one soldier with a meal, telling him that the exercise was over. While he was eating, a door was opened so that he was seen by other members of his unit as they filed down a corridor. His comrades were informed; 'X has told us everything; we have no more questions.' In an atmosphere of fear and deprivation, preferential treatment can quickly breed suspicion and social isolation. As for the meal, it was promptly removed as soon as the subterfuge was completed.

During questioning, the interrogator seeks an initial piece of information, even a lie, which will serve as a hook on which to hang further questions. The lowering of the prisoner's self-respect, combined with demands for an exaggerated respect for his captors, can result in a compulsion to answer the questions that are put to him. Another mistake is attempting to mislead the interrogator. In his book *Living Dangerously*, Sir Ranulph Fiennes, an officer with 21 SAS, recounts his capture during a 'raid' on RAF Lossiemouth: 'under interrogation, I signed a form with the signature Elizabeth Regina and answered erroneously all questions asked of me, including my name, rank and number. Wrong. Resistance-to-interrogation rules demand that SAS men sign nothing under interrogation and say nothing save their number, rank and

In Britain, survival training is followed by evasion and mock tactical questioning (resistance-to-interrogation). (*PMA Pictures*)

name, which should be given accurately.' His penance was a resistance-to-interrogation course, 'After spending ten hours naked, blindfolded, wet and cold, being dragged through nettles and dog messes, and long spells of physical jerks of less than a comfortable nature, I was rehabilitated.'

Every utterance, no matter how banal, will provide the interrogator with more pieces of the jigsaw and some appreciation of the strength of the prisoner's personality. During the Vietnam War, American activists sympathetic to the North, were asked to furnish background information on prisoners held by the Communists. The prisoners were then confronted with a personal dossier so complete that it even contained thumb-nail sketches of their neighbours. Doctored information, designed to lower morale, could also be inserted, apparently to show for instance, that a man's children were on drugs and that his wife, despairing of his ever returning, had taken a lover. The endpoint is the weakening of the personality and the destruction of long established values and beliefs by fear and isolation. Now the interrogator works to implant the seeds of guilt in the prisoner's mind that will lead to self-betrayal and finally the betrayal of country, friends and comrades.

In Soviet psychiatric institutions, drugs were used on political dissidents to hyper-accelerate this process. The techniques and knowledge learnt in these 'experiments' were then taught to doctors who serviced various terrorist groups. Hallucinogens and the major tranquilising drugs not only enable the prisoner to be handled more easily, but deepen disorientation and accelerate the onset of hallucinations and phobias that corrode the structure of the prisoner's personality. More nightmarish are the effects of another drug, Tubocurarine (curare), which is used medically as a muscle relaxant but in higher doses can result in paralysis of the diaphragm. Intubated, and with his breathing supported by artificial ventilation, the prisoner is totally dependent upon his interrogators who, at a whim, can decide not to administer the next life-giving breath; in the hands of today's skilled interrogator, 'resistance' to interrogation is soon broken.

During the Vietnam conflict it became brutally apparent that American Special Forces soldiers would be executed out-of-hand if they responded to questions by reciting parrot-fashion their number, rank and name. A better approach appeared to be the slow release of inessential information, since the value of operational intelligence declines rapidly with time – as the rest of the SF-team leave the area and the supporting agent networks (if any) are folded.

Escape and Evasion

Escape and evasion is an art form that is leavened with commonsense rules. For the highly-motivated individual, successful escape requires imagination, timing, a good plan and a feasible final destination. The literature of the Second World War is replete with successful escapes, both before and after incarceration in prisoner-of-war camps, security police prisons and even concentration camps. Each escape is individual but the common and somewhat more difficult task is remaining free.

Manuals produced for US forces advise the 'evader' not to walk on roads and tracks and to avoid all bottlenecks such as river bridges, where traffic and pedestrians can be stopped and searched. Rivers can be crossed by waiting for nightfall and tying clothing and belongings into a bundle, before swimming or rafting across. Cities and towns are to be avoided if possible, since the evader's ignorance of the local customs will immediately identify him as an 'outsider' and check-points will require identity papers and more than passable language skills. The soldier is also cautioned to avoid children who are often the first to loudly comment on the odd or unusual.

While moving through hostile country, the evader is advised to continue with normal patrol drills: not smoking and burying all excreta and food waste. Better still, the latter can be weighted down and dropped into rivers or streams. Once sighted, the enemy may well use tracker dogs but this is no guarantee of success. The evader is told that tracker dogs and their handlers move slowly and they can therefore be out-run. Dog teams start to lose their usefulness in forest and jungle. Here the evader can slow down his pursuers by doubling back and moving in loops in the hope of tangling the handler and dog who are usually connected by a long running lead. Criss-crossing streams and running on heavily used tracks may also throw the dog off the scent. In his book, *Jungle Warfare*, John Cross, an ex-commandant of the British Jungle Warfare School, relates the story of a group of Communist terrorists who, after carefully covering their tracks, left tiger paw marks to discourage their trackers.

In Vietnam, Viet-Cong guerrillas, pursued by tracker dog teams, would often cross a series of rivers using bridges that lay just below the surface of the water. If the teams proved persistent they were finally led through jungle clearings until, with their concentration lapsing, they were led into a clearing that had been selected as a killing ground by the VC lying in ambush, thus turning the tables on their pursuers.

In contrast, war-dogs such as Alsatians and Dobermanns will be released to run down the evader and, where possible, they should be killed. A British instructor explains:

> In some books you see people pulling the dog's front-legs apart, which is said to rupture the animal's heart. This may work for some dogs but in pulling his legs apart, his jaws are brought closer to your neck and face. A better technique is to let him grab a padded arm, without your being bowled over, and fall on him. That should knock the air out of him and stun him for a bit.

The enemy is also likely to throw cordons in front of the evader but if the latter moves quickly enough, these will fall behind him. Once he has escaped from the hunter/killer teams, the soldier continues on to his destination, using his survival techniques to live off the land.

Continuation training provides the Special Forces soldier with the common core skills in behind-the-lines work. It also provides another level of selection, which rejects the soldier who has survived basic selection but now finds that he cannot master the skills or meet the level of commitment required of him by his unit. He will be required to specialise in one of these tasks and probably cross-train in another. But there are no fully trained soldiers in the Special Forces and, in keeping with this philosophy of ongoing education, the applicants now face training in the many covert means used to place men behind the lines and in the many hostile environments in which they might find themselves.

3

Training for Any Role Anywhere

In James Elroy Flecker's poem *Hassan*, the Master of the Caravan questions a group of travellers,

> *But who are ye, in rags and rotton shoes,*
> *You dirty-bearded, blocking the way?*

The reply, given by Ishak, the minstrel to the Caliph, is inscribed on the 22 SAS regimental clock at Stirling Lines, Hereford,

> *We are the pilgrims, master; we shall go*
> *Always a little further: it may be*
> *Beyond that last blue mountain barr'd with snow*
> *Across that angry or that glimmering sea.*

Small-unit tactics must be employed by forces trained to live and operate on the enemy's side of the fence. These units are small, covert and vulnerable and must rely on invisibility as their primary asset. The man recruited for this sort of unit, who has successfully completed both selection and basic training, is now faced with perfecting both his individual patrol skills and his unit's specialisation. In addition, he must become self-reliant in the skills required to enter and leave hostile territory and, once behind the lines, survive not only enemy action but often a cruel terrain and climate.

TACTICS AND TRAINING: SURVIVING BEHIND THE LINES

In 1759, Major Robert Rogers issued 19 standing orders to his force of Rangers covering operations in French and Indian territory. Examination of some of these common-sense rules demonstrates just how similar they are to today's Standing Operational Procedures (SOPs):

> When you're on the march, act the way you would if you was
> sneaking up on a deer. See the enemy first.
> Tell the truth about what you see and what you do. There is an
> army depending on us for correct information.
> March single file, far enough apart so one shot can't go through
> two men.
> When we camp, half the party stays awake, while the other half
> sleeps.
> Don't ever march home the same way. Take a different route so
> you won't be ambushed.
> Keep a scout 20 yards ahead, 20 yards on each flank and 20 yards
> in the rear, so the main body can't be surprised and wiped out.
> Every night you'll be told where to meet if surrounded by a
> superior force.
> Don't sit down to eat without posting sentries.
> Don't cross a river by a regular ford.
> If somebody's trailing you, make a circle, come back onto your
> own tracks, and ambush the folks that aim to ambush you.

Today, reconnaissance patrolling is just one of the tasks of such units; but covert patrolling procedures are generally used for all long infiltrations. Here, based on experiences in different wars, overall philosophies differ. The relatively large 12-man 'A' Teams can produce a high concentration of fire-power to get the patrol out of trouble and this structure provides all the skills necessary for training indigenous guerillas. In contrast, British Special Forces tend to operate in four-man patrols, on the assumption that the smaller force is more likely to remain undetected. This belief was borne out by SAS experiences in the Second World War and in the jungle campaigns of Malaya and Borneo which were much less intense than Vietnam. The British philosophy requires the smaller module to be more intensively cross-trained, as four men must be able to furnish most of the skills of a larger force.

In Borneo, the New Zealand SAS (NZSAS) deployed with the lead scout in front, followed by the patrol commander, medic and finally the signaller, who watched the jungle behind the patrol, while wiping out any obvious tracks. Three soldiers carried the usual SLR standard infantry rifle or newer American AR-15, while the signaller or last man carried a General Purpose Machine Gun or Bren which, in the event of a contact to the front, could provide heavy covering fire once the other members of the patrol had retreated past him. To the signaller also went the task of transmitting the single coded radio message each day or, in the event of the radio failing, activating the patrol Sabre SAR beacon at pre-arranged times to be picked up on the RAF rescue net.

In thick jungle the first signs of an enemy patrol might be faint sounds or the

Movement is a problem in the jungle. Clearing dropping and landing-zones attracts the attention of the enemy. In Malaya, the SAS pioneered the dangerous technique of parachuting into the tree canopy. (*Imperial War Museum*)

briefest glimpse of a figure or indeed just a zone of unnatural silence. Under these conditions some British SAS patrols placed the signaller closer to the patrol commander and occasionally omitted the lead scout, believing that the movement and noise, however slight, made by the scout walking 20 metres in front of the patrol was an unwarranted distraction. Instead, the patrol relied on its practice of stopping for 10 minutes every half-hour to listen to the jungle noises, and for a further 10 minutes every hour to rest and listen.

The climate and steep mountainous terrain restricted Bergen weights to around 30–40lbs, reducing rations to a minimum. Some food was cached for the return journey and best use of the remainder was made by restricting intake to one evening meal, with lunch and breakfast made up of snacks, usually chocolate, raisins and a mug of tea. At the last rest stop of the day, the main meal was cooked in an atmosphere of well oiled patrol discipline. The soldier left on watch had his meal cooked for him and was replaced by the man who finished his meal first. After the meal, the patrol walked for another 30–60 minutes, clearing the cooking area and the smells that might attract unwanted attention, before moving into dense undergrowth to set up the night's Lying Up Position (LUP). Once the area had been checked for signs of the enemy, the patrol settled down for the night, each man connected to the others by a piece of string tied to his wrist. In the dark recesses of the jungle, the soldier on guard lay awake listening for the sounds that announced an Indonesian patrol moving through the area. If they came too close, a sharp tug on the communication cord had the patrol on its feet and quietly moving down a pre-arranged escape route.

Accidental contact with the enemy resulted in a brief exchange of fire and a rapid backward withdrawal: the so-called 'shoot and scoot' policy. This had the unfortunate consequence of leaving the lead scout out on a limb, a situation not to the liking of Lieutenant Skardon of the Australian SAS, who found himself patrolling with his British counterparts near the Sabah border on 6 August 1964. In thick jungle the British lead scout, suddenly confronted with a large Indonesian patrol, promptly shot the lead man, before being hit himself. As the rest of the patrol withdrew, Skardon went forward to cover the man's retreat but found himself trapped in a sunken creek bed with the dead trooper. Only after abandoning his Bergen and escape belt was Skardon able to slip through the Indonesian cordon and reach safety a day later. The affair resulted in a flurry of recriminations being exchanged between the Australian and British SAS. The Australian position, as expressed by their Commanding Officer, Colonel John Woodhouse, forced the British to rethink their contact drills:

> I believe troops will welcome, and morale demands, an order that if a man is known to have fallen the patrol will remain in the close vicinity until either they see for certain that he is dead or they recover him alive. I think we should expect to fight to the death for this.

Thereafter, Australian SAS patrols laid down an intense barrage of suppressive fire, while using fire and movement to fall back on the rear man. Once the scout had passed the last man, the patrol withdrew until it was safe to form a defensive position, at which point the commander would decide to move to the Emergency RV or, if the situation allowed, return to the point of contact to search for the missing man. Left to his own devices, the able-bodied soldier separated from his patrol faced a long, dangerous walk to a series of alternative RVs. The patrol Emergency RV remained open for four hours after the contact. Missing it meant heading for the Troop RV, usually the previous resting place, which remained open for another 12 hours, the Border RV (insertion LZ) or the War RV (nearest Security Force position). By contrast, if the whole patrol found itself in trouble, the quick transmission of a patrol codeword alerted Squadron Headquarters to send a helicopter to the extraction LZ or, *in extremis*, to home in on the patrol's position by way of the SAR beacon and pluck them from the jungle.

Tactics for the really tenacious enemy who remained in close pursuit were also developed by the American Special Forces and the Australian SAS during the Vietnam War. Some of these involved leaving the direction of march and making a wide loop in the shape of a fish-hook, to a position where the patrol overlooked the trail and could ambush the pursuers. Many such ambushes, often only firing the ubiquitous Claymore mines, were needed before the patrol was able to escape the net that the enemy was attempting to throw around them. So popular was the Claymore or 'mechanical ambush', that some Australian SAS personnel complimented it as the 'greatest thing since canned beer'. Once the pursuers had been caught in a fusillade of small-arms fire, they moved to the member of the patrol responsible for security, the 'Gate-keeper', who, on counting them through and handing them their Bergens, guided them through a carefully prepared escape route. This 'cat and mouse' game would continue until the patrol finally broke contact or reached a helicopter LZ where they could be extracted from the area.

The close reconnaissance of enemy camps and meetings with friendly agents involve particular dangers for the patrol. In his book *Jungle Warfare*, John Cross relates the rules taught at the Jungle Warfare School for the close reconnaissance of targets in Borneo. The patrol was advised to avoid paths, obliterating any tracks they made on wet soil while stopping to listen every ten minutes until the enemy camp was located. The camp was then circled at a distance of 100–200 metres, to locate the sentries. Finally, one man moved closer to prepare detailed drawings, followed by a cover man 5–15m behind. Cross's students were advised, 'If an enemy appears to look straight at you, "freeze" and he will probably not see you.'

Patrols travelling deep into the enemy's territory can be funnelled through a partisan or 'agent' network. Agents can provide a safe covert means of re-supply, providing food and information and replacing damaged equipment. An SAS manual lays down similar rules for meeting agents or partisans. Arriving the day before the pre-arranged RV, the area is watched for signs of enemy activity. On the night of the contact, one man moves slowly towards the RV in ever-decreasing circles, enabling:

> all likely ambush positions to be cleared before arrival at the RV . . . Unless there is a pre-arranged password the decision as to whether to trust the agent must be made on the spot . . . . On NO account however should the agent be given any military information. Indeed if he persists in asking [for] military information he should be regarded with suspicion.

Such are the mechanics and common-sense rules for a war behind the lines,

The foundation for today's desert operations was laid down during World War
Two. Corrugated iron troughs called 'sand channels' were used by Bagnold's
LRDG and proved invaluable in crossing stretches of soft sand. (*Imperial War
Museum*)

but to these must be added the drills and adjustments made necessary by the
many difficult terrains in which specialised units are employed.

The Desert

One-fifth of the earth's surface consists of desert. Best known to the
explorer and soldier is the great 'Dry Belt' which cuts a swath from North
Africa to the heartlands of Arabia. In these countries, the majority of people
live on the coastal fringes, their cities and sea-ports being interconnected by
long stretches of road and railway track, vital not only for the movement of
civilian traffic but also providing ease of movement and re-supply for conventional armies.

Inland lies the desert, areas where the annual evaporation rate exceeds the annual rainfall – on average less than 10 inches per year. Water supplies are meagre and confined to underground wells and oases; beyond them, small quantities of brackish water may be found in wadi beds and dry river courses but these are seasonal. Without adequate supplies of water in the open desert, death comes in two to three days. The first lesson for soldiers in the desert is water-discipline: carry sufficient and drink it sparingly at regular intervals from the water-bottle cap rather than the bottle itself. In an emergency, moisture from the ground or vegetation can be collected as it condenses on the plastic sheet of a solar-still or vegetation bag. When the temperature drops at night, moisture in the air will condense into life-giving water droplets in the form of mists and fog. Further inland, the temperature changes are smaller, there is no condensation and little vegetation. *In extremis*, moving by night and resting in shade by day may extend life to several weeks.

Novices to the desert are taught the advantages of Arab dress. In summer, the noon temperature may exceed 120°F (48°C) dropping to a mild 59°F (15°C) at night. In winter, temperatures may range from 80°F (26°C) during the day to below freezing at night. Light, loose-fitting clothing provides protection from severe sunburn and helps to reduce water loss. At night, the pockets of air trapped in the clothes act as insulation, thereby slowing heat loss.

The merchants' caravans carry their own supplies of meat on the hoof but, in an emergency, the soldier trained in survival is likely to find his next meal in a burrow or under a stone. There are over 5,000 species of birds and animals in desert areas, the great variety of insects and small mammals supporting a range of predators such as reptiles and native dogs. There are also a variety of edible plants, ranging from the fruits and stems of cacti, to millet and wild grasses, as well as fig and date palms.

Two other great problems are movement and navigation. The terrain can vary from seas of rolling sand dunes, whose changing contours defy maps, to salt flats, open scrub, deep wadis, boulder-strewn plains and the remains of ancient sea cliffs, whose escarpments can run unbroken for hundreds of miles. Years of total drought can end in a storm that releases inches of rain in hours. Unable to seep into the parched ground, the water causes flash-floods which sweep through the river courses and flood low-lying ground, carrying away all in their path. Winter also brings blinding sand and dust storms, blotting out the sun and making travel near impossible.

The Long Range Desert Group (LRDG) pioneered the art of long-range patrolling in the desert. The initial LRDG patrols consisted of 30 men and two officers in 11 30cwt trucks. Each man was trained to perform an indispensable service. Vehicle fitters kept the vehicles running, attending to the all too frequent faults caused by the ubiquitous sand which can to infiltrate into every part of the machinery. The signallers were responsible for maintaining radio contact with their base camp; without them, the patrol would have been of little military value. The drivers and navigators worked as a team, plotting and negotiating a course across the often featureless desert.

All long patrols are dependent upon good preparation: too many supplies and the overloaded vehicles would break down; too few meant hardship and death. Consequently, food, water and petrol had to be calculated to the last ounce and gallon, and consumption rigorously regulated. Into the relatively large vehicles were packed all the necessary items to ensure that the patrol could cover distances in excess of 1,500 miles and return safely. Corrugated iron troughs called 'sand channels' were used by the LRDG's commander, Major Ralph Bagnold, in his pre-war expedition across Sinai, and proved invaluable in crossing stretches of soft sand. The heavy loads, rough terrain and intense heat all took their toll on the tyres. Consequently, each vehicle carried 15 or more spares, which competed for space with ammunition, mines, rations and the usual 50 jerrycans of petrol.

The key to long range patrols in the desert has always been navigation. Arriving at the right time at an oasis, petrol cache, small enemy camp or a rendez-vous, which might be no more than a pile of stones on an otherwise featureless expanse of sand might mean the difference between success and failure, or even life and death, as constant corrections to the course meant more consumption of precious petrol and water. For the LRDG, the key to navigation was a thorough knowledge of navigational astronomy. Astro-navigation is a difficult and painstaking science. The positions of several stars and planets, relative to the horizon, are noted at a precise time, usually supplied by a time signal or the navigator's chronometer. Reference is then made to tables in the *Nautical Almanac* and a series of corrections and calculations yields 'lines of position', giving the observer's latitude and longitude. However, navigation involves more than knowing where you are at the end of each day's travel.

A typical day's journey averaged 150 miles and their progress was charted by a careful watch on the vehicle's odometer. The patrol set its initial course by magnetic compass using an intermediate landmark on the horizon by day and a star by night. But once on the move, and in the absence of landmarks, there was a great danger of drifting off course. A mounted compass would have allowed the driver continually to note changes in direction but this was problematic as the particular magnetic-mass of the vehicle had to be compensated for. The long, painstaking compensation procedure involved positioning two small bar-magnets underneath the compass, but the careful work was quickly undone by the constant jarring received in the rough ride across the desert. At the end of the day, the convoy could be tens of miles off course.

A simple alternative was the sun-compass: a simple 'sun-dial' device constructed so that the sun's shadow fell onto an outer ring marked out in the degrees of the compass. Using the knowledge that the sun covers an arc of 15° in one hour, the operator could calculate either the north-south line or the local time. On the move, the sun-compass was adjusted every half-hour to compensate for the sun's passage across the sky. At night, the device could be used in strong moonlight.

LRDG desert lore was passed to David Stirling's SAS and although subject to constant revaluation, has been handed down to today's SAS Mobility Troops. Australia did not share in the desert traditions, its sea-borne raiding forces having operated in the Pacific. When the Australian SASR was fighting for continued existence in the post-Vietnam era, it began to look at a new role: countering threats to the northern areas of Australia. As part of the plan, vehicle-mounted reconnaissance operations, along the lines of the LRDG, were envisaged in the Australian deserts. Sun compasses were considered to be of such importance to this plan that two SASR NCO's were sent to Britain on Exercise LONG LOOK to investigate the instruments and their use for long-range patrol vehicles. They returned empty-handed. Sun-compasses and the rest of navigational astronomy appeared to have been superseded by the enormous range of new technology that culminated in the navigational satellite global positioning systems.

For the ordinary soldier satellite navigation came of age during the Gulf War. Several US manufacturers which produced relatively cheap hand-held positioning systems were deluged with individual credit card sales from US troops in Saudi Arabia. The major function of the Global Positioning System (GPS) is to allow ships and aircraft to obtain their position down to an accuracy of 10–16 metres. The basic principle is relatively simple. The 21 satellites are in polar orbits 20,000 km above the earth's surface. GPS equipment compares the time that each satellite broadcasts its signal to the time at which it was actually received on the ground. This allows an accurate triangulation of the observer's position. The GPS equipment can be carried as a man-pack or vehicle-mounted. The Magellan GPS NAV 1000M is ideal for Special Forces use. Weighing only 0.85kg and slightly larger than a pocket calculator, it updates the observer's position every second, providing an average position accuracy of 15 metres. Various models provide readings using different co-ordinate systems (latitude/longitude for aircraft, Military Grid Reference for ground troops and Universal Transverse Mercator for artillery) and headings in degrees, radians or mils. The device contains 46 map data, plus an additional map which can be chosen by the user. The NAV 1000M can also receive operational data from a computer database, which is compared to the observer's position and the position of his target. Instructions such as 'Steer Left 10 Degrees' guide the user through a series of way-points to his target. Unlike the traditional methods of navigation, GPS is unaffected by adverse desert weather conditions such as sand storms.

At $3,500 per unit, these navigational aids were heavily used by both conventional and Special Forces. Magellan claims to have sold 500 to the 5th Infantry, an unspecified number to the Marines, 600 to the Saudis and another 600 to the British Ministry of Defence. Unfortunately, there was little to prevent the enemy from using the GPS satellites and the Iraqis are reported to have used GPS in aligning their Scud missiles (Allied Special Forces un-doubtedly used GPS in targeting the Scuds for air-attacks). It is possible to downgrade the accuracy of the GPS to 100m by adjusting the satellite's time clocks – a selective adjustment can then be made by friendly forces. However, during the Gulf War the American Department of Defense decided to leave the accuracy unaltered, probably because of the proliferation of small commercial receivers amongst the Allied ground forces.

The British SAS Mobility Troops earmarked for today's desert operations

The Magellen NAV 1000M. (*Magellan Systems Corp.*)

The post-war SAS Landrovers designed for desert operations were camouflaged pink, hence their famous nickname 'Pink Panthers'. (*PMA Pictures*)

are equipped with a range of vehicles including armed motor-cycles for reconnaissance and raiding duties. Like their predecessors in the LRDG, the men of Mobility Troop are expected to become experts in using and maintaining their vehicles, under all conditions. Until recently, the main vehicle was the MkIX Land Rover, originally modified for the British SAS by Marshalls of Cambridge, which came equipped with 'extras' such as suncompasses and were capable of carrying sufficient fuel for 1,000 mile round trips. Originally designed for desert operations in Oman, the vehicles, which were camouflaged pink, (hence their famous nickname 'Pink Panthers') also carried theodolite and machine-gun mounts.

For desert operations the Panther has now been replaced by the 'Light Strike Vehicle'. Among its many assets, this is reputed to climb slopes in excess of 50°, operate effectively in soft sand and turn 360° in a 12m turning circle. Tailormade for desert operations by Longline Ltd, the vehicle is capable of operating within a 200km radius at speeds in excess of 100kph while maintaining a low radar and infra-red silhouette, allowing the penetration of heavily defended areas for reconnaissance/surveillance and raiding tasks. The Strike vehicles also carry GPS satellite navigation and communication equipment but the British manufacturers have wisely avoided the modern computerised engine technology enabling the vehicle to be easily serviced under

Today, the SAS 'Pink Panther' has been replaced by the 'Light Strike Vehicle'. Among its many assets, it is reputed to climb slopes in excess of 50°, operate effectively in soft sand and turn 360° in a 12m turning circle. (*Longline Ltd*)

operational conditions. The basic platform can be adapted to carry a range of weapons also making it ideal for Quick Reaction Force operations (see Chapter 14) and scouting or anti-tank duties. Capable of being para-dropped or slung under transport helicopters, the LSV won the hearts of the SAS and British MOD during a trial in which the vehicle was dropped by parachute. Much to the distress of the observers, the pallet containing the LSV experienced a major parachute failure, with the result that the vehicle lost a wheel on impact. Undeterred the SAS Mobility Troop personnel adjusted the suspension and drove off the DZ to complete the rest of the exercise on three wheels!

Arctic and Mountain Warfare

Britain maintains two specialist sub-units trained in unconventional operations in the mountains and the Arctic: the Royal Marines Cadre and the Mountain Troops deployed by 22 SAS. The parent units themselves also prepare for this eventuality by taking part in a series of exercises in Norway each year.

The snow-shelter not only provides protection from the bitter cold and chilling winds but effectively allows the patrol to disappear from the landscape. (*PMA Pictures*)

Unit instructors in this specialisation are trained on a number of NATO courses. The Arctic and Mountain Warfare Cadre accepts British and some overseas soldiers on its ML-2 course. There is the *Heeresbergfuhrer* (Mountain Guide) course run by the 1st Mountain Division at the German *Gebirgs und Winterkampf Schule* (Mountain and Winter Warfare School) at Luttensee in Bavaria, which is said to be one of the most demanding within NATO but places less emphasis on tactical warfare than the course run by the Royal Marines. The German course concentrates on winter survival, applied medicine, mountain rescue, climbing and long-distance skiing. After initial selection for the course there are five weeks of intensive rock climbing, followed by training in ice cliff climbing in the French Alps near Chamonix. This prepares the men for the serious business of ascending peaks in the Mont Blanc area.

The summer phase of the course ends with more training in the Dolomites and a traverse of the eastern face of the Waltzmann. After Christmas, the training switches to moving and surviving in the mountains under winter conditions. The training in skiing culminates in the obligatory examination for the West German Ski Association's Instructors qualification and prepares the men for a long mountain ski-patrol across peaks in the Gran Paradiso area of Italy. The course ends at Luttensee where the men have to pass a series of tests before receiving their *Heeresbergfuhrer* accreditation.

While most northern Europeans are used to cold winters, soldiers have to be taught how to cope with the extreme winter climate found in regions close to the poles. The ground freezes at night and thaws during the day producing mud and slush. In areas with daytime temperatures below freezing, the environment is said to be dry cold; flesh fuses with metal almost on contact and a soldier can discover, too late, that grenades and rifles easily become welded to his mittens. A cold, but acceptable, ambient temperature of $-29°C$ is reduced to a deadly $-62°C$ wind chill temperature by a 30mph wind.

Winter survival training teaches the men to dress in insulating layers to trap body heat. Mountain and Arctic Warfare Cadre instructors recommend women's tights to Royal Marines preparing for their first exercise in Norway. Clothes must also be kept dry and clean and the outer shell should be windproof. Wet uniforms quickly lose their insulation and can freeze solid. Wet socks produce the numbing pain of Trench Foot that was common in the Falkland's campaign and frost-bite, hypothermia and snow-blindness are constant dangers.

Other arctic survival lessons are not so obvious. In areas of extreme cold, water requirements are greatly increased. Increased body metabolism, breathing the cold dry air and the extremely low humidity can cause dehydration. Dehydrated rations exacerbate the situation, increasing a man's water requirements to about six quarts per day. Although the soldier is surrounded by an abundance of water in the form of ice, snow, melt-water, or water from streams and lakes, the ingesting of ice, snow and cold water is not recommended as it can dangerously lower the body temperature and actually causes further dehydration. The melting of ice and snow, and the purification

The novice discovers that trudging through deep snow with a heavy Bergen quickly leads to exhaustion and exposure. (*PMA Pictures*)

of the water by boiling, require a lot of energy and are a large drain on the precious fuel supplies. Heat from a fire or body heat may have to be used to melt the snow before it can be used.

The novice discovers that trudging through deep snow with a heavy Bergen quickly leads to exhaustion and exposure. Skis are essential for arctic conditions and the experienced man can move at speeds of more than 10km per hour throughout the night. One disadvantage of the terrain is that the virgin snowscape faithfully records the tracks of all who pass through it. Care must be taken to minimise the ski-trails that will alert an enemy patrol to the presence of the SF-team behind their lines. The patrol may move in single file, skiing in the leader's tracks to give the impression of a solitary traveller, such as a hunter or herdsman. Alternatively, they can remain close to the tree-line and seek to break the tracks by moving through cleared areas, but once the patrol's ski-track has been picked up by an enemy force few options are left. They can attempt to out-ski their pursuers, wait in ambush or disperse, leaving the enemy with a multitude of tracks to follow. If the latter course is taken, the patrol must meet at a prearranged RV before dawn, to disappear from the landscape into a snow shelter.

The Jungle

As part of their basic training, recruits to the SAS and other special force units undergo training at the jungle warfare schools where tactics for this terrain have been distilled from the lessons of many jungle wars. Since the Second World War, many of the 'low-intensity' conflicts have been fought in this environment and the jungle is only 'neutral' in that it kills both friend and foe alike. A Second World War SOE manual warned: 'Treat the jungle with respect, even with fear.'

For many soldiers, their first experience of this gloomy, claustrophobic environment **was** a frightening one and much of the early training was designed to familiarise them with the jungle. One SAS man who fought in Borneo described the transition from open scrub to jungle:

> It was like leaving a room with a 1,000-watt bulb and entering a room with a 20-watt bulb. I was very keen to see the wildlife but the birds and animals fell silent at your approach so, as you moved through the jungle, you were immediately surrounded by a zone of silence. Often you didn't see the enemy, you were just aware of another zone of silence moving towards or parallel to you.

He also recalled the high level of anxiety that this new world produced:

> We used hammocks to get off the wet jungle floor and get away from all the creepy crawlies. On the first night, I must have rolled over in my sleep and when I awoke, I was facing an empty clearing. The panic! I thought the patrol had moved out without me!

The soldiers quickly came to appreciate the special problems created by this environment. In areas of primary jungle, 200ft-high trees blotted out the sunlight, making ground cover sparse and movement fairly easy. However, communications were often difficult and the signaller had to make a dangerous climb, carrying the wireless aerial into the canopy, before contact with base could be established. Re-supply or extraction by helicopter often required the same climb in order to attract the attention of the aircraft. Where the rain forests had been cleared by slash-and-burn agricultural methods and then left to regenerate, (secondary jungle) movement was often difficult, slow and noisy. Vines, scrub, creepers and bushes had to be overcome. A large bamboo grove could take days to negotiate and small hills could become ferocious barriers. An old jungle hand recalls his frustration:

> We spent eight days moving through the jungle to relieve an OP [Observation Post] on top of a hill. On the eighth day we arrived on a neighbouring hill. We could see the men in the OP and could have even shouted across to them but it took us another day and a half to reach them!

A small patrol probes for the enemy in his gloomy, claustrophobic jungle sanctuaries. (*Imperial War Museum*)

Before it was suitable for drinking, all water needed to be filtered and sterilised. A cleaner source of water was the condensation that formed in the morning and poured from trees like a fine rain. Other sources of pure water are less obvious and needed to be identified for the students. Water can become trapped within the sections of green bamboo and can be obtained from other plants such as the Water Tree by slashing the bark or from banana plants by making a bowl or 'banana-well' out of the stump.

Probably the most important lessons in jungle survival concern personal hygiene. The hot, wet environment produces excellent conditions for the growth of bacteria and fungi. Abrasions and cuts quickly turn septic and must be cleaned and liberally sprinkled with antibiotics. In Malaya, Borneo and Vietnam, rashes and jungle rot, caused in part by the friction rub of tightly fitting clothes, were prevented by smearing feet, armpits and genitals with vaseline. In Vietnam, many soldiers combated this complaint by throwing away their issue underwear. Carbuncles and boils are also produced by the friction rub of dirty, sweat-ridden clothes.

Mosquitoes and ticks abound and are capable of carrying hideous tropical diseases. Equally nasty pests lurk in the foliage and the water. All six members of an SOE patrol in Sumatra went down with deadly Leptospiral fever after crossing a rat infested pool with abrasions on their feet. Larger parasites, such as leeches, lurk under leaves, awaiting the chance to live up to their reputation as 'the greatest jungle pest.' Sandflys, mites and ticks, hidden in the bamboo groves and swamps, also compete for this dubious title.

The abundant plant and animal life provides a living larder for the individual schooled in plant recognition and trapping, but the larger animals can be a danger in themselves. On 2 June 1965, two Australian SASR soldiers were injured by an elephant, while returning from an infiltration mission along the Sabah/Kalimantan border in Borneo. During the next day and night, the elephant, apparently shrugging off the wounds made by nine bullets, continued to stalk the patrol, cutting them off from the border and the helicopter LZ. Finally, two soldiers ran the gauntlet of the enraged elephant and enemy patrols to get help, leaving the seriously injured man, who had been gored by the beast, in the capable hands of the patrol medic. On 6 June, a rescue party reached the LUP, only to find that Lance-Corporal Paul Denehey had died in agony as the medication ran out.

Tropical swamps are often horrendous areas to cross, being filled with poisonous snakes and, in some areas, man-eating salt-water crocodiles. On 19–20 February 1945, a force of 1,000 Japanese soldiers were retreating through the tidal mangroves of Ramree Island on the Burmese coast. Night found them still snared in the knee-deep mud, vainly attempting to reach high ground; many had wounds that bled liberally into the water. With darkness came the big reptiles, attracted by the blood and the sound of gunfire. British soldiers later described it as a 'night of hell' and reported hearing screams and the sound of heavy thrashing bodies as the giant reptiles grabbed their prey. In the morning, there were only 20 Japanese soldiers left to surrender to the advancing British troops.

4

Covert Insertion and Extraction

'There are very few people who would want to jump out of a perfectly good airplane into an ocean with three to five foot waves during daylight. Fewer still would want to do it at night.'
PH1 Chuck Mussi, 'Sea, Air and Land, Getting There is Half the Battle'; *All Hands*: Magazine of the US Navy.

In the world's inhospitable deserts, jungles and polar wastes, or in the rear of a retreating enemy army, it may be possible to insert SF-teams on foot, or by armed-landrover or helicopter. Here the enemy is scattered and contact unlikely, but a hostile enemy country bristling with troops and defences requires special operational techniques and a long, broken coastline or the unbounded sky may offer the best possibility for covert insertion. Training in modern insertion techniques requires not only a willingness to undertake this often hazardous task but also an ability to cope with increasingly advanced technology.

GETTING IN AND GETTING BACK OUT BY AIR

Static-Line Parachuting

Parachuting is a prerequisite for special operations and the parachute is often a coveted symbol of these troops. The basic static-line parachute course is obligatory for most of the world's Special Forces. In Britain, the course takes the form of extensive ground training that teaches the prospective parachutist the correct way to distribute his weight quickly on landing through of the parachute roll. Elbows and head tucked in, candidates learn to land, whether

While static-line parachuting is no longer possible over the hi-tech battlefield, it remains the method of choice for quick reaction force and maritime operations. (*Special Forces HQ; Australian DOD*)

approaching the ground from the rear, front or side. Outdoor exit trainers simulate the buffeting aircraft slipstream by bouncing the man along 70 metres of wire. Throughout this first period of training, the student learns how to exit from the aircraft, steer away from other parachutists, deploy his reserve parachute and land. The 'jumps' start at ground level and progress from ramps, exit trainers and a 70-foot tower to two actual descents from a balloon tethered at an altitude of 800 feet.

The students then progress to aircraft descents from the C-130 Hercules. The first two are 'clean fatigue' jumps carrying only the main PX-Mk4 parachute and the PR-7 reserve, the latter carried on the chest. Unlike the American T-10, the PX-4 is not steerable, although some control over rate of descent and direction is possible by using the lift webs to spill air from the inflated 'chute. The PX-4 is, however, ideally suited to British operations where sticks of parachutists leave both sides of the aircraft and cross paths behind the aircraft's tail. Under these conditions the deployment of a steerable parachute with a preferred direction would increase the incidence of mid-air collisions.

The last sequence of jumps introduces the students to parachuting with a personal-equipment container and weapon. Thick webbing straps secure the Bergen and weapon sleeve, which are clipped below the reserve. Once in the air, the container is released to hang below the parachutist on a suspension rope. Carrying over 100lbs of equipment, the physical and mental stress of each jump is said to be the equivalent of eight hours manual work. Later in their squadron or company, they may be faced with descents carrying Bergens packed with explosives, ammunition or support weapons. Some men, carrying over 300lb of kit, have to be carried to the door of the aircraft and pushed out into the slipstream. The relatively slow aircraft that transport parachutists to their dropping zones are vulnerable to anti-aircraft defences and enemy fighter aircraft. Consequently, today, static-line parachuting is retained only for humanitarian Quick Reaction Forces and special operations in Third World countries.

LALO Parachuting

Another great problem associated with static-line parachuting is that once the parachute begins to float gently to the ground, the parachutist offers a highly visible target, remaining helpless until he reaches the ground. The obvious answer to this problem lies with a technique called Low Altitude Low Opening (LALO). LALO descents involve the parachutist leaving the aircraft at 300–400 feet, thus maintaining a low profile to ground-fire and reducing the time spent in the air.

Standard parachutes 'breathe' after opening in order to reduce opening shock. This takes the form of the canopy contracting immediately after opening and before assuming a stable configuration. This initial instability is important because it increases the altitude at which most parachutes can be deployed. In order to reduce the minimum safe drop height, both America and

Britain are seeking parachutes with little or no post-inflation collapse. This would allow an operational deployment height of 250ft (76m), reducing the time spent in the air to less than 15 seconds.

Other countries are working on the same problem. The French Army's current assault parachute, the Aerazur TAP 696–26, has an operational drop height of 400ft (125m). The German solution, the T3F, was more unusual: it consisted of three small parachutes and had an operational deployment of only 260ft (80m). This 'chute was designed to be used without a reserve as it was claimed that one parachute would always inflate. Unfortunately the T3F was associated with fatalities and was withdrawn from service. In one instance, one of the canopies wrapped itself around the other two: a common problem when more than one canopy is deployed at the same time. In fact LALO jumps, with all parachutes, require an act of faith on the part of the parachutist as so little time is spent in the air that it is difficult to fully deploy a reserve.

HALO and HAHO Parachuting

Today, the main technique for covertly inserting small groups of Special Forces is known as High Altitude Low Opening (HALO). Here the parachutists leave the aircraft at heights of up to 30,000ft (10,000m) and, on reaching terminal velocity at 120–170mph, fall virtually unseen through the enemy's radar defences. Alternatively, the parachutists may assume a delta position, arching the body into a crude aerofoil to track across the sky at 180 mph. This technique allows the free-faller to move at 35° degrees from vertical and literally fly towards a distant DZ. Once the parachute is opened, the highly manoeuvrable aerofoil canopies used on HALO operations allow the parachutist to land in a very small target area.

High altitudes are a hostile environment. Even above a noon-day desert with ground temperatures of 38°C, the parachutist will experience temperatures of around −21°C (−5°F). As he falls through the air, he will experience a further drop in temperature due to the wind-chill effect. At a 100 miles an hour, the temperature outside his protective suit will be around −90°C. At these temperatures the equipment starts to ice up and any exposed flesh suffers immediate severe frost-bite.

Like a diver, the parachutist must begin to breath an air-oxygen mix as soon as the aircraft is de-pressurised. At 35,000ft, without breathing apparatus, unconsciousness would occur within 60 seconds. However, the breathing apparatus is no guarantee of safety and, if anxiety causes the parachutist to hyperventilate into his mask, a reduction of carbon dioxide in the blood can also result in a blackout.

Unlike the sports parachutist, the soldier carries an inverted Bergen low on his back, slung under the main 'chute. The large amount of equipment necessary for military free-fall makes it difficult to maintain a stable position and opening the parachute while spinning uncontrollably at more than a 100 mph

HALO parachuting has become the technique of choice for covert airborne insertion. (*PMA Pictures*)

is tantamount to disaster. Failure to maintain stability is the chief reason that many applicants withdraw from HALO training. In order to allow the parachutist to concentrate on maintaining stability, the parachute is rigged to open automatically at a set height, the trigger sensing changes in air pressure.

Where it is undesirable for the aircraft to enter enemy airspace, the team may open their parachutes immediately (High Altitude High Opening) and glide across the border to a DZ as far as 30 miles inside the foreign country. This technique also employs highly manoeuvrable parachutes with maximum glide characteristics. The American's use the MT-1X square parachute. Electro-luminescence produces glowing green and white strips that can be seen from above but not from the ground. This enables the parachutists to remain separated in flight.

HAHO poses severe navigational problems for the parachutist, particularly at night. Chest-pack navigational systems, such as the Texas Instruments AN/APS-9A Global Positioning System, have been developed to overcome these problems. The GPS obtains an accurate fix of the parachutist's current position by way of signals from a navigation satellite, such as the Navstar GPS, and calculates a three-dimensional course, through up to 100 way-points, to the predesignated landing zone. The parachutist's position is up-dated every second and the system has an accuracy of 16 metres or less.

Mosquito Aviation

In an interview for *Jane's Defence Weekly*, General James Lindsay, the first Commander-in-Chief of US Special Operations Command (USSOCOM), re-flected current thinking when he suggested that parachutes were 1930's tech-nology and that the American Special Forces were actively seeking alterna-tives. In the mid-1980s other ways of flying to the target were examined by the Soviet Spetsnaz forces, namely Very Light Aircraft (VLA) such as hang-gliders and microlites. This so-called 'Mosquito Aviation' was considered ideal for special operations and deep raids and the Spetsnaz are now reported to have deployed several VLA sub-units and detachments.

In 1981, Syrian Air Force Intelligence procured 12 powered hang-gliders for two Palestine terrorist organisations. In March of the same year, two hang-gliders were used in the abortive attack on the Haifa oil refinery. Armed with bombs and grenades, the pilots took off from Lebanon but soon became lost and were captured soon after landing in Israel. Subsequently, training facilities were set up at Syrian Air Force Intelligence bases in Rayhan and Ayn al-Sabah, where training was overseen by officers of the Soviet Air Force and military intelligence (GRU). Experts from a West German company were recruited by the PFLP-GC to modify their VLAs by installing quieter engines and navigation guidance systems.

Modified hang-gliders were used by the PFLP-GC, in November 1987, to attack Kiryat Shomona. Four hang-gliders were launched from Sultan Yaakub in Syrian-controlled Lebanon and one landed near the Israeli Army base at Kiryat, where the pilot was able to kill six soldiers and wound ten others before being shot. Of the other VLAs that took part in the raid, one was forced by a mechanical problem to return to base and the other two crashed en route. More recently, VLAs have been used by Shi'ite suicide bombers in-volved in Lebanon's sectarian fighting. It is reported that Iran, Libya and the Hezbollah are currently adapting VDLs for terrorist operations.

Helicopters

Post-war military operations have been revolutionised by the helicopter. So-called rotary-wing operations allow a large force to fly dispersed, taking full advantage of the cover offered by the terrain, and converging at the Landing Zone (LZ) to deliver a large combat force close to a surprised enemy. While playing a valuable role in conventional operations, helicopters also provide one of the main methods of inserting and extracting SF-teams. Helicopter insertions avoid the risk of injury associated with military parachuting, esti-mated at about seven per cent. In jungle, swamp or mountainous terrain, where it is difficult for the helicopter to land, the team can leave the hovering aircraft and abseil to the ground, negotiating obstacles on the way. In the rain forests of South East Asia, this proved preferable to attempting dangerous parachute landings into the 150ft-high tree canopy.

Extraction Techniques

Long range reconnaissance patrolling in Vietnam provided the incentive for extraction techniques that would literally snatch patrols from the jaws of the enemy. The Recondo School (Reconnaissance Commando School), 5th Special Forces Group, designed the Stability Operations Extraction System or STABO Rig; in the field the thick webbing harness carried ammunition and water bottles but the 'D' rings sewn into the shoulders could be attached to a rope lowered by a helicopter and the man hoisted to safety.

A more dramatic form of rescue came in the form of the Skyhook, also called the Fulton Surface to Air Recovery System (STAR) after its inventor, Robert E. Fulton Jnr, the grandson of the famous steamboat inventor. Basically this device allowed the team to step onto an aircraft moving at 150 miles per hour. Here the extraction rigs were attached to a helium balloon via a 500ft nylon rope, allowing one or more 'passengers' to be snatched out of a small jungle clearing by an aircraft equipped with a yoke or wide fork attached to its nose, and winched aboard. At night, stroboscopic lights on the lift line allowed the pilot to line up the aircraft with the extraction system. This is obviously not the preferred method of extraction and the system was mainly used to recover sick personnel, prisoners and valuable cargoes. However, in the face of air defences restricting friendly air operations, teams that are inserted by air are often left to find their own way home, crossing the border of a neutral country or making their way towards that other natural border – the coast.

Problems of Sea-borne Insertion

The sea provides not only access to enemy shipping and coastal defences but also holds possibilities for insertion for inland targets and missions. The Second World War saw ample use of these opportunities, with raiding forces

In jungle, swamp or mountainous terrain, where it is difficult for the helicopter to land, the team can leave the hovering aircraft and abseil to the ground. (*PMA Pictures*)

throughout Europe and the Pacific carried to their target by fishing boat, landing craft, submarine, mini-submersible, canoe and the sea-borne equivalent of legs – diver's fins. However, the problems of landing clandestine operatives on the beaches of occupied countries were legion. One submarine commander wrote: 'It is hard to imagine any operation more simple and elementary than this: merely one man to be landed with his stores. Reasonable weather, no enemy opposition, bright moonlight.' But this landing in Malaya took three nights to complete and nearly ended in disaster. On the first night, the operative and his stores were successfully ferried to the beach and the boat party helped him carry them some way inland. A 'boat-keeper' was left standing in the sea, holding on to the canoes. He was without a watch but had been told that the party would return by 0300hrs, precisely one hour after the moon set. But waiting on his own, standing up to his neck in the water, drastically altered his perception of time and his estimate of 60 minutes became a mere 20. Consequently, he returned to the submarine alone and it took two more fraught nights to recover the stranded sailors.

Today, those attempting covert infiltration onto beaches must avoid not only the gaze of the enemy sentry but also the very sophisticated radar and sonar nets that cover the sea approaches to most countries. In effect, this mostly rules out the use of large surface vessels such as fishing boats. The canoe, however, still remains a viable option. The ocean-going Klepper or the more advanced French and German canoes can be parachuted into the sea with the team. Once on a raft or beach, the wooden skeleton is easily assembled and covered with the outer skin, which is drawn taut by inflating the internal buoyancy bags. The 15ft canoe carries a two-man crew, Bergens and equipment and its low visual and radar silhouette makes it ideal for covert coastal and river incursions. Once ashore, the canoe can be dismantled or filled with water and left at the bottom of the river, to await the team's return.

Patrol Submarine

A frequent mode of transport for maritime special units is still a submarine on patrol within the designated operational area. A transport aircraft, such as the C-130, carries the team to a rendezvous with the vessel and makes radio contact with the submarine running at periscope depth. The boat releases smoke or illuminating flares to mark an approximate DZ and a decision is made, depending on operational conditions, whether to surface and risk detection, or remain submerged. The team parachute into the sea on static-line steerable 'chutes carrying all personal kit and closed-circuit breathing apparatus in a waterproofed container. Breathing apparatus is not worn while parachuting as it cannot be used when worn under the parachute harness and the extra equipment makes operation of the reserve parachute difficult. Extra equipment, such as inflatable boats and canoes, is dropped behind the men in containers or on pre-assembled pallets.

Once in the water, the men don masks and swimmer's fins before connecting themselves and their equipment to a rope which is played out to its full length. The two outside divers activate transponder beacons, consisting of two balls in a tube, capable of making sufficient sound underwater to be picked up on the submarines sonar. If the submarine chooses to remain submerged, the captain aims for the centre of the sonar signature and, running at reduced speed, snags the rope, allowing the men and equipment to drift to the

Canoes still provide a viable means of inserting onto an enemy coastline. (*PMA Pictures*)

rear of the boat. Two swimmers dive down to open the stowage hatches and release a rope connected to a buoy that floats to the surface. All containers and equipment are attached to this line and then encouraged to sink so that they can be placed in the stowage boxes. British Teams enter the boat by the 5-man chamber or escape compartment but those of other countries often enter through the more claustrophobic environment of the torpedo tubes.

Once at their destination, 'casing divers' unload the team's canoes or inflatables from under the casing deck and send them back to the surface attached to the rope and buoy. The casing divers then help the team leave the submarine, remaining on the surface until the Special Forces depart.

Combat Swimming

On close reconnaissance and sabotage insertions into enemy harbours, air tanks are exchanged for closed-circuit re-breather equipment. The re-breather removes exhaled carbon dioxide by converting it back to oxygen, without leaving a trail of tell-tale bubbles. Oxygen is fed from a small bottle into a breathing bag which collapses as the diver draws breath. Exhaled breath passes back into the bag and over a chemical carbon dioxide 'scrubber' before being pulsed with oxygen which allows it to be recycled. Ideal for covert swimming operations, the system has the serious disadvantage that it cannot be used below 50ft. At these depths, high levels of oxygen become extremely toxic, poisoning the diver's brain and lungs. Deeper dives require mixed-gas re-breather systems.

On their long swim into the target, the divers have the additional problem of carrying their equipment and explosive charges, usually in the form of magnetic mines, each weighing some 15kg. Some of the mines are constructed of light synthetic material to give them neutral buoyancy under water. Heavier charges are carried in a buoyancy bag which can be partly inflated to make it weightless under water. Swimming in the pitch black water requires total concentration and the diver cannot afford to be festooned with equipment. The problem is made a little easier by the 'attack board' – a small square of light plastic with the fluorescent dials of a watch, depth gauge and compass, arranged in a highly visible triangle.

After completion of the mission, the team again meet the submarine at the pre-arranged RV and, after satisfying the captain as to the authenticity of the men on the surface, re-execute the embarkation procedure.

Dedicated Vehicles

Small dedicated submarines for swimmer insertion are being developed, thus allowing larger missile and hunter-killer boats to remain on patrol. One such craft, the *Piranha*, built by Vickers shipbuilders, has an overall length of only 87ft (27m) and is capable of delivering the seven man crew, ten combat swimmers and two swimmer delivery vehicles close to the operational target. It can negotiate shallow waters and on the surface produces a smaller radar signature than its larger sisters and has an operational range of 1,800 nautical miles on the surface or 70 nautical miles, moving at four knots fully submerged.

The majority of the technical innovations in this area have been concerned with transporting the team between the submarine and shore. One such remarkable boat is the Subskimmer-80, designed by Lieutenant Commander Hugh Oswald, and built by Submarine Products. On the surface Subskimmer is a powerful rigid-hulled inflatable, powered by an 80hp outboard motor. Close to the shore, the outboard's exhaust is sealed and a powerful suction pump is activated to suck the air out of the hull, thereby allowing the boat to sink. Just below the surface, Subskimmer can run at four knots. Close to the target, electric thrusters can carry the craft on a power-dive to greater depths where it has an operational capability as a 'wet' swimmer delivery vehicle capable of covering six miles at two-and-a-half knots. The craft can be left on the bottom of a river while the team infiltrate inland targets and later recovered to return them to the submarine or parent craft. The boat is equipped with a powerful onboard navigation system and additional air supply. With a length of 16ft and an unladen weight of 1,764lbs (800kg), the craft can easily

An American 'wet' SEAL Delivery and Recovery System. Mindful of the need to mount operations in cold northern waters, USSOCOM is seeking a 'dry' delivery vehicle. (*USSOCOM, US DOD*)

be deployed close to the operational area by patrol boat, submarine or helicopter.

Mini-submarines are used as 'dry' delivery vehicles that are capable of deep- and shallow-water penetration. After release from the parent submarine, the mini-sub provides a warm, friendly environment that the combat-swimmers leave only when very close to their target. USSOCOM are currently seeking a delivery vehicle for their Seal Teams. Mindful of the need to mount operations in cold northern waters, USSOCOM will undoubtedly choose a dry delivery vehicle. Currently under evaluation is the 3GST9 (3 in-diameter gas storage toroid, nine metres long) midget submarine designed jointly by Maritalia and Honeywell. This has a quiet, closed propulsion system, that leaves no chemical wake to be picked up by chemical sniffer devices. Its toroidal hull, constructed out of rings of pipes, provides storage for oxygen, fuel and waste gases as well as being sufficiently strong to allow the submarine to operate at depths of 600m. Submerged, it can reach 16 knots; at its cruising speed of six knots it can travel for 1,400 miles.

Sweden has claimed more than 40 incursions by Soviet submarines, in the restricted naval areas around its coast. Some experts believe that these incursions were training exercises for a future invasion of Sweden, spearheaded by Soviet naval Spetsnaz units. In her paper, *Spetsnaz and Soviet Far North Strategy*, Kirsten Amundsen notes that a major incursion, at the Swedish base at Musko in October 1982, involved a number of Soviet submarines including Whiskey class boats (possibly parent craft) and 'three allegedly manned, midget bottom-crawling crafts of a type unknown to Swedish experts'. Earlier a midget-submarine, believed to be part of the same operation, was reported to have successfully entered Stockholm harbour. The possible role of these incursions and other Soviet clandestine operations in Sweden, as part of an overall Soviet battle-plan, are discussed in Chapter 10.

5

The Hidden Heroes of Special Operations

Are you tough? If so, get out. I need buggers with brains.
A sign in the office of Roger Courtney, the first commander
of the Special Boat Service.

In the early hours of 1 August 1945, a Liberator Mark Vc of No 160 Squadron (Special Duties) arrived over the arranged dropping zone above Kota Tinggyi, in Southern Malaya. The area was suspiciously quiet; there was no evidence of the Special Forces reception party, no pre-arranged signal, no 'raging twisting bonfires' with 'figures waving, witches worshipping amid the sacrificial fires, no sweet smell of wood smoke percolating into the cockpit' as Special Duties pilot, Terence O'Brian, described another 'live' reception. Contrary to standing orders, Flight Lieutenant J.A. Muir, circled the area for 85 minutes before reluctantly setting a course for Minneriya. With nearly 2,000lbs of containers still on board, the 16,000lbs of fuel was nearly exhausted when they finally landed in Ceylon. In a vain and brave attempt to support Special Forces ground teams in Malaya, the crew had coaxed the over-loaded aircraft through the atrocious weather systems of the Far East for 24 hours and ten minutes.

One of the lessons of the Second World War was that dedicated aircraft, communications and intelligence were the oxygen of special operations. Today, specialists in these fields are recruited to work as part of the organisational infra-structure of special operational forces. While these civilians and soldiers are frequently killed alongside the clandestine operators, they remain the hidden heroes of special operations.

AIR-SUPPORT

During the war, British clandestine operations in the jungles of the Far East were supported by 357, 358 and 160 Special Duties Squadrons. The crews, drawn from the RAF and from Commonwealth countries, were trained to parachute agents into their operational areas where, once established, the squadrons kept them re-supplied with the necessities of life, including radio-transmitters, weapons and munitions. From their airfields in India, short-and medium-range flights to dropping zones in Burma were covered by Dakota and Hudson aircraft. Catalina flying boats proved admirably suited for coastal landings, thus releasing submarines for other duties. Liberators were used for longer flights but Indo-China could only be reached by refuelling at airfields in China. There the crew and their passengers relied on the good will of the Americans and their Chinese hosts.

Later in the war, a flight of Lysander aircraft were used to ferry passengers to and from jungle air-strips, which had been constructed by the clandestine parties, often with the help of village labour. Many were no more than cleared strips 1,000yds in length and at the mercy of the monsoon rains; others were more elaborate and weather-resistant, having been sturdily built with split bamboo or layers of rock and gravel. The aircrew's greatest enemy was the weather, which accounted for all but one of the 27 aircraft lost by 357 and 358 Squadrons, flak being sufficiently rare to merit a mention in the flight log. But if the aircraft became lost or was forced down by tropical storms, the pilot was frequently met by unbroken mountainous jungle, and few aircrew survived such crashes. Baling out was only marginally better as those aircrew who survived the parachute landing were then faced with surviving the jungle and the Japanese.

In Europe, four Whitley bombers from 419 Flight were initially assigned to parachute agents and supplies into the occupied countries. By 1942 the flight controlled 10 Whitleys and three Halifaxes and was redesignated 138 Squadron with a permanent base at Tempsford in Bedfordshire. Tempsford was shared with 161 Squadron which was equipped with Lysander aircraft, used for pick-ups rather than parachuting. These pick-ups were by far the most dangerous and romantic operations, with the pilot forced to navigate from a map strapped to his knee while he dodged anti-aircraft batteries and night fighters. The makeshift air-strip was usually a field lit by signal fires. Security was maintained by a recognition signal flashed by the reception party. The aircraft was at its most vulnerable on the ground, with the ever present risk that the enemy were close-by awaiting the landing. Later in the war, the strict rules laid down for pick-ups were enforced by RAF-trained personnel working with the Resistance. Once on the ground, the aircraft immediately taxied to its take-off point, the 'Joes', or agents, often having to jump from the moving aircraft. The turn-around time could be less than three minutes. The rules protecting the security of the aircraft were clear: passengers for the flight home approached the aircraft from the left; anybody approaching the pilot from the right would be shot by the pilot who carried a service revolver for his own protection.

As D-Day approached, squadrons from RAF 38 Transport Group and the USAF dropped a vast number of containers to the Resistance forces in France.

Members of an Army Air Dispatch Company dropping supplies over Borneo. Special operations depend upon dedicated air crews prepared to fly the dangerous missions to insert, re-supply and support parties behind the lines. (*Imperial War Museum*)

Longer flights to re-supply the Polish Resistance during the Warsaw Rising were carried out by 1386 Polish Flight, and 624 Squadron RAF. In the closing stages of the Rising, the former braved heavy anti-aircraft fire to drop their containers with pin-point accuracy over Warsaw's blazing roof-tops. The re-supply drops to the Poles were stopped only after 15 of the 16 Polish Halifax crews had been shot down.

Today, Britain has two RAF units supporting the UK Special Forces Group. A Special Forces Flight of 47 Squadron RAF is specially trained in delivering SAS and SBS teams (ocean-drops) by HALO and HAHO insertion and in the low level (300ft) navigation required to penetrate enemy air defences. This unit is supported by LXX (70) Squadron's Hercules C-130 aircraft whose crews are also highly trained in the skills required to drop parachutists.

The AC-130U Spectre Gunship, a modified Hercules, is heavily equipped with armaments and night-sensors to fly interdiction missions in support of US Special Forces. More than 30-years old, the AC-130 has proved its worth in Vietnam, Grenada, Panama and the Gulf. (*USSOCOM, US DOD*)

The Americans were also quick to realise the necessity of dedicated air-support for their 'across-the-fence' operations. Elements of the USAAF were responsible for dropping parties and subsequently re-supplying OSS teams in Europe and the Far-East. At the end of the Second World War the CIA decided that it needed a clandestine air force to service its operations. This was 'Air America', which had grown out of General Claire Chennault's 'Flying Tigers', formed in 1937 to support Chiang Kai-shek's Chinese Nationalist Army. After the war, it metamorphosed into Chinese Air Transport (CAT), expanding into a conglomerate of real and dummy holdings that went under such names as Air America, Inc., Air Asia Co. and Civil Air Transport. Air America provided the transport aircraft which carried mercenaries, supplies and CIA field officers into the CIA's small wars. In Burma they supported the most secret of the secret wars: three attempts by defeated Chinese Nationalist troops to invade Communist China from bases in the Shan States. In 1950, Communist China invaded Tibet and Air America embarked on one of its most dangerous assignments: running supplies and CIA-trained Khamba tribesmen to support the Tibetan rebellion. CIA support was finally phased out as a precondition of Nixon's 1972 visit to China. Meanwhile, the CIA's air force found time between regular commercial flights to support CIA operations in Indonesia, the Congo, Laos and Vietnam.

In Laos, the aircrews of Air America were joined by the 'Ravens', military pilots who flew into battle in civilian clothes, cowboy hats, dark glasses and a 22-carat gold ring engraved with an oriental royal crest. The Ravens were forward air-controllers (FACs) who were drawn from air force personnel in Vietnam and 'sheep-dipped' through the 'Steve Canyon Programme'. Nominally under the command of 56th Special Operations Wing, based at Nakhon Phanom (Thailand), their real posting was Laos. There the Royal Laotian Army, the Special Guerrilla Units of General Vang Pao's Hmong tribesmen and other indigenous units led by the CIA, attempted to prevent the flow of troops and supplies down the Ho Chi Minh Trail and hold Eastern Laos against the seasonal offensives by the North Vietmanese Army and the Pathet Lao guerrillas. Flying slow single-prop aircraft, like the Cessna 0–1 Bird Dog and the T-28 North American Nomad, from air-strips scattered around the Plain of Jars, the Ravens supported ground operations by identifying targets and calling-in air-strikes. When necessary they also organised search and rescue (SAR) missions to pick up downed pilots.

A clandestine American air-transport company still exists to support special operations. Known as Seaspray, it operates under the cover of Aviation Tech Services or, for Army administrative purposes, the 1st Rotary Wing Test Activity based at Fort Eustis (Va), although it is reported to fly small fixed-wing aircraft and helicopters out of Tampa International Airport, Florida. Seaspray was established in March 1981, to circumvent President Carter's Executive Order 12036 which made it illegal for the armed forces to conduct clandestine operations. Consequently, the unit is managed jointly by the Army and the CIA and is reportedly tasked with the transport of US Army Special Operations Forces (SOF), particularly Delta counter-terrorist members. However, in 1982, Seaspray was involved in Operation QUEEN HUNTER, a surveillance mission on behalf of the National Security Agency, which involved the purchase of King Air aircraft through a front company, 'Shenandoah Aerolease'. Modified to carry advanced radio direction-finding equipment, the aircraft are said to have been used to pin-point Salvadorian rebel bases and arms traffic routes between Honduras and Nicaragua.

USSOCOM also maintains the Special Operations Aviation Brigade, tasked with air transport and support missions, while the 160th Aviation Battalion (Task Force 160) provides a fleet of 80 helicopters, manned and operated by SOF personnel, for strike, reconnaissance, assault and transport missions.

The US Air Force (23rd AF, 2nd Air Div – Military Airlift Command) provides the Ist Special Operations Wing, tasked by the Office of Air Force Special Operations with providing USAF unconventional warfare capability. Three Special Operations Squadrons (SOS) maintain six MC-130E Combat

Talon and four MC-130H Talon II for all weather insertion/extraction missions (8th SOS), ten AC-130H Spectre gunships for air-support (16th SOS), and four HH-53H Pave Low and nine MH-53H/J Super Jolly Green Giant helicopters (20th SOS) for insertion/extraction missions. Four additional squadrons are based abroad to provide worldwide support for US forces, with additional Air Force SOF units assigned to the Air Reserve and the National Guard. Most modern American SOF aircraft are equipped with the Adverse Weather Aerial Delivery System (AWADS) that can drop personnel or loads during bad weather or even in conditions of zero visibility.

INTELLIGENCE

Increasingly, intelligence is gathered electronically or from remote sources, such as satellites, unmanned aircraft (drones) and a range of high-performance reconnaissance aircraft. Television pictures ('real-time' intelligence) are replacing the photograph but sources are notoriously vulnerable to weather, range, terrain masking and enemy counter-measures. The alternative is human sourced intelligence (HUMINT) which may come from a variety of sources. In recent years, America planned a new agency, tentatively code-named 'Monarch Eagle', to assume responsibility for the collection and analysis of every type of HUMINT. However, after considerable pressure from the CIA and DIA, its parameters became so limited that the initiative collapsed.

The Special Forces and Intelligence are inter-dependent. The former fields dedicated units such as Long Range Patrol and Surveillance Companies (Chapter 8) capable of providing a continuous flow of 'real-time' human intelligence. Special units are also used by Intelligence for a variety of direct action tasks such as raids, rescue missions and the training of indigenous troops. In return, Intelligence provides the vital processed and analysed information for the successful execution of these special operations and the necessary specialised training to complete 'Int-tasks' in the field. The tight inter-relationship between the intelligence agency and the commando unit is underscored by the fact that until fairly recently, intelligence agencies like the CIA maintained their own 'special forces' in the form of the 'Covert Action Branch'. Meanwhile US military Special Forces have deployed their own undercover intelligence teams for counter-terrorist operations (Chapter 12).

PSYCHOLOGICAL OPERATIONS AND CIVIL AFFAIRS

Psychological operations within the United States are predominantly civilian in nature. Their aim in law is to 'promote a better understanding of the United States in other countries, and increase mutual understanding between the people of the United States and the people of other countries'. It is, in theory at

An intelligence officer de-briefs a four-man reconnaissance patrol. (*PMA Pictures*)

least, entirely overt with no aggressive tendencies. While the United States has continued covert psychological operations in areas of domestic influence, such as Central America, it has reduced considerably its operations in Europe. It has even starved the PSYOPS teams of the resources necessary to support SF-personnel on the ground.

Military Psyops is controlled almost exclusively by 4th PSYOPS Group, consisting of 965 officers and men allocated to one of four battalions (1st, 6th, 8th, 9th). Tasked with the provision of direct overt, covert and clandestine propaganda, and with the provision of advice and hardware for troops on the ground, the Group spends approximately 90 per cent of its time in support of conventional forces and the balance working closely with the Green Berets.

To be effective, psychological operations must meet a number of criteria established by the British during the Malayan Campaign of 1948–60. Operations must be based on thorough research and intelligence; they must be consistent with government, military and political policy; they must stem from a deep understanding of the target audience and must get the right message to the right audience at the right time. Used with tact, subtlety and skill they can assist greatly in the maintenance and credibility of on-going military operations. Used ineptly, they can be wholly counter-productive.

The gaining of support and the co-operation of often politically uninterested locals in an area only nominally under political control has never been easy. As Britain discovered in Malaya and the Oman, and as the United States failed totally to comprehend in Vietnam, it is pointless bringing an area under military control if, in so doing, the social sub-structure of the target group is destroyed. To work effectively psyops must be tied to a policy of hearts and minds. Terror, although acceptable when used overtly against the enemy, must never be employed against the target.

In Malaya, and to a lesser degree in the Oman, Britain relied heavily on Field Intelligence NCOs (FINCOs) to win the support of the local population as a prerequisite to subjecting it to a full psyops programme. FINCOs were drawn from among the senior non-commissioned officers of the British Army's Intelligence Corps. They were taught the language, dialect, religious beliefs and social taboos of the people with whom they then lived, often for months on end. Able to call upon the SAS for medical and logistics support, and upon the resident infantry battalion for aggressive patrolling and ambushing when necessary, they were able, uniquely, to offer their subjects a combination of physical and mental well-being totally at odds with the terror being meted out by the (Communist) insurgents.

Conscious of its shortcomings in Vietnam, the United States has now introduced the 96th Civil Affairs Group tasked with creating friendly groups among the indigenous peoples with whom the US Special Forces will be operating. Four companies and 172 men strong, the CAG is responsible for the creation of civilian and military co-operation and liaison between the United States and host countries at all levels before, during and after hostilities. It exercises executive, legislative and judicial authority in occupied territories and attempts to minimise civilian interference in military activities. It worked with 4th PSYOPS Group in the immediate aftermath of the Grenada intervention and has more recently almost certainly been deployed to Saudi Arabia. Perhaps not surprisingly the Soviet Union has no equivalent of the now extant British FINCO or of the United States CAG.

SUPPORT FOR SOVIET SPECIAL OPERATIONS

The Soviet Army has shown no great willingness to accept *glasnost*, nor do it's leaders see the recent spate of disarmament talks as necessarily leading to peace. The war-planners remain concerned with the possibility of multi-theatre war on three fronts and continue to plan for simultaneous combat in Europe, the Far East and South-East Asia. They accept that any future war would almost certainly be conventional and that victory, if it were to be complete, would have to be gained in the early stages before the divergent enemy had time to rally its forces and mobilise.

Although the Kremlin claims that its new military doctrine is based on 'offensive defence', or reasonable sufficiency, it retains sufficient forces in reserve to strike deep behind the lines of an unwary or unprepared enemy. It continues to regard subversion and psychology as legitimate peacetime weapons in the battle to keep its potential enemy ill-equipped for war.

Potential subversives are often chosen from among visitors to the Soviet Union. Some will be employed by the 2nd Directorate of the GRU to supply information on potential Spetsnaz targets. The majority, however, will be employed by the First Chief Directorate of the KGB. Responsible for so-called peacetime active measures, with particular attention to subversion and disinformation, the Directorate infiltrates individual agents and teams into hostile territory for special missions as diverse as target acquisition and sabotage.

Soviet psychological operations are as uncompromising as they are pervasive. Before the thaw in East-West relations, *Pravda, Izvestia,* the *Tass* news service, periodicals such as *New Times* and *International Affairs,* the *Novosti Press* and *Radio Moscow* were subject to strict control and compelled to follow current propaganda lines. Foreign Communist parties, other left-wing factions loyal to Moscow and unwitting fellow-travellers were subsidised. 'Front' organisations, such as the World Peace Council with its 140 branches, the World Federation of Trade Unions with its claimed 200 million members, and the International Organisation of Journalists all received support and covert funding from Moscow, in their endeavours to spread Marxist-Leninism to anyone with an ear to listen.

Little is known of Soviet military psyops save that there appear to be no specialist units. Internal propaganda, never a popular subject with the conscripts, remains the prerogative of the KGB-appointed political officer (*Zampolit*) attached to every battalion and independent unit. In marked contrast, the West has shown little post-*glasnost* stomach for the continued prosecution of what it sees as Cold War activities.

Part Two

The Military Roles of the Special Forces

6

Helping Your Friends to Help Themselves: Training Anti-Insurgents, Partisans and Mercenaries

'Wars are never fought for one reason', he said. 'They are fought for dozens of reasons, in a muddle. Its the same with revolts.'
Merlyn teaches the young Arthur statecraft in T.H.White's *The Queen of Air and Darkness.*

He had to be played at his own game, by living out in the jungle for weeks on end, by winning hearts and minds of the people and planting our own agents in villages known to be unfriendly.'
General Sir Walter Walker's foreword to Brigadier E.D. Smith's *East of Kathmandu.* 7th Gurkha Rifles Regimental History.

With the development of weapons of mass destruction and the nuclear/chemical stand-off, it is little surprise that governments should rediscover the older form of partisan warfare in order to topple hostile governments. The resulting conflicts were remote and, being fought primarily by infantry, less intense and less likely to escalate into all-out war. What is surprising is that the political creeds of both East and West can be used to support such enterprises. Many of the philosophical and political factors behind today's special operations have been excellently covered in John M. Collins's text, *Green Berets, Seals & Spetsnatz: US & Soviet Special Military Operations*, written at the behest of the American Special Operations Panel as a handbook for Congress and government. Politics and ideology are essential ingredients in the marriage between the Special Forces and their partisan and mercenary allies.

FREE THE OPPRESSED

The United States Declaration of Independence was written by revolutionaries, who had freed their country from British colonial rule. It asserts that all governments instituted by men derive their powers from the consent of the governed and it is therefore the right of the people to alter or abolish a repressive regime. However, today America also acknowledges that many revolutions require outside help:

> History confirms that neither political, economic and social deprivation nor oppressive foreign dictators are enough to incite and sustain insurgencies. Even when conditions become intolerable, headless multitudes remain bound together by blind passion only momentarily, unless clever leaders focus their power on the basic objective, which is to undermine and overide the incumbent regime.

Collins's book identifies the insurgents that will receive American aid:

> The clearest US objective 'is to help people to help themselves' ... US support at this point is very selective. The enemy of our enemy will be assured of our friendship [only] if he shares our values ... and would be preferable to the regime in power.

It is one of the functions of the Special Operational Forces within the intelligence community and the military, to supply those 'clever leaders'. The Special Forces manual FM 31–20 (SF-Operational Techniques) gives examples of 10- and 30-day master training programmes for indigenous forces covering a range of topics from basic navigation, intelligence gathering, selection and organisation of DZs to weapons and demolition training and patrols, raids and ambushes.

Since the end of the Second World War, America has provided support for insurgencies in Guatemala (1954), Cuba (1961), Hungary (1956), Afghanistan (1980s), Cambodia (1980s), Angola (1962–86) and Nicaragua (1980s). For economic reasons, or in order to avoid regional or global conflict, America appointed surrogates or proxies to aid other 'freedom fighters'. The Kurdish separatists' struggle against Soviet-aided Iraq (1970–75) was supported by Iran and operations in Nicaragua have been carried out by the Contras.

However, those wishing to raise revolts must be prepared to find ways of countering them. In a neat reversal of role, Western Special Operations Forces (SOF) have been forced to develop tactics, techniques and technology to counter external threats and internal subversion in friendly countries – Foreign Internal Defence. In these programmes indigenous people have been trained to provide paramilitary forces or specially trained counter-guerrilla commandos to oppose internal subversion and external aggression in Vietnam, Laos, Cambodia, South Korea, Thailand, Tibet, Africa and Central and South America. America's allies, Britain, Australia and New Zealand, have played a similar role in countering subversion and fostering internal defence programmes in Malaya, Borneo and the Oman, and to a limited extent in the Civilian Irregular Defence Group Programme in Vietnam.

SNAPPING THE LINKS

Since the Second World War, the Soviets have supported in excess of 17 insurgencies with training, arms and equipment. Most were not initiated by the USSR but were windfalls to be carefully nurtured. A further 15 insurgencies received aid from surrogates such as Cuba, the Palestine Liberation Organisation, Libya, Nicaragua, South Yemen, Syria and countries of the Eastern Bloc. The rationale for such support is embedded in Article 28 of the Soviet Constitution which guarantees assistance to revolutionaries who seek to overthrow non-socialist regimes.

The early Marxist thinkers would have agreed with the American analysis that repressed peoples have to be helped to revolution by clever leaders. Lenin gave the job of exporting world revolution to the Third Communist International, known as the Comintern. Throughout the 1930s, Comintern agents were active in Europe. However early expectations of 'world capitalism' dissolving into revolution were not realised. Eastern Europe was eventually 'liberated', not from the bourgeoisie but from the German Army, at the end of the Second World War.

Another approach – support for revolutionaries in the Third World – was, at least in part, also inspired by Lenin's teachings. He envisaged the Third World colonies as the weak links in the chain of world capitalism: break them and you break capitalism. In the Far East, the Chinese Communist Party and Comintern representatives, such as Ho Chi Minh, assembled the political infrastructure for revolution.

The conditions for revolution were accelerated by the Second World War. During the period of the Nazi-Soviet pact (24 August 1939–22 June 1941), the faithful were reminded that war was a natural state of affairs for capitalist countries. Their attention was drawn to the Irish nationalists who had taken advantage of the 'imperialist bourgeois crisis' of the First World War to rise against the British. The present conflict offered similar opportunities. After the German invasion of the Soviet Union (23 June 1941), the Party's line changed and they were ordered to stand alongside the other resistance movements in the struggle against fascism. Their fate would be intertwined with the officers dispatched by SOE and the OSS to organise resistance in Europe and

Leading irregular troops in support of conventional operations is not a new
phenomenon. Colonel T.E. Lawrence's account of his guerilla operations
behind Turkish lines in the First World War inflamed the interest of a generation of Englishmen in unconventional warfare. (*Imperial War Museum*)

the Far East. This was the beginning of the modern partisan wars, conflicts
that Professor M.R.D. Foot in his history of SOE, *The Special Operations
Executive 1940–46*, has described as the 'many-sided wars'.

THE WAR WITH MANY FACES

It is not possible here to give a full account of the operations of SOE, OSS and the other clandestine organisations that were charged with raising revolt behind the lines. Happily this ground has been covered by many books that deal specifically with this topic. It is enough to give a short, highly selective account of the complexity of these operations and their post-war consequences.

France

In close proximity to Britain, France was the jewel in the clandestine crown. SOE's F (independent) section is credited with having established nine circuits. The nucleus of each circuit was usually a team of three: radio-operator, organiser and sabotage instructor. General de Gaulle's Free French *Bureau Central de Renseignements et d'Action* (BCRA) established six circuits and the Gaullist country section of SOE R/F Section set up others. Each sent in about 400 agents. The SOE section working from Algiers in North Africa (AMF) sent in a further 600 SOE and OSS agents. To this must be added the Polish officers from SOE's country section for Poles outside Poland (EU/P), SOE's escape apparatus (DF Section) and MI9, a separate organisation that also maintained safe-houses linked into escape lines. Many other agent circuits and resistance groups were formed spontaneously by the French. While this may appear to be a plethora of resistance circuits in one country, albeit the major target of Allied invasion plans, they were spread throughout metropolitan France and were frequently dedicated to one or other of the underground roles: intelligence-gathering, sabotage, propaganda and the raising of clandestine forces to support the liberation. For obvious reasons, propaganda and intelligence functions were best kept apart from sabotage and paramilitary operations which provoked a violent German response.

The German introduction of forced labour sent many young French men and women into the hills, where they lived rough. These groups came to be named after the Corsican word for hill brushwood – *Maquis*. After the Normandy invasion, about 300 Allied officers and NCOs organised into 'Jedburgh' teams were parachuted into France to organise and train the *maquisands*. Each team was composed of two officers and a sergeant signaller of inter-Allied mix. 'Jedburgh' teams in France were drawn from the British, French and Belgium SAS Regiments, American OSS officers and French clandestine personnel.

To arm the underground army, SOE parachuted over 10,000 tons of stores, including arms for half a million men and a large quantity of explosive. Resistance activities were supplemented by Allied SAS units which were parachuted into 42 operational areas of France and Belgium to carry out specific reconnaissance and sabotage tasks in support of the Normandy invasion. Many of the SAS parties also armed and led *maquis* forces on numerous

The German introduction of forced labour sent many young French men and women into the hills, where they lived rough. These groups came to be named after the Corsican word for hill brushwood – *Maquis*. (*Imperial War Museum*)

operations to cut roads, bridges and railway lines, thus delaying German reinforcements rushing to the front.

Most of the French resistance movement was organised into the pro-Gaullist *Etat-Major des Forces Francaises de L'Interieur* (EMFFI). In contrast, the French Communist Party (PCF), maintained an armed wing: the *Francs-Tireurs et Partisan* (FTP). The FTP joined forces with the other resistants in the clandestine National Council of Resistance (CNR) which indirectly controlled day-to-day resistance activities in France. At the end of the war, the Communists expected to be in a strong political position. De Gaulle outwitted them, entering Paris immediately after its liberation, accompanied by his *Missions militaires de liaison administrative* who assumed control of all the regional and national centres of power.

Scandinavia

Finland had fared badly against Russian attacks in 1939–41 and showed a reluctance to become involved in any clandestine activities that might provoke

French parachutists dropped into Brittany to link up with the Resistance, were the first Allied soldiers to land in France ahead of the invading armies. (*Imperial War Museum*)

a German invasion. In Norway, OSS/SOE operators helped organise the resistance or Military Organisation (Milorg) into a force that was 60,000 strong by 1945. Norway saw some notable partisan operations including the raid on the heavy water plant at Vermork and the disruption of the railways that helped trap large numbers of German troops in Norway at the end of the war (see Chapter 10).

Danish army officers and policemen formed 'The Prince' circuit in 1941, passing valuable intelligence to SOE. By 1944, 50 OSS/SOE agents were working with Danish sabotage teams; but it was ultimately a six-week strike by railway workers that prevented six German divisions from reaching the Normandy front in June 1944.

Poland

Invaded by both Germany and the Soviet Army in 1939, the Poles rapidly established more than 100 resistance groups. By 1942 most had combined into the *Armia Krajowa* (AK) or Home Army. SOE (Force 139) organised the insertion of 318 Polish 'fighting parachutists', four British agents, one Hungarian agent, 28 Polish couriers and 600 tons of stores and weapons. Despite the long and difficult flight to Poland, Allied aircraft made 485 parachute drops, losing 73 aircraft, 41 of them shot down over Warsaw during attempts to support the Warsaw Rising.

The men and women of the AK showed themselves capable of extraordinary feats of daring. The SOE agent 'Ponury' escaped capture early in his mission, becoming part of the successful raid on Pinsk prison (see Chapter 9). On another occasion, he stopped a German troop train and, disguised in an SS uniform, walked the length of it removing all the small-arms. These went to arm his several-hundred-strong partisan force.

The underground had more to fear than just the German Army. The Soviets quickly dispelled any pretence that they were allies of the Poles. In Eastern Poland, Soviet partisan bands led by NKVD officers were under orders to eliminate nationalist elements in Poland. AK parties that came into contact with the Soviets were dispersed or incorporated into General Berling's puppet force of captured Poles. The partisan officers enjoyed the same fate as their comrades in the shallow graves in Katyn forest or were sent back to the Lubyanka or Siberian prison camps. Trustingly, AK groups supported the Russian advance into Poland. When Soviet tanks nosed through the Warsaw suburbs, in 1945, the Home Army rose in support and were crushed. The Soviets watched from the other side of the Vistula river. When Berling requested permission to put men across the river to support the AK he was relieved of his command. Poland's fate was sealed.

Italy

After Mussolini was deposed in 1943, the Italian government used a captured SOE radio-operator to establish contact with the Allies. The Germans reestablished control but the Communist resistance undermined their authority in cities such as Turin and Milan. In the mountains there was a myriad of partisan groups of every political persuasion. These were supplied by No 1 Special Force based at Bari. By 1945 there were more than 75 OSS/SOE teams working with the partisans. Immediately after the Allied invasion, SAS parties had been used to attack the German Army's umbilical-cord: the railway lines. Later they and the commandos were used as assault troops but, in December 1944, SAS squadrons were parachuted into northern Italy to organise the partisan attacks in support of the advancing US Army.

The Balkans

Albania had been annexed by Mussolini in April 1939. Resistance was organised along political lines but, unlike Italy, the groups did not work together. In the north there were royalists loyal to exiled King Zog and anti-Communists.

In the south, resistance was under the control of the Communist party leader, Enver Hoxha. By 1943 the rivals were fighting each other to decide the future of Albania after the war. Agent missions and arms were sent to both sides, with the majority going to the Communists on the grounds that they were more likely to kill Germans. When the Germans pulled out the Communists seized power.

Occupied Greece was also a divided nation, with an ongoing war between EDES, an anti-royalist right-wing movement and ELAS – the Greek national army of liberation. ELAS and its political wing, EAM, claimed to represent a national liberation front, but was in fact a front for the Greek Communist Party (KKE). Both sides were given arms and training by SOE and the OSS contributed 30 intelligence and operational group teams. During the war ELAS gave priority to absorbing violently most of the smaller royalist and nationalist partisans. Fortunately, SOE's support for EDES prevented a total take-over. The two organisations worked together only once, to provide cover for the SOE demolition party that destroyed the railway bridge over the Gorgopotamos river used for carrying valuable supplies to Rommel's North African army.

As the Germans withdrew in the autumn of 1944, ELAS made its bid for power and was thwarted by Greek and British forces. The civil war continued with ELAS receiving support from Yugoslavia, Albania and Bulgaria. In 1947, the civil war ended and ELAS guerrillas trickled across the Albanian border after perpetrating a series of particularly barbaric atrocities on the Greek people.

In Yugoslavia, SOE and the OSS initially supported the Royalist guerrillas of Colonel Draze Mihailovic. This changed when signals intelligence suggested that the *cetniks* were co-operating with the Italians, Germans and the local fascist *Ustashe* in attacking Tito's Communist partisans. Politically, Tito seemed to be the less attractive candidate. Before the war, he had been a Comintern agent in Europe, recruiting men for the International Brigade in Spain. Many of these now formed the officer cadre in a partisan army dedicated to revolution. On the other hand, Tito's partisans fought the Germans like tigers, hoping to distract German troops from the Russian front. SOE switched their support to the Communists. The OSS continued to support Mihailovic, whose partisans rescued hundreds of Allied aircrew. The outcome was finally decided when Soviet forces, rather than the Americans and British, liberated Yugoslavia.

Burma

In much of the Far East the Japanese were welcomed as liberators. They were Asians and their Greater East Asia Co-Prosperity Sphere seemed to offer a welcome end to colonial rule and some degree of self-determination.

The Burmese Premier, U Saw, commented 'We Asiatics have had a bad time since Vasco da Gama rounded the Cape', and this view was sympathetically

echoed by his countrymen in the vast central area of paddy fields and forests –
Britain's clandestine forces found little support there. However, in the massive
horse-shoe of mountains on Burma's Indian and Chinese borders there were
other people, hill tribes such as the Chins, Kachins and Karens, who had
traditionally seen the British as protectors against the Burmese lowlanders.
Most welcomed the Force 136 (SOE) parachutists who started dropping into
these areas in 1943. Both SOE and OSS (Detachment 101) established several
guerrilla forces in these regions, tasked with establishing communications
with India, gathering intelligence, reporting Japanese road and rail movements, selecting targets for Allied bombers and harassing Japanese road convoys. As General Slim's 14th Army started to drive down the Sittang and
Irrawaddy river valleys to take Rangoon, parties of guerrillas blocked the
Japanese retreat.

Other parties of guerrillas came from unexpected sources. One group, the
Burma Independence Army (later Burma National Army), had been set up by
the Japanese under Aung San, prior to the country's being given independence. However, when it became obvious that they had merely traded one
colonial master for another, they decided to throw in their lot with the Allies.
While the British civil administration for Burma wanted to treat Aung San as a
war criminal, Slim supplied his units with rations on the understanding that
they would operate in support of the 14th Army.

The other two groups anxious to gain British support were the Communist
Thakin (Master) Party and an assortment of anti-Japanese interests called the
Anti-Fascist Organisation. All supported Slim's push towards Rangoon in
return for the promise of independence. In Northern Burma, two Burmese
SOE operators and their two Chinese radio operators, comprising the
ELEPHANT mission, were dropped to make contact with the AFO in
December 1944. Although they had orders to avoid contact with the enemy,
the clandestines organised a running battle with the Japanese in the suburbs of
Mandalay (8 March 1945) initiating the first open revolt of the BNA.

Operations NATION and CHARACTER were larger missions involving a
total of 17 'Jedburgh' teams codenamed after various animals. NATION's
Jedburghs organised AFO and BNA guerrillas in the Pegu Yomas mountains
between the Irrawaddy and Sittang valleys. Their counterparts in the
CHARACTER operational area raised and organised guerrillas in the Karen
Hills. Throughout Burma, Force 136 was credited with killing 16,879
Japanese and wounding a further 995. The BNA were credited with a further
4,000 kills. On the debit side, 68 British and American officers were lost.

Malaya

When it began to appear likely that Malaya would fall to the Japanese, 45
planters, mining engineers and civil servants, volunteered for the 101 Special
Training School (101 STS) and were organised into eight European stay-
behind parties. The 101 STS had been set up by SOE in July 1941 on an

Although officially captioned as 'Anti-Fifth Columnists', the time and place of this photograph, Singapore Island 1941, and the small-arms pictured here, suggest that these personnel are the 'Left-Behind Parties' undergoing training at the 101 Special Training School in Singapore. (*Imperial War Museum*)

isolated peninsula near Singapore. The clandestine arts taught at the School (demolitions, sabotage, weapons, unarmed-combat, navigation, communications and use of indigenous foods) had attracted a range of American,

French, Danish, Swedish and Portuguese students, who were joined at the eleventh hour by the European civilian recruits, 150 Malayan Communist party members and some ISLD (MI6) teams.

The stay-behind parties inflicted varying degrees of damage to the Japanese road and rail traffic (one party accounted for 500–1,000 Japanese) but most had too little time to prepare and were very quickly captured or killed. Four graduates, including Chapman Spencer, avoided capture and fell in with the Anti-Japanese Union and Forces (AJUF). This group had been established by the Malayan Communist Party which, well organised into cells and committees, had attempted to sabotage the British war effort until Russia joined the Allies in 1941.

In May 1943, the first of the GUSTARVUS parties was landed. Operation GUSTARVUS, a series of submarine landings on the west coast of Malaya, had a number of objectives: the creation of a submarine serviced link between Ceylon and Malaya and a local intelligence network: and the establishment of links with indigenous guerrillas and the survivors of the stay-behind parties. What they found was a nationwide guerrilla army commanded by capable leaders, one of whom, Man Wa (code name Chen Ping), would later become familiar to thousands of British servicemen as the leader of the Communist guerrillas during the post-war Emergency. By the summer of 1945, clandestine operators awaiting the expected Allied invasion included 3–5,000 AJUF guerrillas, 90 Force 136 officers and 48 wireless operators. The OSS also launched 17 sorties and the ISLD (MI6) had at least two agent circuits ('Moon' and 'Mud'). In fact the war ended before the Allied invasion could take place.

Siam (Thailand) and Sumatra

Politics marred the activities of the clandestines in Siam. The Siamese Government was allowed to remain in office after the Japanese invasion and Siam formally declared war on Britain and America on 25 January 1942. Some government ministers encouraged the formation of resistance groups such as the 'XO Group'. Both Force 136 and OSS established contact with the resistance and, by 1945, SOE trained officers had supervised the construction of roads and landing strips in readiness for the invasion. Ultimately, these preparations served as an effective deception for the Allies' projected next move: the invasion of Malaya.

In Indonesia the Dutch left stay-behind parties who attempted to organise guerrilla groups in the jungle. Winston Churchill proposed an Allied invasion of northern Sumatra during the monsoon season (May to August) in 1944 (Operation FIRST CULVERIN). This was to be supported by clandestine teams sabotaging the Japanese lines-of-communication, organising rebellion and spreading rumours to create panic in the enemy's rear areas. In the event, Force 136 activities were limited to carrying out a series of reconnaissance missions, identifying possible sites for proposed Allied airfields. There was little local support for Allied instigated rebellion. The Indonesians had little interest in risking their lives assisting the Dutch in retaking their colony. Indeed, potential agents who were to be trained and sent back into the country had to be press-ganged by Allied parties landing from submarines. This situation was made worse by the inability of the Dutch to understand the difference between high-profile commando raids and quietly and patiently organising resistance networks. In spite of local difficulties Force 136 carried out a series of reconnaissance missions, identifying possible invasion landing sites. By 1945, Sumatra was the only island without an SOE presence. In August 1945, the Japanese ignored the Dutch and surrendered to the Indonesians. The Dutch East Indies descended into armed chaos, placing at risk not only the surrendered Japanese but Allied prisoners of war and women and children interned by the Japanese. In many places the Japanese recovered their weapons and re-established order. They were shortly supported by British forces who took over the role of policeman until the country was formally handed back to the Royal Netherlands Army.

French Indochina (Vietnam, Cambodia and Laos)

French forces remained loyal to the Vichy government and continued to run the country, although some elements favoured de Gaulle and open resistance. Consequently, the Japanese installed a 40,000-strong army of occupation to keep watch on their new allies. From 9 May 1944, Force 136 started to parachute agents into the country to contact the French forces. They returned to report that there was a resistance movement and that it would co-operate with the French High Command. By February 1945, 60 men and 21 active radio transmitters had been infiltrated into the region, together with 3,400 Sten guns, 6,000 grenades, 800 pistols, 94 Bren guns, 250,000 shells and more than a million rounds of ammunition.

Further efforts to support the resistance movement was marred by the conflicting British, American and Chinese political aspirations for the region. When the Japanese seized control of key installations and massacred French troops and civilians in March 1945, efforts to drop the French 5th Colonial Infantry Regiment (*Corps Léger d'Intervention*) to bolster resistance were thwarted by politics. Sporadic fighting continued in areas of Vietnam and Laos close to the Chinese border. The Allies sent in further OSS and SOE officers and Jedburgh teams and the resistance received further support from Ho Chi Minh's Communist partisans but the rebellion was over. When the 5th Regiment landed in Indo-China in November 1945, the war had been over for three months and the Japanese were still in control.

POST-WAR PARTISAN OPERATIONS

In the post-war years the so-called Iron Curtain cast its shadow across Europe and the former Allies became enemies again. Behind the Curtain a series of coups brought Hungary, Czechoslovakia and Romania into the Communist bloc. The OSS and SOE were disbanded, their mantles assumed by the CIA and MI6 respectively. The latter basked in the glory of its ENIGMA SigInt coup which had enabled the Allies to read the German signals traffic throughout the war. Both organisations may have thought that they could do better than their two amateur wartime predecessors but they were sadly mistaken.

The CIA and MI6 responded to events in Eastern Europe by recruiting exiles to build up underground armies in the Baltic States and the Ukraine. Inserted by parachute or fishing boat, most were quickly liquidated by the NKVD which had heavily infiltrated the resistance networks. Others survived for months and even years in the frozen forests, until betrayed by double agents or killed in ones and twos by NKVD hunter/killer units. The CIA missions to Romania and Albania were even greater failures.

In the Far East, China began to present a more serious threat. Chinese Communists had finally beaten Chaing Kai-shek's nationalist troops, who retreated to the island of Taiwan and the protection of their powerful American allies. In the summer of 1950, the North Korean army invaded South Korea. When the UN forces sent to support South Korea advanced to the Manechurian border, Chinese troops entered the war, crossed the Yula River and attacked General MacArthur's forces, driving them back into the South.

The CIA looked for ways to draw Chinese forces away from the Korean battlefields and the opportunity presented itself when Chinese troops invaded Tibet in the same year. Within 12 months the country was under Communist control and the CIA began training the Dalai Lama's Khamba tribesmen in guerrilla warfare at a secret base in Colorado's Rocky Mountains. Once trained and equipped with modern weapons, they were flown to India and Nepal and allowed to infiltrate back across the Himalayas. The rebellion spluttered out in the late 1950s, reduced to raids led by CIA contract mercenaries, supported by a secret air force. While the operations netted valuable intelligence on the momentous events inside China, they did little to liberate Tibet.

In the same year, the Agency conceived another way to distract the Chinese: a direct invasion of mainland China. When the Nationalist Kuomintang (KMT) Army had retreated from the mainland, 4,000 KMT troops, cut off from Chang Kai-shek's main forces in the south, escaped into the Burmese Shan States. There they joined the tribesmen in the old OSS/SOE operational areas, who had been in a constant state of rebellion against Rangoon's authority since Burma became independent in 1948. Here was the perfect springboard for an invasion of China's westerly Yunnan province, an invasion that was expected to gather momentum as the Chinese peasants rushed to join the colours.

The 'CHINAT 'LI MI' operation, named after the Chinese general who commanded the army, was launched in April 1951; it lasted a week. The KMT was driven back, taking heavy losses; support from the Chinese peasants was noticeably lacking. Undeterred, the CIA began a build-up of arms and regular KMT soldiers from Taiwan. Suitably impressed, 8,000 hill tribesmen flocked to join the CIA's army, creating one of the largest armed groups in the country. In August 1952, the third and final invasion of China was launched. The insurgents penetrated 60 miles before being stopped by the Chinese Red Army.

With all hope of liberating China gone, the mixed army of Nationalist Chinese and Kachin tribesmen turned their attention to eastern Burma, consolidating their hold over the region and its lucrative crop, opium. The Burmese government used three élite army brigades to contain the rebels, while making representations to the United Nations. A Four-Nation Military Commission, composed of representatives from the United States, Burma, Thailand and Taiwan, was appointed to oversee the KMT withdrawal. Many of the 2,000 fighting troops repatriated were members of the Burmese hill tribes; there were also 7,000 camp-followers, mainly women, children and wounded. Attracted by the money and power associated with the opium trade, more than half the guerrilla army decided to stay in the hills until an offensive by the impatient Burmese army drove a further 4,000 guerillas across the Thai border. Throughout the late 1950s, there was another build-up of KMT forces in Burma and Communist China and the Burmese Royal Army launched a series of joint offensives throughout 1960–61, overrunning airfields and factories refining opium into its morphine base.

Currently, the area produces 80 per cent of the Golden Triangle's output of opium, the poppy fields being protected by Kachin and Shan guerrilla armies who form the National Democratic Front, with an approximate strength of 17,000 combatants. The Burmese Communist Party's force of 10,000 guerrillas control the north-east border region with China, again financed by drug traffic. In addition, powerful war-lords maintain independent armies controlling the drug distribution networks that run through Thailand to staging posts such as Hong Kong, where it is shipped to the West to be processed into heroin. This is the legacy of covert guerrilla operations in Burma.

MALAYA: FROM POACHER TO GAMEKEEPER

The Special Forces had long left Malaya when their Communist guerrilla comrades returned to the jungles and swamps. The guerrilla leader was Chin Peng, hero of Force 136 whose Communist underground army had fought the Japanese alongside the Allied SF teams. After the war, he had received the OBE and marched in a victory parade in London. This was mere window-dressing as British efforts to institute a Malayan Union which would have given the Chinese, 38 per cent of the population, some rights and power, had failed. The Federation of Malaya, established in 1948, preserved essential Malay rights to land and government jobs, although the Malays constituted only 49 per cent of the population.

After the Second World War, the Malayan Communist Party, almost totally Chinese in composition, had gained political recognition and, in an

An Iban tracker advises a patrol commander in Malaya. The skills of indigenous personnel again proved valuable in the post-war counter-insurgency operations. (*Imperial War Museum*)

attempt to initiate political change, had fomented strikes and unrest in the essentially non-Communist workforce. When these measures failed the guerrillas returned to the jungle as the Malayan People's Anti-British Army (MPABA). Many of the old arms and supply dumps were still in place and the extensive anti-Japanese supply and intelligence apparatus was re-activated; the war continued.

For their plan of campaign, the guerrillas used Communist revolutionary theory. Phase one was a campaign of terror against planters and government officials in rural areas. In the early morning of 16 June 1948, three Chinese guerrillas cycled into Elphil Estate in Perak and shot dead a British planter, Arthur Walker. A few miles away another assassination squad tortured and killed Ian Christian and his manager, Mr J. Alison. The executioners then harangued the Chinese and Malay workers on the need to struggle against imperialism. The 'Malayan Emergency' (1948–51) was declared the next day.

The campaign of terror was to lead to the second phase-the creation of 'liberated' no-go areas under guerrilla control; the third and final phase envisaged the MPABA leading the population in an uprising to overthrow the colonial administration. Vital support for the guerrilla army was provided by a clandestine group of approximately 7,000 non-combatants: the *Min Yuen*. This organisation formed a link between the guerrillas and the large Chinese squatter population who had fled into the rural areas to escape the Japanese. They were the ultimate source of intelligence, recruits and supplies for the 1,200 strong guerrilla army. Volunteers swelled the insurgent's forces, which at their peak, fielded 5,000 combatants, optimistically changing its name to the Malayan Races Liberation Army.

From 1948–50, police and army counter-insurgency operations were conducted under the Malay Federation's Commissioner of Police. British army units such as the Gurkhas, Devons, Seaforths and Inniskillings were brought into Malaya to harden the security around potential terrorist targets. Units of guerrillas, pinpointed by chance sightings or intelligence, were pursued and ambushed. In the towns and villages, the police Special Branch spearheaded efforts to identify and eliminate Communist cells and their terror apparatus, the *Lie Ton Ten*, which comprised assassination and sabotage squads.

Despite these efforts, the jungle still provided a sanctuary for the main guerrilla force and their extensive network of bases and supply dumps. In July 1948, a special force was raised, from veterans of SOE's Force 136 and a few volunteers from the Regular Army, to take the war into the jungle. They were joined by 47 Dyak trackers from the Iban tribe in Borneo – head-hunters who had already put their blowpipes and poisoned darts to good use against the Japanese. During its short existence, 'Ferret Force' was credited with identifying 12 enemy bases, proving that military guerrilla units could re-adapt their role to play an important part in counter-guerrilla operations.

By March 1950, 1,138 Communists had been killed and 645 captured; another 359 had surrendered to the security forces. In the same period the Communists had killed 863 civilians, 154 soldiers and 323 police officers. By 1951, the war had intensified and the guerrillas were credited with killing seven civilian or security force personnel a day.

About this time an ex-Special Forces officer, Mike ('Mad Mike') Calvert submitted a detailed analysis of British counter-insurgency efforts in Malaya which would form the basis of a revolutionary new approach in COunter-INsurgency (COIN) operations. Under Calvert's plan (known as the 'Briggs Plan' after Sir Harold Briggs, the British High Commissioner) half-a-million Chinese squatters from 410 villages were resettled in new fortified villages called Kampongs, complete with schools, clinics and agricultural land. This effectively isolated the guerrillas from their source of recruits, intelligence and supplies. These efforts were consolidated by the creation of a Chinese political party, the Malayan Chinese Association, intended to give the Chinese community a stake in the coming independence of Malaya.

The 'Briggs Plan' also directed efforts to break the Communist organisation in the unpopulated areas, dominating the ground and forcing the guerrillas into battle with the security forces. Mindful of the success of Ferret Force, Calvert formed a new special force, the Malayan Scouts (SAS), to operate for long periods in guerrilla sanctuaries. The Scouts were initially composed of three squadrons: A Squadron, recruited in the Far East from a variety of ex-Special Forces and Regular Army personnel; B Squadron recruited from Britain's territorial unit, 21 SAS; and C Squadron, consisting of Rhodesian volunteers, the so-called 'Happy Hundred'. The Scout's became Britain's Regular 22nd SAS Regiment in 1951. By 1956 the Regiment had been enlarged to five squadrons with the addition of D Squadron and the Parachute Regiment Squadron.

The SAS were re-formed to support the 'Briggs Plan' in a number of highly specialised ways. The Regiment ran long-range reconnaissance patrols into the sanctuary areas to locate guerrilla bases; an activity that required infinite patience as it was calculated that it took 1,800 man-hours to establish one contact with the enemy. The patrols, which could last three months, were often inserted into virgin jungle by parachute – a dangerous operation that forced the parachutist to abseil down from the 200-foot tree canopy. As always, the RAF undertook to resupply the patrols, losing over 100 men in crashes resulting from the often appalling flying conditions.

The identification of a large force of guerrillas was the prelude for a large follow-up operation by ground troops. Where the main guerrilla force could not be found, the SAS let the guerrillas come to them, by ambushing well-used jungle tracks, supply caches and jungle clearings used by the guerrillas to grow their own food once the 'Briggs Plan' had begun to bite. To support these missions, the Regiment also took over the Ferret Force role of training and operating with the Iban head-hunters who had been formed into the Sarawak Rangers.

Other operations used ex-guerrillas. Security force successes were followed up with anti-Communist propaganda and offers of bribes and amnesty for guerrillas who surrendered. Surrendered Enemy Personnel (SEPs) were then used to guide British patrols back to their former jungle camps. Other rehabilitation centre graduates joined the Special Operational Volunteers conducting covert operations against their estwhile comrades. These operations took many forms. Doctored and booby-trapped ammunition, infiltrated into guerrilla supply lines, sapped morale, while money and documents left at dead-letter drops suggested that key Communist officials were in fact government agents. Captured enemy radio transmitters were fitted with homing devices to allow the RAF to pinpoint and bomb jungle camps and were then re-introduced into guerrilla supply caches. The survivors from one of these operations left the jungle and surrendered to the army, still clutching their valuable radio-transmitter!

Northern Malaya, the stronghold of the country's Aboriginal minority (one per cent of the population), was the Communists' most secure area and represented a formidable challenge to General Sir Gerald Templer's 'Hearts and Minds' policy. Here the Communists had replaced the Malay authority, maintaining a friendly paternalistic relationship and often intermarrying and learning to speak the Aboriginal dialects. The SAS first began to dominate the area

The gains made by the security forces in Northern Malaya were consolidated by
the creation of a civilian irregular defence programme. The *Senoi Praak* gave
the indigenous tribes a large measure of self-determination and provided them
with a militia for their own defence. (*Imperial War Museum*)

with a chain of jungle forts from which the soldiers distributed free food and
medical care, enticing the Aboriginals into the well-defended encampments.
Learning the language was the key to success, which was measured in terms of
transferred loyalties rather than body counts.

First encounters were often highly dangerous and required great tact and
sensitivity. One village chief's wife had recently given birth to a child who was
obviously dying. The chief cunningly struck a deal with the patrol commander;
if they would save his son's life, his people would move into a fortified village; if
not, they would hand the patrol over to the Communists. While other members
of the patrol were taken into 'protective custody', the patrol medic worked on
the child, which was refusing to suckle. With great patience the medic was able
to persuade the child to suck reconstituted powdered milk from his fingers. He
then transferred the paste to the woman's nipples and the child began to suckle.
The deal was honoured and the village moved to a more secure area.

The programme received an unexpected boost in 1956, when the NZSAS arrived in Malaya to replace Rhodesia's C Squadron. It was discovered that the Maoris amongst the New Zealanders, and a contingent of Fijians from 22 SAS, made a very favourable impression amongst the Aboriginals, helping to close the rift between the indigenous people and the security forces.

The successful 'Hearts and Minds' programme was consolidated by another ex-Special Forces officer, Dick Noone, who had served with the ISLD (MI6), and who helped create the *Senoi Praak* – the Department of Aborigines' (*Orang Asli*) para-military organisation that gave the indigenous tribes a large measure of self-determination and provided them with a militia for their own defence.

When the Communists used terror to dissuade the people from supporting the government, the SAS and other units, such as the Gurhkas and the Royal Marine Commandos, mounted pursuit operations. Li Hak Chi's guerrillas pulled a suspected Chinese informer from a bus on the Seremban-Kuala Pilah road and hacked him to death. They were finally tracked down by the NZSAS Squadron and eliminated in August 1957, in the Negri Sembilan mountains, when they broke cover to search for food. An Hoi, who had disembowelled an informer's pregnant wife, went the same way, cornered in the Telok Anson Swamp in February 1958.

The Communist insurgency failed, many of the guerrillas leaving Malaya to seek sanctuary in Thailand. There, 40 years after the 'State of Emergency' had been declared, the sporadic fighting finally ended. In late December 1987, as part of a negotiated surrender, elements from three Regiments of the Malayan Races Liberation Army left the jungle, bringing with them a mass of ammunition, weapons and anti-personnel mines. As part of their resettlement, each guerrilla family was given 37 acres of land and, for the first year an allowance of $0.50 a day.

Lessons were learnt from this rather special and restricted insurgency war. Specialised military units capable of operating for long periods in the jungle, working with indigenous people, were well suited for such 'low-intensity' wars, fought mainly between infantry and guerrillas but as demanding as any conflict on the battlefield and requiring 'a whole new kind of strategy, a wholly different kind of force'. They were said to require 10–12 government troops to each guerrilla, resettlement and civilian irregular defence programmes and a 'Hearts and Minds' approach, all vital to military success. By isolating the population from the guerrillas and bringing alienated communities back into the country's political life, the counter-insurgency forces removed the *raison d'être* for revolution.

BORNEO: THE BORDER WAR

In the early 1960s Singapore, and Sarawak and Sabah in British Borneo were all British colonies awaiting independence. The British proposed that the three amalgamated with the Federation of Malaya, to form the new state of Malaysia. However, Sukarno, President of Indonesia since independence from the

Dutch in 1949, had his own plan to absorb the British colonies into Greater Indonesia. After an abortive attempt to overthrow the independent sultanate of Brunei in 1962, he declared *Konfrontasi* (Confrontation) and dispatched forces across the 970-mile border between Indonesian Borneo (Kalimantan) and the British colonies in the north of the island.

At first the Indonesians fought the war by proxy. Civilians were trained as guerrillas and sent across the border to raid isolated village police-posts and treat the locals to a large dose of political rhetoric. These were known to the security forces as Indonesian Border Terrorists. As the war intensified, Indonesia started using regular troops including Indonesian Special Forces (para-commandos and marines). These forces received some support from inside the country, notably from the Clandestine Communist Organisation, mainly supported by the Chinese populations in coastal towns and Indonesian labourers in the timber trade along the southern border of Sabah. The aim was to spread revolution throughout the colonies and bring them into union with Indonesia.

To counter these incursions, the British employed some 15,000 troops, mainly infantry supported by the full range of logistical units such as artillery, signals, engineers, Army Air Corps and, of course, the Royal Navy and RAF. For the most part, Borneo was a patrol war where British units attempted to 'out-guerrilla' the enemy by reconnaissance patrol and ambush. It was a war perfectly suited to special operations. Some of the most valuable operations, the Top Secret CLARET patrols, were designed to force the Indonesians to move their bases further back from the border, without escalating the war or inviting intervention by the United Nations.

Other operations were concerned with developing civilian irregular defence programmes and intelligence networks amongst the 20 or so tribal groups in Sabah and Sarawak. These projects brought problems unique to Borneo. Faced with a multitude of languages and dialects, the SAS actively trawled other units for soldiers with an aptitude for languages, who became attached to the Regiment as specialists. The fortified village system pioneered in Malaya was unnecessary in Borneo. While the Indonesian insurgents sought to alienate the locals from the British and the Malaysian government, they did not rely upon the local population for supplies or recruits. The indigenous people were mainly pro-British, although some were quite introverted and resistant to outside influences. Others, like the Punans, were hard to find, migrating back and forth across the border. In this tightly-knit 'world within a world' few events in the jungle went unnoticed and the 'bush-telegraph' would often give advance warning of Indonesian incursions.

Indonesian incursions had to contend with a range of defences: a thin line of forts, surveillance and reconnaissance patrols dotted along a 700-mile stretch of the border, watching the mountain passes and well-used tracks. Some escaped to be faced with a 2–4-week walk through the jungle to their target areas. The aim of the 'Hearts and Minds' programme in Borneo was to turn the jungle villages into a deeper defence network of eyes and ears that would report the slightest indication of an incursion.

The aim of the 'Hearts and Minds' programme in Borneo was to turn the jungle villages into an intelligence network of eyes and ears that would report the slightest indication of an incursion. Some tribesmen were recruited for intelligence gathering and para-military operations. (*Private Collection*)

The usual 'Hearts and Minds' system required a patrol to live close to a village, providing medical services while encouraging the natives to pass on information. In his masterly history of the Australian SAS Regiment, *SAS Phantoms of the Jungle*, Lieutenant Colonel Horner quotes the patrol logs from these operations:

> The babies are one hell of a mess, they have sores all over their bodies and are covered in warts. I suspect this is from malnutrition and the parents not keeping them clean ... We look like having a bit of a 'flu epidemic. Chicken pox is rife at the moment, 50% of the kids in the longhouse have it ... 3yr old boy with an infected penis due to having a bamboo splinter forced up the eye, cured him with penicillin ... The women have queer ideas about having kids. When they are ready to drop the kid, they sit as close to fire as possible, drink rice water as hot as they can stand and massage the stomach with a hot stone. They lose on average one out of eight mothers this way ... The locals reckon we are number one because we will go just about anywhere to look at their sick ... since they did not care about the Indonesians one way or the other, events could take place and they would not mention them.

At night, the patrol withdrew to a secret LUP in the jungle to maintain security; in theory a good system, but a trifle embarrassing when the natives' morning sick parade formed up in front of the hide. As contact increased, gifts of portable radios, medical kits and even Christmas hampers from Fortnum and Mason sealed the friendship. The villagers were persuaded to clear helicopter LZs for the sheer excitement of seeing the aircraft land in the village or for the promise of other delights that arrived by air. An old Borneo hand recalls one such adventure:

> We had promised the village chief two cases of Tiger beer if they would clear the LZ. Next day, as promised, an aircraft flew in low over the clearing and the supplies were kicked out of the door. Suddenly there was a shout and I looked around in time to see the Chief run out to catch his beer. Fortunately, I was quick enough to bring him down in a rugby tackle. The villagers would not have been very impressed if the Chief had ended up being driven into the ground like a tent-peg!

While the helicopters played a large part in the life of the village, ferrying rice and livestock, they also provided a rapid response to reports of enemy sightings and the cutting edge to the British promise to protect the jungle peoples.

Some tribesmen were trained as Border Scouts. Their primary role was to move between the villages gathering intelligence on Indonesian incursions from the natives' bush-telegraph – 'bare-arsed ears and eyes that could go anywhere'. Unfortunately, having received basic military training, many were used in the static defence of villages as civilian irregular defence militia. This was a role totally unsuited to their temperament or training, as evidenced by the events in September 1963, in Long Jawi. A detachment of 21 Border Scouts and six Gurkha NCOs were manning the Scout post unaware that a company of Indonesian regulars had slipped across the border, just 30 miles away. The Indonesians attacked one morning at dawn, killing all but three of the security forces before looting and burning the village. While most of the insurgents were hunted down over the next two months, the Scouts' reputation and morale received a crippling blow. The problem of adequately defending the villages was solved by bringing in the Australian and NZSAS and using the Gurkha and Parachute Regiment Independent Parachute Companies in the SAS role.

In the summer of 1964, 22 SAS took over training the Border Scouts in camps in northern Borneo and Western Sarawak, returning them to their original role of intelligence gathering. Some of the graduates of this programme were used as trackers, joining other Dyaks from the Sarawak Rangers who had served in the Malayan Emergency. There were still many more SAS patrols than trackers and as a consequence, the Dyaks became the teachers, passing on their skills to SAS soldiers with an aptitude for this art. This scheme was almost marred by the distrust between the Dyaks and the Malay administration, which was unwilling to supply automatic weapons to the jungle tribes for fear of arming future insurgents. Fortunately, many were quite pleased to be issued with shot-guns, which were proving excellent weapons for the sudden close quarter combat in the jungle.

Other camp graduates were selected for cross-border operations with the SAS or were sent to camps run by the British MI6, These establishments trained guerrillas for covert, deniable raids and intelligence duties deep inside Indonesia. The guerrillas were all indigenous tribesmen, trained and controlled by British Army Special Operations teams, commanded by seconded British Army officers and civilian MI6 officers. This was little more than tit-for-tat response to the Indonesian civilian guerrilla raids but these operations must have caused Sukarno a considerable headache before he was replaced as President by General Suharto, in an appallingly bloody coup mounted by the Indonesian Army in October 1965. This was in response to an uprising by the Indonesian Communist Party, possibly orchestrated by Sukarno himself, in an attempt to eliminate rivals within the Indonesian officer corps. A year later, and with some 600,000 dead inside Indonesia, the Indonesians lost interest in their Borneo quarrel and signed a peace agreement – 'Confrontation' was over.

THE OMAN: HEARTS AND MINDS

In Malaya, the 'Hearts and Minds' programme had become a central pillar of the British COIN operations but the unusual and restricted rebellion by the Chinese population had not really tested the philosophy. In contrast, the Oman proved to be an acid test of the embryonic COIN doctrines. A mountainous desert sultanate on the south-east edge of the Arabian Peninsula, it had, by a quirk of history, come to control the tip of the Musandam Peninsula – a natural choke-point on the Straits of Hormuz, through which 50 per cent of the West's oil passed on its way to European and American markets.

The Oman was in every sense an anachronism. Its people were impoverished and disease-ridden, and education and Western consumer goods were banned as being a threat to the country's Islamic religion and its absolute ruler, Sultan Sa'id bin Taimur. To make matters worse, the Sultan ruled not from the capital Muscat but from his palace in the coastal town of Salalah, in the southern desert province of Dhofar. There, the country was governed by radio-telephone or through expatriates. No man could even repair his house without permission of the Sultan and infringements were punished by floggings, imprisonment or the destruction of the village well, with obviously catastrophic consequences.

The SAS first found itself in the Oman in 1958. A tribal rebellion, simmering since 1955, was fanned by outside interests and threatened to

The core of the British counter-insurgency efforts in the Oman was a 'hearts and minds' programme that wooed the desert peoples away from the guerillas. (*Imperial War Museum*)

overwhelm the sultanate. In 1957, Britain committed forces to help restore order and the tide was finally turned by a classical SAS commando raid on a natural fortress that had withstood seige after seige for at least 900 years.

However, commando operations have limited success against scattered guerrilla forces and do nothing to counter the social conditions that allow insurgency to develop. In 1965, Iraqi-trained Dhofari tribesman began a campaign of ambushes, raids and assassinations, which gathered momentum two years later, when the British withdrew from Yemen's southern neighbour, Aden. The government of the now Marxist People's Democratic Republic of Yemen (or South Yemen) began openly to support the war in neighbouring

Dhofar. Soon the war began to tax the Sultan's Armed Forces (SAF), which, by arrangement with the British Government, was commanded by British officers.

A fundamental change in the Oman's fortunes resulted from three events: the discovery of oil; a palace coup which toppled Sa'id in favour of his son, Qaboos; and the return of the SAS in 1970 to spearhead the British counter-insurgency campaign. Organised into British Army Training Teams, a cadre of 50–100 SAS soldiers immediately put into effect the lessons learnt in Malaya. Psychological operations, promising an aggressive civil aid programme and offering amnesty and money to surrendering guerillas, reaped a harvest of Surrendered Enemy Personnel (SEPs). These men were screened and the most useful trained and integrated into counter-guerrilla units known as *firqats*. By 1975, the SAS administered 1,600 men deployed in 21 separate *firqat* units. By living in close contact with the irregulars, the SAS team leaders overcame the problems of command and control that not infrequently resulted in mutinies. With skilful handling, the *firqats* became a key element in operations to recover lost territory and win the hearts and minds of the Dhofari tribesmen.

Penetration into guerrilla controlled territory began when areas promising underground water and access were taken in large-scale conventional operations. Once the local guerrillas had withdrawn, units of engineers arrived to construct buildings, roads and water-points. The *firqat* base, held by the irregulars and a small number of the Sultan's soldiers, now dominated the surrounding area and, once taken, an area was never relinquished.

The water supply had an almost magnetic attraction for the people living in the surrounding areas. When they drove their cattle into the base, they discovered a mosque, a school, government shops and clinics dispensing medical and veterinary services. Other specialists within the Civil Action Teams provided advice on crops and animal husbandry. For the keen farmer, model farms had been set up, with stock imported from Britain. The *firqat*, intelligence and psyops personnel moved amongst the people, many of whom had regular contact with the *Adoo* (guerrillas), gathering intelligence and counselling the tribesmen not to allow the guerrillas to interfere with the Sultan's gifts. Totally dependent on the goodwill of the tribesmen, the guerrillas lost the ideological battle.

Those that refused to accept the government amnesty were left to their own devices and hunted by SAS/*firqat* units supported by the 15,000 strong SAF. Barbed wire barriers running for 30 or more miles were constructed and guarded by booby traps and electronic surveillance devices. These severed the supply-lines that ran from the guerrilla units to their supporters in South Yemen and forced the insurgents closer to the border, where the final bitter battles were fought in 1976.

7

Hearts and Minds: Indo-China

*Political activities were more important than military activities,
and fighting less important than propaganda.'*
General Vo Nguyen Giap, *People's War, People's Army.*
Hanoi, 1961.

It could be argued that the most recent conflicts along the western borders of
Laos and Cambodia began with the moonlight landings of Free French and
American parachutists in 1944. Three wars spawned a cluster of sub-
conflicts, fought across five countries for nearly 50 years by 'international
brigades', complex wars in which the protagonists often changed sides for
tangled political reasons. France fought the Japanese to recapture her
colonies, which the Communist Viet Minh fought to keep. The Americans,
mindful of their own revolutionary heritage, were philosophically opposed to
both the fascist dictators and the old European colonialists. OSS Teams
armed and led the Communist Viet Minh against the Japanese and Vichy
French puppets and were on hand to lend support for their struggle against the
tripartite British-Japanese-French caretaker administration which prepared
Indo-China for the return of the French. Thus, the wars against the Japanese
and French blurred into a continuum that the Vietnamese Communist Party
called the 'First Indo-Chinese War'.

The Geneva Accords which ended the French war divided Vietnam into two
regimes, North and South, but called for national elections as a prelude to the
country's eventual reunification. The political situation in North Vietnam
looked bleak after the Communists assumed power. Nine hundred thousand
refugees fled south to escape the 'People's Courts' and a regime that had little
time for their many and various religions. Nobody had any doubt as to the
ability of the Communists to successfully manipulate the outcome of national

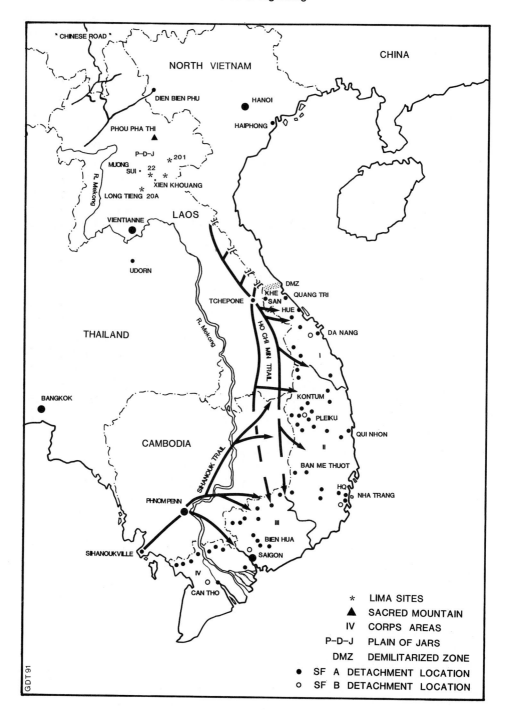

"CHINESE ROAD"

NORTH VIETNAM   CHINA

DIEN BIEN PHU   HANOI

PHOU PHA THI ▲   HAIPHONG

P–D–J
                   * 201
MUONG
SUI • 22
       *   *
LONG TIENG * XIEN KHOUANG
            20A

LAOS

R. Mekong

VIENTIANNE

UDORN   DMZ
                                    XHE   QUANG TRI
                         TCHEPONE   SAN
                                         HUE

THAILAND   R. Mekong   DA NANG

                                    HO CHI MINH TRAIL   I

BANGKOK   KONTUM

                                    PLEIKU
                                              QUI NHON
CAMBODIA   II

                  SIHANOUK TRAIL   BAN ME THUOT

PHNOM PENH   HQ
                                              NHA TRANG

                                    III

SIHANOUKVILLE   BIEN HUA
                          SAIGON

                   IV
              CAN THO

                                    *   LIMA SITES
                                    ▲   SACRED MOUNTAIN
                                    IV   CORPS AREAS
                                    P–D–J PLAIN OF JARS
                                    DMZ   DEMILITARIZED ZONE
                                    ● SF A DETACHMENT LOCATION
                                    ○ SF B DETACHMENT LOCATION

GDT 91

elections and, in May 1955, President Diem of South Vietnam refused to participate. America, now more concerned about the fall of the Far Eastern 'Dominoes' to international Communism than Old World Colonialism, backed Diem with military aid.

In May 1959, the 15th Plenum of the North Vietnamese Communist Party launched the 'Second Indo-Chinese War'. Rejecting the North Korean model of an overwhelming assault across the Demilitarised Zone, the Communists spearheaded their war with political cadres working in the South, charged with waging an ideological struggle among the people. Some 90,000 veterans from the South were persuaded to return home. On their way, they activated further revolutionary networks that had lain dormant in the South. Back in the North, the 599th Transportation Group began to build a complex series of roads on the Laotian side of the Annamite Mountains. This would become the Truong Son Strategic Supply Route, a communications link with the war in the South that the Americans would called the 'Ho Chi Minh Trail'.

America's war in Vietnam has been compared unfavourably with the British campaigns in Malaya and Borneo. However, Vietnam was no simple counter-insurgency campaign. North Vietnam would prove willing to 'pay any price, take any risk' for final victory, while America, faced with the realities of a distant, brutal and frustrating 'television war' would renege on President Kennedy's promise to defend America's allies. Equally, the British never experienced infiltration on the scale made possible by the Truong Son Supply Route. By 1967, there were 400,000 American troops in South Vietnam, fighting approximately 200,000 Viet-Cong guerrillas, 20,000 North Vietmese Army regular troops and 20,000 political cadres. It has been calculated that to have achieved a 6:1 superiority over the enemy, a mere half of that employed by the British in Malaya, almost the entire American Army would have needed to be stationed in Vietnam.

One central core of this conflict that rarely reached the television screens was the ideological struggle or 'People's War' – a clandestine conflict fought with revolutionary fervour and terror by the Viet-Cong, Pathet Lao and Khmer Rouge guerrillas backed by the North Vietnamese, Chinese and Russians. It would be countered by the CIA and US, Nationalist Chinese, New Zealand, Australian, South Korean, British and Thai Special Operations personnel. Together the clandestine operators would raise and train armies of indigenous tribesman, fuelling the nationalist and tribal aspirations that are being pursued on the battlefields of Laos and Cambodia today.

VIETNAM: THE OTHER WAR

The revolutionary offensive to capture the countryside ('Peoples War') began in 1959. From the outset the Communists targeted government officials, village chiefs, teachers and other educated élites who might provide an alternative leadership to the Party. The aim was to spread fear and dislocate

The spearhead of America's 'other war' for the Vietmanese hamlets. The People's Self-Defence Forces were created to protect the hamlets from communist tax-collectors, political cadres and murder squads. (*TRH Pictures*)

the workings of everyday Vietnamese society. Political cadres were then well placed to blame all the peasants' misfortunes on the Diem Government. While the Vietnamese Government and American military became mesmerised by the violence, some CIA officers were more concerned with the revolutionary infrastructure; an invisible 'octopus' spreading its subversive tentacles throughout the villages. The battle for the Vietnamese villages, what President Lyndon Johnson called the 'other war', was being lost.

In his book, *Lost Victory*, ex-CIA Director William Colby presents the nature of this 'other war' and the enemy that they faced:

> The main problem Washington faced was strategic – its efforts to fight its kind of war, a soldier's war, instead of the people's war the enemy was fighting. In this situation, the Communist thrust went under the American military effort in South Vietnam. The American forces, trained to 'find, fix, fight, and finish the enemy', could not even find him, so their enormous power expended itself against the jungles – or the peoples of the rural areas who were the real objective of the enemy ... American military commanders, and consequently their intelligence officers, were concerned primarily with intelligence about enemy military units that might attack them or that they saw as their targets. Their focus, therefore was the Communist military enemy rather than the civilian activists who inhabited the rural communities or visited them to conduct the basic elements of the people's war strategy – proselytising, taxing, conscripting. Military interrogators of prisoners thus would ask every detail of the activities of a main force unit or local force unit in the neighbourhood, or even of a guerrilla squad, but ignore the identity of a local tax collector or *agitprop* activist.

Communist violence was applied selectively to subdue the villagers without attracting the attention of the military. Government agents and hostile village headmen were publicly beheaded or ritually disembowelled. Official projects aimed at improving life in the villages and bridging the gulf between the Government and the peasants came in for special attention. A prime example was the programme to eradicate malaria which withered under a hail of bullets. While the Party complemented itself on its propaganda victory, the village children continued to die from this far older killer.

The failure of other South Vietnamese Government projects were self-inflicted wounds. President Diem's 'agricultural cities' failed to motivate the villagers and became a mere resettlement programme; the peasants returned to their bamboo huts. Other attempts to resettle villagers in protected hamlets ignored their strong cultural and religious links to the land and failed to provide adequate protection. Unlike the British COIN tactics of clearing, holding and dominating areas, the Americans and Vietnamese would 'sweep' through selected areas. Once the Americans left, the Communist infrastructure quickly reappeared.

From 1960–63 the CIA started to work on its own solution of motivating selected communities into organising their own self-defence forces and initiating development programmes. The British style 'Hearts and Minds' programme was seen as too passive in treating the population as an 'inert audience'. The American solution became pacification and Vietnamisation: programmes to engage the population in its own common national effort. In 1966, the American civilian agencies which were involved in different aspects of the rural defence and development programmes (CIA, United States Information Agency, United States Agency for International Development) were unified into the Office of Civil Operations (OCO). A year later, the OCO was combined with Military Assistance Command Vietnam's (MACV) Rural Development Support Division, into an integrated approach to pacification under the title, Civil Operations and Revolutionary Development Support (CORDS).

CORDS mounted its campaign for the war in the countryside under 15 sub-programmes that formed four broad fronts: firstly, the support of police and Self-Defence Forces at the regional and village levels; secondly, the funding of Rural Development Cadres (to revive village government), various village improvement projects, information and community centres and much needed land reform; thirdly, the care and support of highland tribal groups and refugees; and the fourth front was an amnesty programme to attract Viet-Cong defectors, harnessed to the *Phuong Hoang* or Phoenix counter-terror programme to kill or capture the Viet-Cong infrastructure. Colby provides convincing evidence for the success of these initiatives, whether measured by figures from the CIA's computerised 'hamlet evaluation system' or the mere fact that the programme's senior officers were increasingly able to drive around remote areas of countryside after dark. If the battle for the countryside was finally won by this multi-pronged approach to counter-revolutionary warfare, it was lost again when American forces withdrew from Vietnam. Ironically, the anti-war movement in America gorged itself on horror stories ascribed to the Phoenix counter-terror programme (see Chapter 12), stories that fed the growing American revulsion with their war in South East Asia.

THE BATTLE FOR THE CENTRAL HIGHLANDS

The fact that the Central Highlands of Vietnam provided a strategic barrier of mountainous jungle between the Communist supply route and the lowlands of South Vietnam was not lost upon the CIA. To penetrate deep into South Vietnam, Communist forces had to pass across land occupied by 32 mountain tribes known to the French as Montagnards or mountaineers. These tribes were of two distinct ethnic backgrounds: Malayo-Polynesian and Mon-Khmer. Most lived in appalling conditions and American Special Forces medics were to discover that approximately half the 1.5 million tribesmen suffered from tuberculosis and dysentery, while some 10 per cent showed signs of leprosy and nearly all suffered from malaria. Only two of the tribes, the Rhade and Jarai, had any form of written language. To the South Viet-

An American Special Forces camp in the Central Highlands. The aim of the CIA's Civilian Irregular Defence Group Programme (CIDG) was to provide armed territorial units that would protect local settlements from Communist infiltration. The next step was to place fortified camps inside contested areas. (*TRH Pictures*)

namese they were savages (*Mois*). The Americans and Communists came to see them as mercenaries. All failed to take account of these people's perception of themselves and their world – a mistake that would cost all parties concerned very dearly.

Some of the indigenous peoples employed in American special operations could be described as mercenaries. About 500,000 Chinese Nungs lived in Saigon and the coastal towns. Some of these were recruited by Military Assistance Command Vietnam Studies and Observation Group (MACVSOG) for covert operations outside Vietnam. Others were recruited by the Special Forces to serve alongside the hill tribes. In contrast, the Montagnards saw themselves as descendants of the Champas, a kingdom that embraced central Vietnam and parts of Cambodia and Laos around 200 AD. Conquered by the Mongol Emperor Kublai Khan and then by the Viets, the Champas retreated into the Highlands and descended into poverty. Like many partisan forces during the Second World War, the Montagnards sought to ally themselves with any group that would support their independence movement.

Under French rule the tribesmen lived in an autonomous zone, many of them rising to senior positions within the army and colonial administration. When the French left, the Montagnards found themselves persecuted by President Diem's government, which seized their land and gave it to Vietnamese immigrants. Many tribes were resettled along the coast at gun-point as part of Diem's divide-and-rule policy. In 1959, the political cadres appeared in the hills, joining the thousands of Viet Minh soldiers sent to live with the tribes after the French defeat. Revolt followed swiftly and Diem's search-and-destroy expeditions were met first by cross-bow and then modern weapons in the hands of Montagnard Second World War veterans. While tribes such as the Kor, Sedang and Bahnar turned to massacring South Vietnamese garrisons, the Hre went over to the Viet-Cong. Strategic areas such as Darlac Province, north-west of Ban Me Thuot, fell into Communist hands. Provincial road traffic was stopped at will by guerrilla bands and a 'road tax' levied on the passengers. Any Americans unlucky enough to be stopped on the roads were summarily executed. Finally, the Communists over-reached themselves, when they attempted to purge the tribal leadership. The kidnap and murder of thousands of former Montagnard colonial soldiers resulted in many tribes abandoning the so-called National Liberation Front.

It was against this background that CIA teams started working with the Rhade tribe in 1960. The aim of the Agency's Civilian Irregular Defence Group Programme (CIDG) was to provide armed territorial units that would protect local settlements from Communist infiltration. The next step was to place fortified camps inside contested areas. Once established, the CIDGs dominated the area around them by aggressive patrolling, always spreading outwards, in William Colby's words, 'like ink on a blotter'. Over the next three years, the CIA teams were supplemented by 'A' Teams from the 1st, 5th and 7th Special Forces Groups. In mid-1963, the CIA's paramilitary groups were handed over to MACV under Operation SWITCHBACK. The CIA's Covert Action Branch faded into the background to provide logistical support and direction.

At the end of 1963, the Special Forces had trained 43,000 hamlet militia. A further 18,000 highly-trained, indigenous personnel were organised into Strike Forces and used for more offensive operations, such as the recapture of fortified Montagnard villages held by the Viet-Cong. By 1964, the 5th Special

Forces Group, now permanently assigned to Vietnam, started to expand its offensive indigenous operations. Under the Border Surveillance Programme, patrols composed of CIDG troops and Special Forces operated against the Communist supply lines on the Ho Chi Minh Trail.

The Viet-Cong sensed that they were losing the battle for the Highlands and responded by attacking the Montagnard bases. While remote, the bases were well defended and contained air-strips that enabled the garrison to be resupplied by air. The Viet-Cong's tactic was to launch surprise assaults under cover of darkness, overwhelming the surprised defenders with massed-wave attacks. Some bases were swept away in a night. The Americans countered by recruiting the most able indigenous personnel from the CIDG camps and forming them into battalions called Multipurpose Reaction Forces or Mobile Strike Forces (Mike Forces). Capable of being deployed by parachute or helicopter, Mike Force companies rapidly reinforced besieged bases, turning the Viet-Cong's military sacrifices into bloody defeats.

The Americans were quick to see the possibilities of the Mike Force philosophy. Now, instead of waiting for the Communists to attack the Special Forces bases, Mike Force would lure the VC into carefully constructed traps. The enemy saw small reconnaissance patrols as easy targets and LRRP teams frequently needed a larger force to get them out of trouble and capitalise on their intelligence gains. Mike Force would provide that support but would additionally operate with its own combat recon-unit which could be deployed behind enemy lines as a stalking horse. In 1966, Mike Force strength was increased to three battalions and two years later it was reorganised into the 5th Mobile Strike Force Command. At the close of 1968, the 5th Special Forces Group controlled 7,000 Mike Force troops and 27,000 other CIDG personnel, many of whom were also organised into aggressive Mike Force-type units such as the Guerrilla Strike Force.

Other countries contributed Army Training Teams to the CIDG Programme, notably Australia, whose teams included SAS and Military Intelligence Commando personnel. Britain made a small contribution in the form of a team composed of Borneo tribesmen commanded by the MI6 officer Dick Noone. Dick Noone was one of a number of anthropologists who made significant contributions to this area of covert operations. As specialists on indigenous peoples they were admirably suited to organising and training partisans and CIDG troops. During the Second World War, Dick Noone and his brother, Pat, also an anthropologist, had run an intelligence network amongst the Malays in southern Thailand, and his contribution during the Emergency in Malaya and 'Confrontation' have already been recounted. Perhaps not surprisingly, the man who had made a sizeable contribution to British COIN operations in Malaya by fostering a sense of political and tribal identity amongst the Aboriginals, was cold-shouldered by the Vietnamese. A brief account of Dick Noone's adventures are to be found in Barry Petersen's fascinating book, *Tiger Men*.

INDIGENOUS SUPPORT FOR CONVENTIONAL OPERATIONS

The Special Forces' Mike Force concept was attractive to the conventional forces forced to do battle with an elusive enemy. By July 1968, the 5th MSFC (5th Special Forces Group) had been joined by another four Mobile Strike Force Commands, attached to I, II, III, and IV Corps Tactical Zones in Vietnam. This brought the total Mike Force strength to around 11,000 personnel deployed with 35 Mike Force companies. Mike Force irregulars performed scouting and combat reconnaissance tasks for units such as the 1st Air Cavalry and the 173rd Airborne Brigade. Patrolling forward of the conventional units, Mike Force companies would invite attack and then attempt to engage and maintain contact with the enemy until the airmobile brigade arrived.

Other indigenous support units were appropriately accorded titles that recalled America's earlier Indian Wars. Captured enemy guerrillas and regular NVA soldiers were rehabilitated and used as Kit Carson Scouts'. Whether they were used to demonstrate the apparent ease with which a Viet-Cong sapper could penetrate barbed-wired minefields or as scouts on reconnaissance patrols, their special knowledge and background was invaluable to American troops adjusting to guerrilla warfare.

Apache Force was a training/advisory unit made up of Montagnard CIDG personnel and their Special Forces advisers. Their students were newly-arrived American troops about to start their 365-day tour in Vietnam. Apache Force instructors were given the difficult task of orientating these soldiers towards operations, where the primary form of contact with the enemy would be restricted to ambushes, sniping and a lethal array of booby-traps. To reinforce these lessons, Apache Force personnel accompanied the troops during their first few days in a combat zone. Later in the war, Apache Force was reabsorbed into Mike Force as combat reconnaissance platoons. Other units, known as Eagle Scouts, were also used in the combat reconnaissance role.

THE WAR WITHIN THE SPECIAL FORCES CAMPS

The CIDG Programme faced two major enemies: the Communists and the South Vietnamese Government. Both dismissed the Montagnards as savages and mercenaries but the latter heaped on further indignities by misappropriating American aid and depriving the tribes of education, medical care or any voice in local government. To the Montagnards, the singular difference between the two was that they were encouraged to kill Communists – and occasionally, the South Vietnamese helped blur even that distinction. In 1962, Montagnards from the Rhade and Jarai tribes were forced to leave their village, given some antique weapons and resettled deep within Communist controlled territory at a place called My Tach in Pleiku Province. Within two weeks, the Viet-Cong had over-run the 'Strategic Hamlet' twice, burning the barracks and killing many of the tribesmen. When the 'savages' asked to be returned to their village, the Province Chief ordered 60 of the Montagnards to be executed. With many of the men already killed by the Viet-Cong, the firing-parties are reported to have made up the numbers with women and children.

The American Special Forces attempted to redress this balance but were forced to run the camps with their protégés: the South Vietnamese Special Forces or *Luc Luong Dac Biet* (LLDB). The parallel command structure was part of America's policy of Vietnamisation. At best this was no more than 'helping our friends to help themselves'; at worst, it provided a sanction for the Vietnamese habit of oppressing ethnic minorities. To make matters worse, the LLDB showed a lack of enthusiasm for the dangers of small-group warfare, which earned them the contemptuous American title 'Look Long Duck Back'. Consequently, in most camps the Vietnamese LLDB were relegated to running the camp's administration, while the Americans retained operational control.

On 20 September 1964, Montagnard rebels seized control of seven Special Forces camps, disarming the American advisers before slaughtering their LLDB counter-parts. Four large groups of rebels then closed in on the vitally important town of Ban Me Thuot, selected by the Diem government as an emergency capital if Saigon should ever fall to the Communists. By-passing loyal Montagnard troops, the rebels managed to kidnap Y-Bham Enuol, the unofficial head of the Montagnards, and occupy the airport. In adjoining Quang Duc Province, near the Cambodian border, a force of 500 Rhade and M'nong over-ran a Vietnamese Civil Guard outpost and massacred the occupants. During the next four days the rebels killed a total of 84 Vietnamese, sparing a few administrators who were kept as hostages.

With the area now open to Communist infiltration, more than a little panic ensued. A Vietnamese airborne unit was hurriedly sent to reinforce the crumbling defences in Ban Me Thuot, followed by a number of American and Vietnamese officials. A meeting was arranged with the rebel leaders, who presented their demands for regional autonomy. In effect, the war could continue but with Montagnard soldiers led by their own officers, fighting for a regional state under Montagnard control. Unfortunately, politics and self-interest muddied a negotiated cease-fire and 3,000 hard-core rebels decamped for Cambodia where they formed the *Front Unifié de Libération des Races Opprimeés* (FULRO) – the Front for the Liberation of the Oppressed Races. Y-Bham Enuol was named as the first President of the High Plateau of the Champa.

Subsequently, the American Special Forces were able to persuade 600 of the rebels to return to the Highlands and, in one of the strangest operations of the war, American helicopters collected the heavily armed tribesman from a base in northern Cambodia. The war continued but now American patrols were being fired upon by villages previously thought friendly and in some American bases the Vietnamese flag was replaced by FULRO's three-starred banner. Unlike their SAS counterparts in other theatres, the Green Berets had kept their distance from the indigenous soldiers. This was partly due to their

An American Special Forces sergeant instructs Montagnard tribesmen in the use
of the 60mm mortar. (*TRH Pictures*)

rotation system. Until 1964, the Green Berets had spent six months with a
particular tribe before being replaced. A new system assigned Special Forces
personnel to a particular camp for a year, after which they were rotated out as
individuals, rather than teams, to ensure continuity. As a result the American
relationship with the Montagnards deepened.

In September 1965, trouble broke out again. The South Vietnamese considered the Special Forces camps to be hotbeds of rebellion and sent troops to
pacify the Montagnards. The Americans resisted and General Ky threatened
to have the camps bombed if his troops were denied access. The Americans

capitulated and were forced to watch as thousands of suspects were arrested – and several fully-armed FULRO companies went over to the Viet-Cong. Approximately 400 members of the Rhade, Jarai, Bahnar and other tribes were executed. The journalist, Kuno Knobel, described events:

> Alleged and real members of the rebel movement were herded together and publicly shot. Government execution squads swept through the highlands and took revenge on the 'savages'. In Plei Me, Sergeant Duke said to me, 'If the Vietnamese had fought as passionately against the Communists, there would be nothing for us to do now'.

The Vietnamese and even the CIA blamed the American Special Forces for the FULRO rebellion. The Americans blamed the Viet-Cong and French. This was only partly true. Two of the principal leaders, Chau Dara and Les Kosem, were double agents, working for both the Cambodian secret service and the French SDECE. The former served Prince Sihanouk who, while attempting to ally himself with both sides in the war, had a particular dislike of the CIA and their projects. Likewise, his French intelligence associates, the French, had not forgotten that American OSS Teams had supported the Viet Minh in their war against France, and throughout the Vietnam War, the SDECE maintained an intelligence network in Indo China made up of planters, diplomats and some Jesuit priests. There is evidence that they procured arms for the Communists and even engaged in the assassination of American intelligence officers. In contrast, the upsurge of nationalism amongst the Montagnards, did not serve the interests of the Viet-Cong, who marked the FULRO leaders for assassination and merely manipulated events to profit from the rebellion. The real culprits were the South Vietnamese.

Prince Sihanouk saw the FULRO leadership as an important political pawn in his plans to play one side off against the other. When, in 1968, it was rumoured that the FULRO chiefs intended to return to Vietnam, they were arrested and held in Phnom Penh. In 1975 they fell into the hands of the victorious Communist Khmer Rouge forces and are believed to have perished along with two million others in the 'killing fields'.

The CIDG programme managed to survive the FULRO episode. During the Tet Offensive of January 1968, Mike Force units stationed in Ban Me Thuot and Nha Trang inflicted severe casualties on the guerrillas. Following Tet much of the CIDG effort was directed against Communist border infiltration routes. In 1968, the process of turning the CIDG camps over to the Vietnamese was accelerated, aided in no small part by the efforts of Special Forces Detachment B-51 to increase the training standards of the Vietnamese LLDB. In early 1971, the CIDG programme was officially ended and the indigenous troops absorbed into the Army of Vietnam (ARVN), though approximately 37 of the CIDG camps were retained as ARVN Ranger Camps. These Border Rangers and their CIDG component continued to operate against the Communist infiltration routes. After the Communist victory in Vietnam, many Montagnard leaders and CIDG members found themselves in extermination camps.

CROSS-BORDER OPERATIONS

The role of the Military Assistance Command Vietnam Studies and Observation Group (MACVSOG), often more accurately paraphrased as the 'Special Operations Group, was to conduct the full spectrum of special operations, either inside North Vietnam or in countries with which there was no formal declaration of war, such as Cambodia, Laos and China. Its personnel were an amalgamation of army, air force and navy special forces, with a smattering of professional intelligence officers from the various American agencies (CIA, DIA, NSA). At the height of its activity, MACVSOG employed around 2,500 Americans, including members of the 5th (Special Operations Augmentation), 1st and 7th Special Forces Groups on six-month temporary duty attachments. These were augmented by members of the Vietnamese LLDB, 8,000 Vietnamese and an unknown number of Cambodian and Laotian ethnic groups.

MACVSOG operations were planned and executed by a number of 'Study Groups', each responsible for a particular area of activity. Ground Studies Group (OPLAN 35) conducted a range of cross-border intelligence operations (see Chapter 8) such as KITCAT (North Vietnam), SHINING BRASS/PRAIRIE FIRE (Laos) and DANIEL BOONE (Cambodia). Ground Studies Group also monitored the location of Prisoner-of-War camps for BRIGHT LIGHT combat rescue missions (see Chapter 9). The Psychological Studies Group (OPLAN/OPS 33) sent false radio broadcasts into North Vietnam from transmitters in Hue and Tay Ninh. The Air Studies Group (OPLAN 32) provided air support for MACVSOG operations, using their own clandestine air-force: the 90th Special Operations Wing. The Wing is reputed to have used Nationalist Chinese and CIA Air America pilots. The Maritime Studies Group conducted sea-borne reconnaissance and raiding missions along the North Vietnamese coast and in the Mekong delta (OPLAN 34A/OPS 31).

Control of these many and varied activities centred on MACVSOG's headquarters in Pasteur Street, Saigon, radiating out to encompass three Forward Observation Bases or later, Command and Control (CC) sites. Command and Control North, based at Da Nang, was responsible for operations into Laos and North Vietnam. The area where the borders of South Vietnam, Laos and Cambodia meet (Tri-Border Region) was covered by Command and Control Central based at Kontum, while Command and Control South (Ban Me Thuot) ran operations into Cambodia. In addition, Mobile Launch Teams at Ban Me Thuot, Kontum, Khe Sanh and Da Nang handled particularly sensitive operations such as the free-fall insertion of teams into North Vietnam.

Many of its activities involved indigenous troops. Authorship of the most sensitive 'deniable' operations was concealed behind mercenaries such as the dependable Chinese Nungs and North Vietnamese expatriates like the Muong hill-tribe. MACVSOG also aided and employed a range of indigenous regular and irregular forces in Laos and Cambodia, including the anti-Communist Cambodian Khmer Serei (Free Khmer) and the Khmer Kampuchea Krom – a Cambodian faction attempting to gain autonomy for the Khmer Krom people living in South Vietnam's Mekong Delta.

LAOS: THE SECRET WAR

Situated below the belly of China and bordered by North Vietnam, Laos was President Eisenhower's first 'Domino' in Indochina. Laotian partisans, armed and led by Allied parachutists, looked towards independence after the Second World War but their hopes, embodied in the Free Lao nationalist movement, were dashed when the French reclaimed Laos in 1946. Fleeing first to Thailand and then Vietnam, a faction of the Free Lao movement, under Prince Souphanouvong, joined forces with the Communist Viet Minh, becoming the Communist Laotian guerrilla forces or Pathet Lao.

The years that followed the French withdrawal were pocked with right-wing coups and uneasy coalition governments. Amidst this political flux, one event was more dependable – the dry-season Pathet Lao offensive across the strategic Plain of Jars in north-east Laos. Each year the Communists and government forces shuttled back and forth across this area of rolling grassland that had traditionally sheltered the capital, Vientiane, from the Laotians' Chinese and Vietnamese neighbours.

Other elements fought a war more to the CIA's liking. The French had left a legacy of rural *Auto Defénse de Choc* militia units. Of these the most effective were village self-defence units composed of Hmong mountain tribesmen who, believed to be of Mongolian or Eskimo extraction, had ferociously resisted Viet Minh incursions onto their territory. Capitalising upon this in the early 1950s, a French Special Forces team under Colonel Roger Trinquier, had forged the Hmong into mobile groups adept at fighting the Viet Minh with their own tactics of guerrilla warfare. Trinquier's 20,000-strong army was surreptitiously financed from the Hmong's principal cash-crop, opium, which was bought by the French and resold to the Vietnamese Emperor, Bao Dai, for 50,000 francs a kilo. With the Hmong, the CIA counter-insurgency experts would discover another asset beyond riches – the charismatic commander of the Hmong militia, Lieutenant Colonel Vang Pao, who had served with a range of commando and guerrilla units and had been commissioned in both the Laotian and French armies. Under American control and using US aid as an inducement, the stocky Hmong peasant would forge the most effective fighting force in Laos.

In 1959, the CIA started work on its counter-insurgency programme, severely hampered by the 1954 Geneva Accords that forbade overt American military assistance to Laos. Free of American military interference, the CIA's tactics were as simple as they were effective: Laos would be defended by

The experience gained advising and instructing South Vietnamese forces was put to good use in Laos and Cambodia. (*TRH Pictures*)

mobile guerrilla units and air-power. Using Air America helicopters, indigenous assault groups stormed Communist strongholds throughout Northern Laos. Once the area was secure, rough air-strips, known as Lima Sites, were built to allow the clandestine airforce to ferry in food, medicine and 'hard-rice' – weapons and munitions. CIA operations now had the benefit of air-support, albeit home-made bombs and napalm fashioned from petrol and domestic washing powder. More effective air-support would become available in 1964, when US fighters were allowed to accompany unarmed reconnaissance fighters on YANKEE TEAM missions over Laos. After the loss of several aircraft on these euphemistic 'air-sorties against targets of opportunity', the National Security Council authorised twice-weekly bombing strikes codenamed BARREL ROLL.

Within a year the CIA was joined by Special Forces personnel operating under the civilian Programme Evaluation Office (PEO). Working closely with the *Armée Nationale de Laos*, the advisers built training facilities, distributed military equipment and trained the Laotians in counter-insurgency operations. Eight teams concentrated on Van Pao's irregular tribesmen, organising them into mobile forces known as Special Guerrilla Units. Other companies received counter-insurgency training in Thailand and were reorganised into Special Operations Teams charged with raising and training static village militia units. In April 1961, already heavily involved in the fighting, the PEO was officially transformed into the US Military Advisory and Assistance Group, Laos.

As in Vietnam, the war in Laos was fought by an 'international brigade'. Thailand worried about events on it borders, sent volunteers from their Police Aerial Reinforcement Unit to help train the CIA's Hmong army. When the war turned in the Communists' favour, Thailand committed volunteer 'UNITY' infantry and artillery battalions. When it was reported that North Vietnamese soldiers were crossing the Chinese border in 1962, the CIA went to see their old Nationalist Chinese comrades. Once again pushed out of their opium plantations by the Burmese Army, they were easily persuaded to patrol the Chinese border with Northern Laos. Special Forces teams joined them to train Yau tribesman at a secret base at Nam Yu. From there patrols were sent on reconnaissance missions deep into Red China.

The Special Forces teams, now WHITE STAR Mobile Training Teams, expanded their activities to raise other unconventional units amongst the Lao Theung tribesmen on the Bolovens Plateau in Southern Laos. Central and southern Laos were increasingly falling under Communist control as the Ho Chi Minh supply routes proliferated. In August 1962, another coalition government signed a new set of Geneva Agreements compelling the WHITE STAR teams to leave Laos. The Communists paid no attention to the new agreement, and consequently neither did the CIA.

American Army Special Forces returned in 1966 under diplomatic cover as part of Project 404 which also implemented a programme to improve the Laotian Air Force (WATERPUMP). Laotian and Thai pilots were trained by the Air Commandos who were forced to pay lip-service to the Geneva Accords by shuttling back and forth across the border with Thailand. Over the combat zones, the air strikes were directed by American Forward Air Controllers from another clandestine airforce known as the Ravens. Throughout the conflict in South-East Asia, American thinking was dominated by memories of the Chinese invasion in Korea. A limited 'invasion' did finally materialise in the form of road construction crews, guarded by anti-aircraft batteries and thousands of Chinese troops. The resulting all-weather roads marched relentlessly east and west, cutting off 15,000 square miles of northern Laos and creating a supply network to support Communist offensives in Laos, Thailand and South Vietnam (Chinese troops helped administer Laotian sections of the Ho Chi Minh Trail). The 'Chinese road' was ordered off-limits to all US personnel. Instead it was attacked by American Air Commando T-28 single prop fighter bombers flown by Thai pilots.

The 1968 seasonal Communist offensive was different. Losing patience with their Pathet Lao allies, the North Vietnamese took control. Now the Laotian forces were forced into the situation of fighting a guerrilla war against conventional forces well supplied with Russian tanks and artillery. Over-confident, instead of withdrawing at the start of the wet season, the NVA held their positions. Hmong guerrillas cut their supply lines. The starving army was then routed by mobile guerrilla regiments and the Vietnamese retreated, abandoning tanks and other assorted combat vehicles. By 1972, the Communists had moved seven divisions into Laos and launched dual offensives in the north and south of the country. The Hmong guerrillas, still led by CIA field officers and Special Forces advisers, were exhausted.

Air power no longer stopped the Communist offensives. Fifty thousand tons of bombs were dropped on northern Laos. The Air Force used B-52 strikes and other sorties by T-28 fighters and F-4 Phantoms operating out of bases in Thailand. Frequently, these were directed by 'Fast FACs' flying high-speed jets, high above the battlefield and consequently, much of the bombing was indiscriminate, hitting villages and friendly forces.

In 1973, the Paris peace talks resulted in an ostensible cease-fire in Laos. The Americans chose to accept the charade and withdrew from South-East Asia. Vientiane fell to the Communists a few months after Saigon. Even in defeat, the Hmong continued to fight. In 1977, their last stronghold on the Phu Bia massif fell after severe aerial bombardment. Many fled to refugee camps on the Thai–Laotian border; others stayed to continue their struggle against the Communist Lao People's Democratic Republic from mountain sanctuaries in north-east Laos. The Hmong divided into two groups; one, the Lao United Front, is still led by General Van Pao. The world knows the other as the Ethnic Liberation Organisation of Laos but its guerrillas call themselves the *Chao Fah* – Lords of the Sky.

CAMBODIA: THE SHADOW WAR

Cambodia remained neutral throughout much of the war in Vietnam. This suited the Communists who blithely ran their supply-lines through eastern Cambodia. Other supplies were landed from Russian ships at the port of Sihanoukville. At times the so-called 'Sihanoukville Trail' handled more than 80 per cent of the Communist supplies destined for the war in South Vietnam. Prince Sihanouk maintained the neutrality by means of a political dance that accommodated Vietnamese forces within the country, while giving tacit approval to US 'hot pursuit' operations. In 1967, the Cambodian Communist Party decided it was time to end the pretence and launched an armed revolt. Soundly crushed by paratroops, the Party activists scattered to re-think their doctrine. They re-emerged as the Khmer Rouge guerrillas, whose hall-mark was a primitive agrarian form of Communism, and whose notorious activities resulted in the deaths of millions of Cambodian peasants.

In 1970, Sihanouk was deposed while on a state visit to China. Within days the *Forces Armées Nationales Khmere* (FANK) went into action against the NVA in their border sanctuaries. At this eleventh hour in the war for Indo-China, Cambodia's new leader, General Lon Nol, looked to America for military assistance. This was no longer a simple matter. Attempting to prevent further escalation of the war in South-East Asia, in 1971 the Congress had formulated rules preventing US military personnel from advising or supporting forces inside Cambodia. The letter of the law was maintained by means of creating several organisations derived from MACV and United States Army in Vietnam (USARV). One was the United Individual Training Group (UITG) created in February 1971 to conduct 13-week training cycles for FANK units at bases inside Vietnam. Most of UITG's personnel were Special Forces experts including members of the Australian Advisory Training Teams, the NZSAS, the American 1st SFG (Okinawa) and the US Marine Corps. During its short existence, UITG is reputed to have trained a total of 85 Cambodian battalions, ranging from airborne and Special Forces units to light infantry and marines.

Additional training was provided by US Special Forces personnel in Thailand. Khmer Special Forces teams were trained at the Royal Thai Army Special Warfare Centre at Lopburi under Operation FREEDOM RUNNER. In turn, the Khmer Special Forces opened their own Recondo (Reconnaissance Commando) School in Battambang and, true to American doctrine, began seeding a programme of village militia. Other special units were trained in Indonesia as para-commandos and the Cambodian Navy was encouraged to raise its own SEAL units. The MACVSOG programme, CEDAR WALK, which used indigenous Cambodians against targets on the Ho Chi Minh Trail, was handed over to the Cambodian intelligence service in October 1971. Other MACVSOG Cambodians of the Khmer Seri (White Cambodian Forces), fighting in Laos as part of Project COPPER were repatriated to help contain the ever-growing Communist stranglehold on Cambodia's north-eastern provinces.

After the Americans and their Allies withdrew from South-East Asia, history repeated itself in Cambodia. Despite American equipment and training, the Khmer forces buckled under the overwhelming offensives by irregular and conventional Communist forces. The Khmer special units, too small to make a difference, were often used as shock assault troops to shore up crumbling defences. In the very last days of the war, Special Forces units continued to fight. Faced with certain death at the hands of the Khmer Rouge, some commanders called-in friendly strike missions onto their own positions, rather than retreat. In April 1975, the last Special Forces units, surrounded in Phnom Penh, attempted to break out towards the South Vietnamese border. It is not known how many survived.

THAILAND: THE LAST DOMINO

On 25 of May 1962, the NZSAS Squadron was deployed to Thailand, joining units from Thailand's other SEATO Allies America and Australia. The developing conflicts in Borneo, Vietnam and Laos overshadowed the Thai Government's call for assistance but to the forces fighting to contain revolution in

America and her allies used the tactics of unconventional warfare to blunt the Communist guerilla offensive. The North Vietnamese were forced finally to use overwhelming conventional force to capture South Vietnam, Cambodia and Laos. (*TRH Pictures*)

South-East Asia, the situation in Thailand realised their worst fears – another 'Domino' was falling.

Since the 1930s the Communist Party of Thailand (CPT), leavened with Chinese and Vietnamese cadres, had plotted revolution. In 1961, the Third Party Congress declared a 'Peoples War' and established a 'North-East Region Jungle Headquarters' and a civilian support infrastructure. In the south of the country, the Malayan Races Liberation Army, responsible for the 'Malayan Emergency', switched their attentions to Thailand. In the north, the CPT guerrillas were supplied by the Chinese via their new road system in Laos. To the north east, the Pathet Lao and North Vietnamese also proved willing allies. Together, they built a supply network to feed the insurgency and gave it the formal title of the 35th Platoon, 95th NVA Company. It put the

Thai Government on notice: the revolution would not stop at the borders of Laos.

As always, the Communists looked for recruits amongst the 'outsiders' of the society and once again they discovered an attentive audience in the disadvantaged hill-tribes. Soon the recruiting teams were made up of tribesmen who had attended guerrilla-warfare courses in China, Laos and Vietnam. Their call was as seductive as it was dishonest – 'Join with the traditional *oa phoa thay* – the rebellion to make a king'.

The Security Forces, led by officers of the 'old school', saw counter-insurgency in terms of 'body counts' and 'search and destroy' operations. Fruitless conventional operations often achieved little, while incurring large numbers of casualties from booby-traps. Then, in October 1973, student demonstrations toppled the military government and things began to change. The new counter-insurgency programme owed much to British COIN doctrines and the approach of the American Special Forces. The political and economic inequalities that made revolutionary Marxism appear attractive were identified and development teams sent in to correct them (Accelerated Rural Development). Protected by powerful conventional forces, the villages were strengthened and developed and the people encouraged to elect their own leaders. Village self-defence militias and regional mobile strike forces, or 'Rangers', were formed and led by Thai Special Forces. These units pursued the guerrillas and finally blunted the Communist offensive. Regular troops or 'main forces' also undertook counter-insurgency operations but these were conducted as part of 'Advanced Training', removing the impetus for over-zealous officers to see the operation in terms of 'body counts'.

Ironically, it was Thai democracy that finally achieved the Communists' stated aims of putting guns into the hands of the people to bring about political change. If the low intensity conflicts proved nothing else, they demonstrated that paramilitaries and the tactics of guerrilla warfare are not just instruments of revolution but can be used to protect and foster national stability.

8

The Long Range Reconnaissance Patrol

The Reconnaissance Poem
Who controls reconnaissance watches the enemy;
Who watches the enemy perceives the threat;
Who perceives the threat shapes the alternatives;
Who shapes the alternatives determines the response.
From *Deep Black* by William E. Burrows

All infantry units conduct 'recce' patrols in their area of operations to identify the enemy that faces them across the front-line. The Long Range Reconnaissance Patrol (LRRP) differs from the infantry patrol in its depth of penetration. The LRRP employs covert patrolling skills to penetrate deep into enemy-controlled country (Deep Reconnaissance) and gather information about enemy units far from the front-line (Deep Intelligence). Currently, the planning ranges for American LRRP missions are 150km in front of the 'Forward Line of Own Troops' (FLOT) for teams tasked at corps level and 50km forward of FLOT at divisional level. Within these respective 'areas of influence', multiple LRRPs can allow the corps/divisional commander to see deep into the enemy's rear as well as accomplishing such additional tasks as acquiring targets for air and artillery strikes or follow-up raids by ground forces.

THE AMERICAN EXPERIENCE

The Americans originated the term Long Range Reconnaissance Patrol, which derived from the provisional 'recon' companies formed to support the US Army in Germany in the early 1960s. While deep reconnaissance pre-dates modern warfare, the Americans can lay claim to embracing the concept wholeheartedly and raising it to an art form, if not a cult, in Vietnam. There, a mainly conventional US Army, expecting to fight another Korean War, found itself faced with a variety of guerrilla and regular enemy units that switched between set-piece battles and guerrilla warfare with apparent ease. Often unit commanders were called upon to launch operations in the many Communist strong-holds or contact NVA units reported crossing the border, without any idea of Communist strengths or dispositions. All too frequently, the enemy managed to melt away, striking again at a place and time of their own choosing. It soon became clear that there was a need for a system of attached 'recon' units to 'enable the [area] commander to employ troops and/or firepower in the most advantageous manner'.

A memorial to one of the first British officers to be killed on a long range reconnaissance patrol. Lieutenant Colonel Roger Townshend was killed at Fort Carillon, in July 1759, while attached to Roger's Rangers. The influential Townshend family later befriended Robert Rogers and chose to include in their son's memorial the effigies of two Indian irregulars. (*By Courtesy of Dean and Chapter of Westminster Abbey*)

VIETNAM: LRRPS FOR ALL SEASONS

During the American military build-up in South Vietnam in the mid-1960s, the 5th Special Forces Group became increasingly burdened with the job of running LRRPs to acquire targets for conventional forces (tactical LRRPs) and collect intelligence which would allow the staff planners some idea of the enemy forces threatening the different tactical zones (strategic LRRPs). This, as we shall see later, not only diverted Special Forces assets from their own projects but was seen as a basic misuse of these highly specialised troops.

In order to train other units to carry out long-range patrols, the 5th SFG opened the MACV Recondo (Reconnaissance Commando) School at Nha Trang in September 1966. There the students were given an introduction to 'common core' SF-skills such as survival training, map reading, navigation, intelligence, communications, emergency first-aid and patrolling. Throughout the lectures, the candidates were exposed to severe physical conditioning. This was vital for men operating on their own, who might be forced to escape over long distances, while carrying heavy loads, in an effort to break contact with enemy forces. Seven-mile speed marches, road-runs and obstacle courses led to exercises in which the patrols were tested on their specialised contact, insertion and extraction drills.

While much of the School's curriculum covered high-grade infantry skills, some of the basic problems associated with such activity were not immediately obvious to commanders of conventional formations. One such problem was the lack of traditional support, and the vast amount of specialised equipment that needed to be carried on such missions. Among the basic tools of the students' new trade were rucksacks and Stabo-rigs: a waistcoat designed to carry slung ammunition and water bottles and equipped with snap-links that enabled the wearer to attach himself to a harness dropped from a helicopter and be snatched from the jungle. The rucksack and rig provided a home for additional ammunition, together with a first-aid kit, signal mirrors, mini-smoke and phosphorus grenades, Claymore mines, radios to contact ground and airborne relay-stations, SAR beacons, albumen plasma expander, compass, maps, survival knife, mosquito net, sleeping mat and assorted escape and evasion kit.

With rucksack weights around 50–100lbs, a further loading of normal C-Rations (2lbs/unit) resulted in an unfavourable equipment/weight ratio – a vicious circle where additional weight requires additional energy-producing food. In Vietnam, this problem was partially solved by designing freeze-dried LRRP rations but while weighing only 11 ounces, these were 'energy depleted' (1,200 calories) compared with the 2,400 calories provided by C-Rations. Consequently, the extra calories were scavenged from C-Rations, in the form of carbohydrate and protein-rich foods (canned fruit, peanut butter etc.) and rice, seasonings and dehydrated meat from the Indigenous Personnel Rations.

Even so, most soldiers running LRRPs experienced marked weight loss and some American Rangers attributed the later development of chronic illness to the physical deprivation they had experienced in Vietnam. In the concurrent war in Borneo, the Australian SAS were recording losses of 6–8lbs after 12-day patrols. James England's text, based on experiences in Vietnam notes:

> . . . missions very much in excess of 7 to 14 days can be hard to justify. A team could become immobile due to the weight of needed supplies. When planning mission length, allow for a minimum of three pounds of weight for every day of deployment.

Even with the establishment of the Recondo School, there were still more applicants than training slots for these dangerous missions and the 5th SFG started three-week courses in LRRP skills in which the final exercise was an actual combat patrol. Soon most of the major American units had their own LRRP platoon.

In August 1967, there was another change in philosophy when, starting with the 9th Infantry Division, each division expanded their platoons to company strength, attaching a 'recon' detachment to each brigade. The specific tasks of each company reflected both their area of operations and divisional tasks, the 5–6 man patrols being known as either LRRPs or Long Range Patrols (LRP). The 2/17 Cavalry, 101st Airborne Division used their LRRP for short-term reconnaissance, evaluating air-strikes and providing security for downed aircraft (BRIGHT LIGHT missions, see Chapter 9), the 3rd Battalion, 22nd Infantry, 25th Division pioneered the use of motor-cycles for deep reconnaissance, while the 74th Infantry (Airborne), 173rd Airborne Brigade used their teams to identify targets for the air force and raid enemy bases. Additionally, the armies of other countries involved in the conflict fielded dedicated Special Forces units: South Vietnam (ARVN LLDB and Rangers), Australia (SAS company plus one New Zealand SAS troop), South Korea (Reconnaissance Battalion, Capital 'Tiger' Division).

In the summer of 1968, a Lieutenant Colonel from the 173rd Airborne Brigade used his departure from Vietnam to criticise the Army's use of LRRPs and to call for their abolition. In an outspoken interview with journalists, he claimed that their one primary value was warning against surprise attack but that over a six-month period his brigade's LRRPs had generated only two worthwhile contacts. He believed that the patrols tied up valuable transport helicopters and gunships and claimed he found himself ordering helicopters to extract teams '. . .because they hear bushes snapping; I extract them because they hear voices talking, I extract them for all kinds of things'. Finally, he felt that the field units should have been platoon or company size and the tasks carried out by ordinary infantrymen and not specialists.

The contact/man-hour ratio was not unusual for these patrols. During their operations in Malaya, it was estimated that the British SAS spent 1,800 man-hours for each contact, killing or capturing on average only ten guerrillas a year. A major problem, as the Colonel himself admitted, was the lack of a reaction force, often the result of brigade headquarter's insistence that most of the patrols be deployed most of the time. With no reaction force to exploit intelligence and contacts, it only remained to extract the teams as quickly as possible but, all too frequently, the patrols received the terse radio signal; 'Break contact and continue mission'. Even when finally extracted, the teams often found themselves back in the field within days. Morale and trust in the command structure suffered and undoubtedly some teams did avoid moving into areas where a contact was likely.

Few commanding officers had experience of these deep patrols, where within a short time the situation could change dramatically. Many action reports brutally illustrate this point. Recon Team OPEL was inserted into mountainous jungle along the South Vietnamese border to pin-point a North Vietnamese force responsible for previous contacts. On the first day they found evidence of the presence of an NVA unit in the area but this was only distant voices and lights in the jungle. That night, without warning, a large NVA unit of company or battalion strength moved through the immediate area of their LUP. When an NVA soldier with a flashlight actually stumbled into the patrol hide, both sides were so terrified of the consequences of opening fire that he was allowed to disappear back into the jungle. Throughout the night the patrol was left alone, presumably because the enemy did not want to attract the attention of larger American units. However, at some point, NVA troops crept towards the patrol perimeter, sabotaged the Claymores, turning others inward, as a prelude to a dawn attack. Once the attack finally materialised, OPEL found itself being driven into a killing ground carefully prepared overnight by the NVA but were saved at the last moment when the cavalry quite literally arrived in the shape of the 'Blue Ghosts' reaction force (Troop F, 8th Cavalry).

Another of this officer's complaints was that the teams were often without experienced leadership. This was an inevitable consequence of the lack of a permanent experienced command structure, given the 365-day tour periods in Vietnam. Many of the Recondo School graduates were also Ranger-qualified but the Rangers themselves had been disbanded by an Army which was inherently anti-élitist. During most of the war, only the Ranger School at Fort Benning remained and was used as an advanced leadership course, producing highly trained infantry soldiers and preparing them for combat in Vietnam. Thus, while recognising the need for special assets, the Army distributed them throughout the infantry with the aim of giving each platoon at least one Ranger-qualified officer and sergeant. It was hoped that their 'special skills' would percolate through the command, while giving each unit special operational capability in the form of Recon units – a classic case of wanting to have one's cake and eating it.

Like all special operations, LRRPs work most effectively when controlled, planned and led by experienced specialist personnel. The US Army went some way towards recognising this fact when, in January 1969, it appointed the 75th Infantry Regiment as the LRRP's parent unit, reorganising them into 13 Ranger Companies designated C-I and K-P. While the Army was happy with

The small lightly-armed LRRP employs covert patrolling skills to penetrate deep into enemy-controlled country and gather information about enemy units far from the front-line. (*PMA Pictures*)

this consolidation, it made little difference to the 'recon' units in the field, except that they could now call themselves rangers. Following the withdrawal from South East Asia, and on the basis of lessons learnt, the Rangers were formally reactivated in 1975, becoming the 75th Ranger Regiment. Originally given two battalions (1/75 & 2/75), a third (3/75) was added in 1984. Still an integral part of the US Army component within USSOCOM, one of the Ranger's operational roles remains LRRPs.

5TH SPECIAL FORCES GROUP: THE GREEK LETTER PROJECTS

The 5th SFG also ran 'in country' LRRPs but these were different in that they used indigenous personnel. They also differed from the MACVSOG patrols, which also employed a range of partisan/mercenary allies but in operations directed towards Cambodia, Laos and North Vietnam. The most famous of the 5th SFG LRRPs were the so-called Greek Letter Projects: DELTA, SIGMA, OMEGA and GAMMA, which grew out of Operation LEAPING LENA and were designed to train the hill tribes in the art of long patrolling and provide MACV with a constant supply of high-grade intelligence.

DELTA, activated in June 1964 and run jointly with the South Vietnamese LLDB and Green Beret Detachment B-52, consisted of 12 'recon' teams composed of two Green Berets and four mercenaries. Delta also ran six (later 12) Roadrunner Teams, each consisting of four native operators. While the 'recon' teams' survival depended upon their moving unobtrusively through the network of roads and tracks that made up the North's supply artery, the Roadrunner Teams openly travelled along the trails disguised as Viet-Cong guerrillas. This very dangerous work required an élite and aggressive reaction force to capitalise on the intelligence gains and rapidly reinforce the field units. To this end, DELTA was assigned the 91st ARVN Ranger Battalion which was flown into action by another dedicated asset, the 281st Assault Helicopter Company. DELTA's other role was to supply instructors to the Recondo School. At its peak, the Project employed over 1,200 indigenous personnel drawn mainly from the Chinese Nungs.

In 1966, Detachment B-56 was ordered to initiate Project SIGMA to help cope with the increasing demand for intelligence from the border areas. Consisting of eight 'recon' teams, three Mike Force companies and one camp defence company, SIGMA employed ethnic Cambodians and Chinese for its missions. Among SIGMA's many tasks were the BLACKJACK operations conducted by the Mobile Guerrilla Force. A BLACKJACK would start with the insertion of a 'recon' team into a VC/NVA sanctuary area where the team identified targets of opportunity over a period of 30–60 days. As re-supply was pressing, food and equipment caches were dropped along their route by Vietnamese Skyraider jets, inside dummy napalm canisters. A real napalm strike close by would complete the deception. If the enemy closed on the 'recon' team, the situation was exploited by a reaction force.

A number of SIGMA operations initiated major combat actions. The first operation with a Mobile Guerrilla Force, BLACKJACK 33, was carried out between 27 April and 24 May 1967, and was credited with killing 320 enemy troops. In the spring of 1967, BLACKJACK 41, resulted in two Mike Force companies parachuting into the Seven Mountains area of IV Corps to liberate Communist POW camps. In August 1966, recon patrols identified the VC 96th Division licking its wounds in an area close to the Special Forces camp at Soui Da (III Corps), near the Cambodian border. As the Viet-Cong prepared to attack the camp in October–November, a Mike Force company crippled a VC battalion, subsequently resulting in a pitched battle south of the Don Dien Michelin plantation between the 96th Division and more than 22,000 American troops from 196th Infantry Brigade and 27th Infantry (OPERATION ATTLEBORO).

OMEGA was established by Detachment B-50 for missions in the 1 Corp areas. Operating out of Ban Me Thuot, OMEGA consisted of eight Roadrunner Teams and eight 'recon' teams which saturated areas of the Ho Chi Minh Trail with LRRP missions. As usual the recon elements were supported by three Mike Force Companies to exploit their contacts and perform reconnaissance-in-force operations. The last project GAMMA, was directed

A Rhade LRRP returns to the safety of its base near Ban Me Thout in the Central Highlands. The covert patrolling skills of indigenous personnel were a central part of the Greek Letter Projects and MACVSOG 'out of country' operations. (*TRH Pictures*)

against NVA infiltration into Cambodia. Formed by Detachment B-57, GAMMA used ethnic Cambodians and Chams for its missions launched from bases in II, III and IV Corp tactical areas.

MACVSOG: ACROSS THE FENCE

At its peak, MACVSOG fielded around 70 Spike Recon Teams, which were the primary operational unit within the three Command and Control units. Taking their codenames from American states or snakes (eg RT WEST VIR-GINIA; RT RATTLESNAKE), the 'recons' were based on the Special Forces 'A' Detachment, consisting of an American team leader, assistant team leader, radio operator and 6–9 indigenous personnel, including an indigenous team leader. Unlike the 5th SFG, SOG preferred Chinese Nungs, partly because of the FULRO rebellions and partly because there were fears of large-scale VC infiltration within the tribes. The RTs had their own reaction forces, known as Hatchet Force, consisting of five Special Forces personnel and up to 300 mercenaries. While SOG's 'recon' patrols were still aimed at intelligence gathering, the information formed the basis of later ambushes, strikes, assassinations, seizure of prisoners, raids on enemy bases, sabotage, BRIGHT LIGHT missions and other covert operations. The teeth of these clandestine follow-up missions were the four SEARCH-LOCATE-ANNIHILATE-MIS-SION (SLAM) Companies drawn from Hatchet Force.

Both MACVSOG and the 5th SFG operated in the border areas and ran 'recon' operations on the Trail. Asked for the rationale and difference between the patrols run by the two organisations, a veteran of these operations replied: 'You assume that there was one [rationale]! People didn't talk to people over there. If we had, we might have won.' One essential difference was that SOG ran operations deep inside Cambodia and Laos, two countries with which America was not at war. These were deniable operations; they and the operators were deemed not to exist and if the men were captured they were more likely to be killed than listed as a POWs. Their deaths would be recorded in some other part of the theatre; for example, 5th SFG personnel attached to SOG were officially to be found 'Attached Headquarters 5th SFG'. Regular equipment was worn on missions but some teams preferred plain cotton-poplin fatigues, sprayed with black paint and worn with an outer survival vest that doubled as a sleeping bag. This 'low-profile', that might enable them to pass at a distance for a VC, was maintained with captured Communist weapons.

THE BATTLE FOR THE HO CHI MINH TRAIL

The Ho Chi Minh Trail was both the alpha and omega of the American war in Vietnam. This was a complex of routes that stretched from North Vietnam through a series of staging areas along the Laos and Cambodian borders, emerging on South Vietnam's southern border with Cambodia, to threaten the South's capital, Saigon. At first a mere series of tracks that meandered through the wild mountainous jungle of the border regions to by-pass the hi-tech minefields on the Demilitarised Zone, the Truong Son Strategic Supply Route soon became a central pillar of Ho Chi Minh's vision for the 'liberation' of the South.

The Trail was cut, maintained and developed by the Truong Son (High Mountains) brigades, composed of 300,000 soldiers and peasant labourers. Another 200,000 peasants provided a part-time labour force. Under the watchful eye of their commander, General Vo Bam, army engineers organised the clearing of jungle in the mountainous passes. The weather was both an ally and an enemy. While the heavy mist hid them from the Americans, the rain in the Wet Season washed away the tracks. These were quickly rebuilt and paved with bamboo or even asphalt to provide 9,600 miles of all-weather roads. Along them came an array of vehicles carrying ammunition and weapons to the war in the South. Fleets of pack bicycles, strengthened by wooden supports and carrying 100kgs a piece, completed the entire journey in 10 days. Trucks took only seven days, so the Truong Son infrastructure built 3,000 miles of aluminium pipeline to carry petrol, storing the precious fluid at each staging-post in underground tanks, each capable of holding 1.5 million litres.

Regular NVA units marched down 'Uncle Ho's' road to join their VC guerrilla comrades of the 'South Vietnam Liberation Army'. As the war progressed they came with heavy artillery and tanks. The supply trucks only carried munitions, so the Truong Son workers grew rice and maize along the route to feed them. They also built underground factories, hospitals, command-posts and air-raid shelters. Soon the supply artery that fed the Communist forces in the South was also an 'open wound' through which the 'life-blood' of the American commitment and military effort drained away.

When first faced with placing teams along the Communist highway, the Americans turned to the classical insertion techniques but discovered that parachuting, particularly night-time HALO descents, was too dangerous and fraught with problems. Helicopters provided an excellent alternative for inserting and extracting the teams from LZs close to the Trail. In response, the Communists created their own special-purpose force to combat the patrols; GROUP 565. This complemented the 25,000 guards permanently stationed at the check-points and artillery positions.

By 1968, most of the helicopter LZ's had been identified, mined or placed under surveillance, apparently securing the area. When they discovered that the American dehydrated rations made their enemies exceptionally dependent upon fresh water, wells and streams were booby-trapped or watched. As a consequence Americans started to carry extra water-bottles and their rucksacks became even heavier, creating a bigger problem. The extra water bottles were sufficient for five days normal patrolling but if the Americans found themselves in a running fire-fight, the water was likely to run out before the ammunition.

Their experience in Vietnam forced the Americans to seek solutions in firepower and technology; the LRRPs were no different but in this instance the solution was ingenious. Several days prior to the mission, the patrol commander would fly over the area to build up an overall picture of the insertion site. Immediately prior to the mission, the patrol would be fully briefed on the available information derived from his study of available maps, friendly agent reports, airborne radar, infra-red satellite surveillance, listening devices placed in the jungle and previous patrol reports. On the day of the insertion, the Air Force dropped 10,000lb (4,500kg) bombs over the area, punching out multiple helicopter sized holes in the jungle. As dusk approached, decoy helicopters pretended to insert teams at many of the new potential LZ's, providing a decoy for the flight of aircraft that was actually carrying the LRRP team. As many as five helicopters descended upon the chosen LZ, the first flying at 1–2,000ft and several minutes ahead of the next two choppers, which were actually carrying the team. Behind them came helicopters carrying fire-support teams, which could be called upon if the team was ambushed by the VC or NVA on the LZ.

The Special Forces directed their efforts towards two types of operation in their attempts to halt the Communist traffic feeding the war in the South. Firstly, units leaving the trail were tagged for air-strikes, ambushes and raids.

Those that survived would hopefully be re-acquired by the 'recon' teams deployed by conventional units operating on the South Vietnamese side of the border. These operations often invited contact with the Communists and an ex-MACVSOG operator, asked what these patrols were like and how they compared with the British experience in Borneo, replied that they ranged from the routine to experiences beyond nightmare. Pressed harder, he told the following story about an SOG patrol detailed to locate an NVA Main Force, which had been mauled in Vietnam and had recrossed the border to lick its wounds in a sanctuary area within the Tri-border region.

> My friend's patrol had tracked this unit for some days and finally found them early one morning on the far side of a hill. They were just rising and thinking about breakfast, and from the relaxed way they were going about things, you could see that they felt safe. As he watched them, one of his Indigs tapped him on the shoulder and pointed to the plain of Elephant grass they had just crossed. When he looked back, he saw waves in the grass moving towards them, just like waves on a sea-shore – a large VC force had picked up their trail and were tracking *them*. He considered his options: cut left or right along the hill and the VC would link up with the regulars and the patrol would become one of the many that had disappeared in that area. So they slipped the weapons on automatic and charged down the hill, cutting a swathe through the NVA camp with automatic fire. Bodies, kit and equipment was scattered to the four winds. They all made it through the camp, turned left and ran for their lives. Behind them, there was chaos and panic, as the regulars opened fire on each other. Well, the VC unit was sure going to think twice about following them down that hill in a hurry. After a while they stopped to get their breath and my friend noticed that everybody kept looking at the top of his head. He ran his hand through his hair feeling for a wound and found that it was standing on end!

The second type of mission was to identify the natural choke-points on the network of roads such as river crossings, mountain passes and track junctions as well as large convoys, supply-dumps and staging-areas, for the Air Force's LOC (Lines-of-Communication) aerial interdiction strikes. By 1967, the United States could put 300 aircraft a day over the Trail areas and each one over the target for 30 minutes. In total, they dropped more than 1,100,000 tons of bombs on the supply routes. The most formidable of these raids were the B-52 ARC-LIGHT strikes. At 40,000ft the flights of 3–6 planes were silent and invisible and death came without warning. To correct for the curvature of the earth, each aircraft was equipped with Combat Skyspot radar that enabled the pilot to place his 50 750lb bombs within 700 yards of the designated target. Later versions of the Stratofortress carried more than a hundred 500lb bombs.

Rivers represent a serious hazard to the covert patrol. In Borneo, several Australian SAS soldiers were drowned crossing the island's deep, fast flowing rivers. In addition, the enemy may be waiting in ambush on the opposite bank. This Gurkha is attached to a safety-line. His kit is packed into a buoyant bag and two rifles strapped either side allow a quick response to enemy contacts. (*Imperial War Museum*)

However, finding these vulnerable points was another matter in the wilderness areas of Cambodia and Laos. The area abounded in paths and trails but most showed little sign of recent use. The only signs of the recent passing of an NVA battalion might be piles of elephant dung (the Communists occasionally used elephants for transport), foot prints, tyre tracks, rile-pits and abandoned equipment. Often the patrol was forced to interpret the tracks to ascertain the intelligence indicators encompassed in the mnemonic SALUTE: Size, Activity, Location, Unit, Time and Equipment. No interpretation was required to ascertain the direction of travel, it was almost always south or east – towards the war zones in South Vietnam.

Time was of the essence as the tracks often revealed that the enemy unit had passed through the area some days previously. To enable the teams to transmit their intelligence back to headquarters, the Americans used a range of dedicated aircraft. By day, a communications relay was provided by forward air controllers flying single-engined spotter planes or C-130 airborne command centres permanently on station high above the jungle. Southern Laos was serviced by a command centre codenamed HILLSBOROUGH, which was relieved at night by MOONBEAM. In turn, the aircraft relayed the coded messages to dedicated ground stations, like the MACVSOG signals installation on Da Nang's Monkey Mountain. The intelligence staff then assessed the significance of the report and sometimes attempted to re-acquire the target by photograph reconnaissance or by intercepting Communist radio transmissions. High priority targets were then passed to Air Force Intelligence for air-strikes. Small, well-defined targets were usually pursued by fighter bombers such as the Douglas Skyraiders, while larger, well-concealed targets were treated to ARC-LIGHT carpet-bombing strikes.

Frequently, spoor-marks provided insufficient information on the volume and type of traffic passing through the border areas. Roadwatch surveillance teams might be placed along trails thought still to be active. Other trails would be covered by 'mechanical trailwatchers' under Project IGLOO WHITE. Camouflaged to look like small trees, and cunningly concealed along the edge of tracks, these seismic probes and microphones faithfully recorded the vibrations produced by enemy vehicles or sizeable infantry units and transmitted the information to circling aircraft to be passed to the 'antenna farm' at Nakhon Phanom in Thailand. Often whole areas would be saturated by probes dropped from low-flying aircraft. Finally, their very frequency along parts of the Trail became their undoing. Once recognised, Trail workers moved them to 'inactive' areas and used recordings of vehicles to dupe the American Air Force into bombing their own devices.

The Trail also held bitter surprises for the LRRP teams that discovered Communist supply bases. There amidst the Soviet and Chinese equipment, were sacks clearly marked, 'A gift from the American people'. In a country where corruption was rife, aid given to the South Vietnamese often found its way to the Communists. A more disturbing story is related by Kuno Knobel in his book, *Victor Charlie*. A French Army Lieutenant, 'Jacques Blanchard', part of a French military advisory group, was allowed to visit the Trail and was conducted through a Laotian section by Pathet Lao guerrillas. Finally, he was led to a camp of underground bunkers run by North Vietnamese and Chinese soldiers. The Communists appeared to be using American POWs as slave labour.

> At first I thought they, too, were Chinese because they towered over the small Vietnamese. But then I saw they were Whites, Americans, captured soldiers who were wheeling heavy loads of earth on bicycles. They were emaciated and exhausted and scarcely looked at me. They were bound by iron chains around their wrists to the bicycle frames. My Vietnamese escort told me they were prisoners paying for their crimes against the Vietnamese people.

A veteran of American special operations, asked for his opinion on Knobel's story, was reluctant to discuss it beyond the comment, 'Yes there were Chinese on the Trail in Laos. The prisoner story is possible.' In his book *The Bamboo Cage*, British journalist Nigel Cawthorne provides convincing evidence that American prisoners were sorted into various groups. Some were released after the war, others were kept as hostages to impel America to pay war repatriations, while technical specialists were forcibly sent to China and the USSR. The last group were held at sorting camps inside Laos.

A man-hunt frequently followed any inadvertent contact with Communist forces in these areas but the immediate seriousness of the patrol's position could be gauged from the enemy's contact drills. A Green Beret explains:

> If the enemy force immediately broke contact after the first exchange of fire and continued to track you from some way back, they were usually VC guerrillas. But if you heard enemy on your flanks, attempting to surround you, they were NVA regulars.

Once a long-running fire-fight developed, the patrol's only hope was a speedy extraction, but even on the extraction LZ they could still find themselves mere bait to catch the slow vulnerable helicopters sent to rescue them. To protect patrols that found themselves ringed by enemy on the LZ, the American's deployed a range of dedicated aircraft. The C-130, codenamed LAMPLIGHTER, could illuminate the area with flares for attack aircraft carrying bombs and napalm. Formidable and precise fire was provided by the AC-130 Spectres, with their miniguns, 20mm Vulcan cannons and 40mm Bofors cannons capable of encircling the patrol in a close ring of fiery steel.

Intelligence gathered by the LRRPs resulted in some bitter political wrangling back in Washington. Unlike bombing missions in support of operations in South Vietnam, the effect of the air-strikes, was difficult to assess. While Special Forces teams were often asked to go back into these areas to report on the damage, the thousands of workers and soldiers who formed the Trail infrastructure worked around the clock to obliterate all traces of the bombing. The US Air Force favoured the bombing of choke-points to increase the effectiveness of the strikes. Roadwatch teams to the south of the target were then asked to count the vehicles that passed in front of them. The estimated 'truck kills' were then passed back to the American military bureaucracy, where it joined the 'body-counts' and 'hamlet evaluation figures' in the great military 'fruit-machine' which spat reports at Washington designed to show that the war in Vietnam was being won.

Throughout the late 1960s, the CIA, with a different perception of the war, was warning the administration that the war was being lost. Intelligence estimates suggested that the infiltration rate was doubling or tripling every year. In the peak years, approximately 90,000–150,000 personnel were travelling south along its length. Other calculations claimed that 300 bombs were dropped for each infiltrator killed: in effect the American bombing was killing around 1,000–2,000 infiltrators each year at a cost of $2 bn.

In this respect, the bombing of targets on the Trail brought the Agency into conflict with the Air Force. Intelligence collected by the 'recon'-units was passed to the Air Force, which used it to select targets for bombing missions. However, subsequently, the CIA was reporting that the trucks were still getting through; the bombing had failed and implicitly the Air Force had failed. When a wounded Air Force requested access to overhead reconnaissance assets such as spy-planes, satellites and drones, to assess the effectiveness of the ARC-LIGHT strikes, the request was denied: checkmate.

However, the CIA underestimated the tenacity of Air Force Intelligence Chief, Major General Keegan, who surreptitiously arranged for Air Force Intelligence to obtain Communist signals-traffic intercepts. Nobody would decipher them for the Air Force so Keegan had his own people break the codes. The intercepts revealed that 90 per cent of the enemy's supplies were passing through two key mountain passes on their journey from North Vietnam to the start of the Trail in Laos. In fact, there were at least three; the Kao Neua Pass, the Mu Gia Pass and the Ban Karai Pass. Once through the passes, the trucks entered Laos, an area of the Trail so heavily used that parts of it were described as being as busy as the 'Long Island Express-Way – during rush-hour'. Chinese Nungs and other MACVSOG personnel operated from the Laotian side, penetrating the heavily-guarded buffer-zone that defended the roads to set up Roadwatch bases. These were used for up to six months at a time and served as a base for patrols that pushed further into the Trail structure to observe the road traffic and occasionally sabotage depots. So perilous were these areas, that the teams kept constantly on the move. There were added complications. As many of the Nungs were illiterate, the CIA/Special Forces equipped them with special transmitters. Instead of carrying the standard buttons with the alphabet printed on them, the keys showed pictures of military hardware such as tanks, trucks and artillery-pieces. The appropriate button was pressed each time the corresponding vehicle passed in front of the Nung observer.

In order to ensure that these passes were blocked, Keegan targeted them for three weeks of air strikes. The CIA learned that something was afoot and put its spies in the Air Force targeting organisation but Keegan found them and got rid of them. So the CIA had the Special Forces insert Roadwatch teams into the area, which sent back reports listing the numbers of trucks still getting through the passes. Reconnaissance photography refuted this, so Keegan parachuted Air Force Intelligence teams into the area to decide the issue once and for all. At great risk, the teams moved deep into the Trail structure and discovered that the passes were indeed blocked. A large number of trucks were moving east and west in a vain attempt to discover a way to the south. The Roadwatch teams had been counting vehicles **heard** as vehicles **seen** and assuming that all this traffic was travelling south.

The Americans' refusal to invade Laos in force and sit astride the Communist supply route effectively lost them the battle for the Ho Chi Minh Trail. Air interdiction proved futile against an enemy who demonstrated cleverness, tenacity and a willingness to take casualties. While the Americans rotated through their tours in Vietnam, the strategic highway was run by dedicated cadres whose homecoming would have to await the end of the war; 10,306 of them lie buried in a 40-acre cemetery and thousands more lie somewhere in the jungle. When the Special Forces entered these areas on their reconnaissance missions, the Truong Son Brigades deployed their own Special Forces to hunt them down. When the American aircraft appeared, the convoys were shunted into caves, while their drivers took refuge in underground shelters. The Americans bombed the river bridges but within a week ferries took their place, disguised as floating islands. More than 10,000 anti-aircraft batteries were hauled across the mountains and placed on hill tops, with the result that about 40 per cent of American aircraft had to be diverted to 'flak suppression' missions. On average, the Americans destroyed only 25 per cent of the traffic and, for many pilots, bombing missions on the Trail became a one-way trip to prison in the 'Hanoi Hilton'. Long after the Americans had reduced the Trail areas to a moonscape, the Communists used the highway for their final assault on Saigon.

MODERN DEVELOPMENTS: LONG-RANGE SURVEILLANCE

Today, Long-Range Reconnaissance Patrolling remains an important task for the Special Forces of America and her NATO allies. At NATO's Long-Range Reconnaissance Patrol School at Weingarten, West Germany, Dutch Marines, British SAS, Belgian Para-Commandos, German *Fernspaeh* troops and US Special Forces from the 1/10 Special Forces Group (Bad Toltz) come together to learn modern techniques and lessons from the past. These skills are then tested on realistic annual NATO exercises such as TRISTAR, originally devised by Britain's SAS.

In recent years, the LRRP teams have been joined by another intelligence-gathering specialist. While the climax of a successful patrol may be the close reconnaissance of an enemy target, LRRPs lack the wherewithal to maintain extended periods of surveillance. To fill this gap the Americans have created Long-Range Surveillance Companies (LRSC) and Detachments (LRSD). The 189-strong LRSCs are attached to army corps and are part of the Military Intelligence Brigades (Combat Electronic Warfare Intelligence). The LRSDs are assigned to divisional armoured battalions, deploying 53 men to armoured and mechanised divisions and a further 41 men to light divisions. The primary function of these LRS units is to gather battlefield (tactical) intelligence, reporting 'enemy dispositions, movements and activities, and battlefield conditions', using a range of visual and electronic devices. The LRS units are solely concerned with intelligence-gathering, 'boom and bang' follow-up missions being the responsibility of the Rangers and Special Forces. Like their colleagues in the Green Berets, they are trained in all the covert infiltration/exfiltration techniques, as well as being intelligence and communications specialists. However, because their operational area is immediately behind the battlefield, they may use an uncommon form of insertion known as stay-behind (see Chapter 6; Malaya), remaining in well-concealed positions while friendly conventional forces retreat and the enemy vanguard rolls past, before emerging to conduct their tasks.

INDIGENOUS RECONNAISSANCE/SURVEILLANCE UNITS

Wilderness provides every opportunity for covert insertion. While such areas have been turned to our advantage in foreign wars, the presence of a wasteland on the edge of one's own continental land mass, provides an 'open door' for drug-runners and the clandestine forces of hostile powers. The security of such areas falls between two stools. Conventional units are unused to long operations in wild country but such routine patrols would be felt to be a misuse of the élite Recce-commando unit's skills. Equally, using regular forces to close this geographical 'door' can be expensive, and very unpopular with the troops themselves. In recent years, two countries have solved this problem by recruiting the local people into army special warfare reserve units.

The Eskimo Scouts were raised as part of America's Alaskan Army National Guard. This 1,500-strong force is organised into Scout Battalions which deploy companies to cover individual regions within Alaska's immense tundra. The idea behind these indigenous formations is not to turn Eskimos into soldiers but to harness their scouting abilities to 'reconnaissance/surveillance duties'. In effect, this means issuing the Scouts with M-16 rifles, radios and a few snowmobiles and asking them to gather information during their hunting and fishing trips. Recently, the Eskimo Scouts became enmeshed in a rumour that the unit had found evidence of Spetsnaz incursions along the Alaskan coastline, though this has been strenuously denied by both the US Government and academics investigating the claims.

Australia has also raised three Regional Surveillance Units (RSU) to watch the scrubland and coasts of its 'Top End': the Pilbara Regiment (North Western Australia), the 51 Far North Queensland Regiment (North Eastern Australia) and NORFORCE (Northern Central Australia). The RSU concept grew out of a Second World War formation, the 2nd/1st North Australia Observer Unit. Raised by anthropologist Professor W.E.H. Stanner and composed of local bushmen, police, surveyors, clerks and miners, this 'phantom army' was to provide a surveillance force behind Japanese lines in the event of an invasion.

The North West Mobile Force (NORFORCE) is of particular interest, being trained, equipped and organised along SAS lines. NORFORCE consists of a Regimental Headquarters (including Signals Troop) and four Regional Surveillance Squadrons (Darwin, Arnhem Land, Alice Springs and Kimberley). A Base Squadron provides specialist support and is made up of a Quartermaster Troop, Transport Troop, Medical Troop and Technical Sup-

America and Australia are both using civilian indigenous personnel in their 'national guard' units which keep watch on their respective wilderness areas. NORFORCE mounts two-week surveillance patrols in Australia's 'Top End', during which the soldiers are expected to live off the land. (*Australian DOD*)

port Troop. The Force has a total peacetime complement of 43 Regular Army staff, 430 Reservists, 105 Aboriginals and 48 women.

Each of the four Surveillance Squadrons conducts short patrols at weekends and longer 16-day patrols throughout the year. In any one training year, NORFORCE deploys about 12 patrols for two-week periods. Soldiers are expected to be expert in survival techniques and receive rations sufficient for only half the duration of the patrol. Regimental Headquarters provides a range of the usual SAS courses including basic and advanced Patrol Courses and four specialist courses. The six-man patrols are commanded by an officer or senior NCO with the additional personnel being cross-trained as signallers, medics, drivers and small-boat handlers. Aboriginals are expected to reach the same standard as other personnel but those living in remote stations in the Outback are provided with a further two weeks of continuous training every four months by mobile training teams. The problem of the tremendous distances is overcome by a wide range of insertion and extraction vehicles including Landcruisers, helicopters, boats and aircraft.

Apart from its primary role of reconnaissance and surveillance, NOR-FORCE collects geographical and military information, provides guides and information for conventional units and maintains regular friendly contact with stock stations and Aboriginal communities. The local civilians are encouraged to report unusual events, thus enlarging the unit's intelligence-gathering potential. In wartime, NORFORCE would operate in a stay-behind capacity.

TARGETING THE WEST: SOVIET URBAN RECONNAISSANCE

Traditionally the Soviet Spetsnaz consisted of three sabotage regiments (one each for the Western, South Western and Far Eastern Theatres), 24 diversionary brigades (one each for the 16 military districts, four groups of forces and four fleets), some 40 independent companies and an undisclosed number of agents. Although the sabotage regiments and independent companies were recruited from the professional army, the diversionary brigades, which accounted for 90 per cent of the 30,000 active personnel involved, were drawn from conscripts serving for no more than two years. Even taking into account the fact that the conscripts had all received prior training with DOSAFF, and were in many cases competent parachutists, their standard was inevitably far below that of the regular element. Furthermore, many diversionary brigades were vastly under strength, leading the American Defence Intelligence Agency to suggest that the overall pre-mobilisation combatant strength was in fact no more than 12,000. Spetsnaz was, in effect, incapable of carrying out its duties.

This problem was compounded in the 1980s by the introduction in the West of far more sophisticated intelligence support. Likely drop zones, beachheads, assembly areas and approach lines were logged and watched. Vulnerable and key points, which might be lucrative targets for sabotage teams, were catalogued, studied and guarded. Aggressive patrolling, once limited to the front line, was extended far to the rear. Intelligence and operations networks at divisional and corps level began to liaise closely to identify potential enemy ingress and egress air routes.

Soviet Military Intelligence, the GRU, then attempted to diminish the potency of NATO's counter-insurgency forces either by neutralisation or by inserting agents into Western society. The term 'agent' has always been applied by the Soviets to a foreigner recruited by the intelligence services, specifically excluding Soviet citizens executing spying missions abroad. Most agents recruited by the GRU were talent-spotted from among the visitors to the Soviet Union who then returned home to recruit others. Some attended a highly secretive training camp, possibly in the Odessa area, where they were taught communications, security and, where necessary, the theory and practice of demolitions and firearms. They were not encouraged to mix nor did they learn anything of the structure either of the GRU or Spetsnaz. Most were mature, preferably involved in restricted or classified work, and able to move about freely. Some were idealists whilst others worked for money. A few were even blackmailed into service.

Some agents are immediately employed in intelligence or reconnaissance duties. Others become part of a 'sleeping network', *zamorozhennye* (frozen) in Soviet idiom. As such they were destined to continue their normal lives, their only contact with their controllers being coded radio transmissions, such as the incessant stream of numbers that used to emanate from East Germany, known colloquially as 'Magdeburg Annie'. At times of need or during transition to war, the 'sleepers' may be awakened to conduct intelligence tasks, minor industrial sabotage or, rarely, support Spetsnaz operations by identifying targets or maintaining 'safe-houses'. It has been estimated that some European countries still harbour between 50–500 *zamorozhennye*. This agent structure is serviced and controlled by career intelligence officers with diplomatic accreditation ('Legals') or by officers using carefully constructed covers ('Illegals').

Generally, Spetsnaz operators themselves did not attempt peacetime reconnaissance of restricted areas but instead relied upon the 2nd Directorate of the GRU to supply its agents with sufficient funds to move to areas in the proximity of likely targets. Much of this information was piecemeal and large parts of it irrelevant. Nonetheless, painstaking analysis of thousands of facts must have enabled the GRU to compile sufficient data on a range of targets to make a potentially successful attack at least possible.

9

Combat Rescue

Blessed is the match consumed in kindling flame
Blessed is the flame that burns in the secret fastness of the heart.
Blessed is the heart with strength to stop its beating for honour's sake
Blessed is the match consumed in kindling flame.

Hanna Szenes

Parachuted into Hungary in 1944 officially to organise the rescue of downed RAF pilots and unofficially to save Jewish refugees; captured and shot by Hungarian fascists shortly before the end of the war, Hanna lit a fire in the hearts of the later Israeli paratroops, who memorise her poem.

Greek legends tell of the launching of a thousand ships to recover Helen of Troy – a very willing hostage; to recover an 'agent' on a TA exercise in Belgium, they sent a four-man patrol. That particular legend is enshrined in a cartoon that hangs on the wall of a London parachutists' mess. According to the exercise intelligence report, the 'agent' was due to be transferred between prisons and the most direct route involved turning left at a T-junction and travelling down a heavily wooded road. Acting on this information, the patrol parachuted into Belgium on a Friday night and, evading 'hunter-killer' units of the Belgian Para-Commandos, set up an ambush on the left-hand turn, just short of the T-junction. It had been a long walk in to the target and, tired and anxious, the patrol hurriedly set their 'charges' on two large trees, to drop them fore and aft of the prison vehicle, thus effectively cutting-off any escape route. Quite soon a blue prison van approached the T-junction but, much to the soldiers' dismay, it failed to take the left-hand turn and continued happily on into the Belgian countryside.

After a long and bitter walk to a coastal extraction RV, the patrol returned on the Sunday afternoon to analyse the failure. The de-brief revealed something of the story: the van driver had made a simple navigation error. Nevertheless Sunday evening passed amidst clouds of cigarette smoke, as the exercise was analysed in fine detail to discover a way in which the four-man patrol might have covered this eventuality.

If, in retrospect, the patrol had been in a position to assess the outcome of historical agent/aircrew rescue operations, much *angst* might have been spared. Rescue operations have proved to be the most complex, dangerous and the least successful of all special operations. As with all such enterprises, a good plan, surprise and a well-picked team goes a long way but the other essential ingredient, recent and accurate intelligence, is far more important. Unlike an enemy headquarters or a similar target scheduled for reconnaissance or demolition, prisoners are likely to be moved, dispersed or killed. At the very least, because of their importance, they will be heavily guarded. After the rescue, wounded or sick prisoners require immediate evacuation. In the absence of special evacuation procedures, the two qualities that protect teams behind-the-lines, speed and stealth, are dangerously compromised.

What sort of personnel merit these special operations to bring personnel back across the lines? All military and civilian prisoners are deserving of rescue but, within the limitations of war, two categories merit special pleading: aircrew and intelligence agents. Both are likely to find themselves escaping and evading in the enemy's backyard. The former are expensive to train (a fighter pilot cost £15,000 to train during the Second World War) and difficult to replace, while the agent may hold information that, if revealed under interrogation, could cost the lives of tens or even hundreds of other agents or soldiers.

Operations to bring them out fall into two broad categories. The first, of which the TA exercise was an example, is the relatively high-profile and 'active' commando operation to rescue personnel from prisoner-of-war camps and security prisons; the second type of operation is 'passive' and seeks quietly to net evaders and successful escapees who are then funnelled to safety along chains of 'safe-houses'.

ESCAPE LINES

With the outbreak of the Second World War, the British SIS saw the need to revive an escape organisation. This became MI9 which, under Brigadier N.R. Crockatt, assumed the two functions of interrogating and vetting enemy prisoners (MI19) and organising the escape of prisoners-of-war (IS9(d)). The task of the latter department was to train servicemen in escape and evasion, provide them with escape-kits (forged papers, compasses and maps etc.) and establish escape lines in occupied Europe.

However, as the survivors of the British Expeditionary Force (BEF) trickled across the Spanish frontier after Dunkirk, it soon became clear that many had been helped by French and Belgian families. Some were simply Good Samaritans; others, determined to resist the German occupiers, organised

Combat-rescue requires the speedy evacuation of wounded or sick prisoners. (*PMA Pictures*)

themselves in teams and prepared 'lines' of safe-houses and guides that stretched from Brussels, Paris and Marseilles to neutral Spain. Some expatriates resident on the French Riviera, and soldiers and airmen on the run from the Germans, forfeited their chance to escape and became helpers and organisers. Many leaders such as Captain Ian Garrow, Pat O'Leary, Mary Lindell and Andrée De Jongh became legends for their fortitude and daring. But these were the mere tip of the iceberg. It has been estimated that 12,000 escape-line personnel survived the war, with another 500 being shot by the Germans or dying in concentration camps. With such a groundswell of support, it only remained for MI9 to supply money and radio-transmitters, give advice on security and organise pick-ups by aircraft and boats.

In Western Europe, approximately 7,000 American, British and Commonwealth servicemen made it back to Allied front-lines, while another 5,143 took refuge in neutral Switzerland. All returning British servicemen were classified by MI9 as 'evaders' or 'escapers'. With the exception of several hundred soldiers from the BEF, most of the evaders were aircrew shot down behind the lines. In the areas covered by escape lines in north-west Europe, 3,000 airmen successfully avoided capture. The majority arrived in Spain, having been assisted by escape lines. After D-Day, operational rescues recovered another 500–600 from the battle zones.

A further 1,248 British and Commonwealth returnees from Germany and Italy were classified as 'escapers'. Most were soldiers and very few were lucky enough to make contact with organised escape lines. Prison camps in Germany, in the midst of a hostile population and facing a well-oiled security apparatus, represented the most severe challenge. MI9 escape aids such as dock passes, button compasses, silk maps and money arrived in more than 7,815 special parcels or, on at least one occasion, appeared as 'novelties' in doctored Christmas crackers. Armed with these gifts, approximately 150 escapers made their own way to Sweden, Switzerland, Spain or Russia. They were joined by 713 Americans, many of whom, escaping later in the war, made their way towards the advancing Allied armies. Another 13,768 escaped and 4,416 successfully evaded capture in the Mediterranean theatres.

The Americans had their own version of MI9 – the US Military Intelligence Escape and Evasion Section (MIS-X) – but their most outstanding escape lines were provided by the Balkan Air Terminal Service (BATS) and the Air Crew Rescue Unit (ACRU) of the 15th Airforce. BATS was an aircrew construction unit that specialised in building airstrips in the most unlikely places, including the high mountain valleys and coastal plains in Yugoslavia claimed by Tito's and Mihailovic's partisans. While the airstrips were primarily intended to supply the partisans, they became vital collection points for aircrew shot down over Yugoslavia and central Europe and Americans released by the fascist government of Romania when it surrendered in August 1944.

Attached to BATS were OSS teams which made contact with the partisans. Their aim was to round up evaders, whose only training in SERE was often merely a verbal instruction to make contact with the partisan forces if shot down. These teams were later joined by ACRU teams comprising a doctor, radio operator and an OSS officer under the command of an air force captain. This widened the net and provided prompt medical treatment for injured evaders, greatly increasing their chances of survival. In addition, SOE officers attached to the partisans provided rescue teams and guides for evaders who wandered into their area of operations. The combined operation rescued 3,870 aircrew and approximately 2,000 other nationals on the run from the Nazis.

On arrival at the BATS airstrips, the steady flow of evaders were repatriated

Yugoslav partisans, Allied Special Forces and the Balkan Air Terminal Service combined to form one of the most successful escape-lines of the Second World War. (*Imperial War Museum*)

by aircraft or patrol boat. Air evacuation was conducted with a particular thoroughness that has characterised American air force commitment to special operations. A Dakota transport aircraft was used to pick up passengers from the BATS airstrips. This was covered by a Wellington bomber, its rotating machine-gun turrets providing fire-support against any enemy infantry that might decide to attack the airfield while the Dakota was on the ground. The two aircraft were, in turn, supported by up to 36 Lightning fighters, which provided ample protection against German air attack. Such was the efficiency of this joint operation that one B-17 Flying Fortress crew was back at its home airfield a mere four days after crash-landing in Yugoslavia.

Both the OSS and the British RAF sent teams into Romania to provide guides and escape lines for the long journey to Yugoslavia. Many parachuted into areas held by Tito's partisans and made the difficult and dangerous journey into Hungary and Romania by foot. These parties included Jewish men and women from the camps in Palestine, recruited by the RAF but under orders from the Jewish Underground to extend the operation to Jewish refugees. In Hungary, most of the teams, like the Hanna Szenes party, were caught and imprisoned or shot. In Romania, some OSS teams survived long enough to supervise the evacuation of POWs in the interim between the fall of Antonescu's fascist government and the arrival of the Russians.

In the Far East, the jungle, immense distances and sometimes the island nature of the war made escape and evasion much more difficult. Some evaders were rescued by partisans or Special Forces. A dedicated escape line existed in China: the British Army Aid Group (BAAG). This netted some evaders after the fall of the British colonies but by 1943 BAAG no longer served this function. Instead it turned to supplying high-grade intelligence to the 14th USAAF, while serving as a cover for SOE.

The remote location of many Japanese POW camps, and the Japanese habit of executing recaptured prisoners, discouraged escapes. Japanese ferocity, particularly the machine-gunning of 20,000 Chinese subsequently disposed of in Singapore harbour, was responsible for the joint SOE (Force 136)/OSS (E Group) operation mounted at the end of the war to prevent the possible slaughter of Allied POWs. In August 1945, 50 four-man SOE teams were briefed to move close to the major camps, which held an estimated total of 100,000 Allied POWs. They were instructed to wait until 26 August 1945 (12 days after Japan's surrender) before making contact with the Japanese administration. As a consequence an orderly evacuation of the POWs was achieved, with the Japanese continuing to administer the camps while the Special Duties Squadrons and other attached aircraft dropped containers of food and medical supplies to the prisoners.

RESCUE: INSIDE JOBS

One of the most difficult aspects of 'active' operations to spring prisoners is the need to get in and out of occupied territory. Operating without support and without the possibility of extraction, to avoid follow-up operations by the security forces, requires great daring and more than a little luck.

Four partisans of the Polish Home Army, and another four agents parachuted into Poland by SOE, managed to break into Pinsk prison on 18 January 1943, armed only with light machine-guns (Sten-guns). The security prison, 100 miles east of Brest-Litovsk, was holding Polish resistance activists under sentence of death. Four of the team, one wearing the uniform of an NCO in the SS, drove up to the main gate and used bluff to gain entry. Once inside, they shot the guard, forced open the inner gate and entered the prison courtyard. Here they were joined by the rest of the team who used a ladder to scale the back wall of the prison. A quick search of the administration block revealed the commandant, whom they killed before removing his keys to the men's block and releasing over 40 prisoners, including the parachutist and his two companions who were the object of the raid. The Pinsk operation has been hailed as 'a classic example of the tactics of a small commando group, led by well-trained and selected parachutists equipped with modern weapons'.

A similar operation to the Pinsk rescue took place in the Philippines, conducted by one of the great unhailed heroes of the Second World War, Richard Sakakida. Sakakida was born in Hawaii of Japanese parents and, like many of the Nisei (first generation expatriates), volunteered for service with the American forces at the outbreak of the Second World War. Working for the American Counter-Intelligence Corps (CIC) in the Philippines, Sakakida was captured by the Japanese. After convincing his captors that he had worked for the Americans under duress, Sakakida was given a job in the Japanese Judge Advocate General's office. This work brought him into contact with the wife of Ernest Tupas, a guerrilla held by the Japanese in Muntinglupa prison. Sakakida suddenly saw the opportunity to continue his intelligence work behind the lines. He would break the guerrillas out of prison and use their radio-transmitter to send regular reports back to the Allies.

The Muntinglupa jail-break was almost a carbon-copy of Pinsk. Sakakida met the guerrillas very early one morning in October 1943 and, donning the uniform of a Japanese officer, complete with medal ribbons and sword, marched a contingent of four guerrillas to the gate of the prison where they impersonated the night security guard from the local barracks. Sakakida barked some orders at the guards and Japanese well-oiled discipline did the rest. When the guards bowed low in respect, they were swiftly clubbed on the back of the head. The main raiding force of 25 guerrillas were then let into the prison, where they overpowered the guards and released nearly 500 Filipino prisoners in the second biggest gaol-break of the war.

Sakakida then coolly returned to his barracks and continued to pass information to the guerrillas for the rest of the war. When, in 1945, the accurate bombing of well-camouflaged Japanese headquarter units suggested the presence of a spy in the camp, Sakakida escaped and survived in the jungle, finally emerging two weeks after the end of hostilities.

THE FIRST MODERN COMMANDO RESCUES

At the end of the Second World War, Britain's MI9 was not disbanded but underwent transformation into a series of reserve army units (POW Rescue, Recovery and Interrogation unit; Intelligence School 9; Joint Reserve POW Intelligence Organisation; Joint Reserve Reconnaissance Unit [TA] and the Reserve Reconnaissance Unit [TA]), before the role was allotted to 23 SAS (TA). Behind this metamorphosis was the implicit understanding that passive networks of escape-lines, which were dependent upon resistance forces, had little place in the post-war world. Henceforth personnel behind the lines would be rescued by specially-trained commando units. However, this begs the question as to how successful such operations had proved in the past.

Operation JERICHO was unusual; today, it would be termed an 'Air

Commando' or Air Force special operation. During the early months of 1944, as the Allies prepared to land in France, Amiens prison, in north eastern France, held over 100 resistance workers under sentence of death, including four important Allied agents. Gestapo chief Brauman decided to start shooting large batches of prisoners to make way for those rounded up in the German counter-intelligence sweeps during the winter of 1943–44. On Saturday, 19 February, 120 Resistance workers and agents were scheduled to die. The prison, defended by thick stone walls, was heavily guarded and, in desperation, the French Resistance requested British intervention.

The British decided to send in highly-manoeuvrable Mosquito fighter bombers to blow gaps in the walls and prison block and release escaping prisoners, who would be met by resistance personnel waiting outside the prison. On Friday 18 February, 19 Mosquito bombers of 21 and 987 Squadrons and the Australian RAF 464 Squadron, took off in two waves and headed for the French coast. With them went 14 Typhoons of 198 and 174 Squadrons to provide protection against any intercepting German fighters. Despite leaving England in snowstorm conditions, the first wave arrived over Amiens at 12 noon precisely, to hit the German canteen which was packed with guards eating lunch. The second wave arrived a few minutes later to continue the job of demolishing the outer walls, and they were heartened to see prisoners running away from the shattered prison. The blast from the bombs opened many cell doors, allowing some to escape and disappear back into the resistance networks, including at least four of those destined to be shot the next day. Unfortunately, the bombs killed many of the prisoners, the fuses being set too short to allow sufficient time for the prisoners to take cover. Others were killed by machine-gun fire as the guards rallied after the air-raid. Many of those who failed to escape were discovered in a mass grave after the liberation.

The raid was marred by tragedy. As well as the prisoners killed, four Mosquitoes were lost, including that of the operation's commander, Group Captain Pickard. On the way home, Pickard altered course to investigate the site of a crashed Mosquito and was hit by anti-aircraft fire. Limping towards the French coast, Pickard's disabled aircraft was pounced on by German FW 190 fighters and both he and his navigator were killed. Pickard, one of Bomber Command's outstanding pilots, had conducted other RAF special operations, including the raid by the Parachute Regiment at Bruneval (see Chapter 10).

The success of JERICHO should not be assessed merely on the number of escaped prisoners or downed aircrew. Some resisters reported that the raid at Amiens irreparably damaged the German counter-intelligence effort and allowed the Resistance in northern France to re-group prior to the Allied invasion of Europe.

Two real commando rescue operations took place almost simultaneously in Italy in the summer of 1943. The first was the rescue of the Italian dictator, Benito Mussolini, imprisoned by an Italian interim government dithering

RAF Mosquitoes blow an escape route for Resistance workers held in Amiens prison. The operation was timed to catch the German prison guards at lunch. The photographic reconnaissance Mosquito needed three passes over the target to secure this photograph. (*Imperial War Museum*)

between surrendering to the Allies and continuing to fight with the Germans. On 26 July, Hitler gave this extraordinarily difficult mission to the German Special Forces Commander, Otto Skorzeny. In almost total secrecy, Skorzeny assumed control of every aspect of the operation, assembling a group of 50 parachutists and setting out personally to locate Il Duce. The search led him to the island of Ponza and then to Sardinia, where Mussolini was being held in a villa on the edge of La Maddalina. On 18 August, Skorzeny conducted an aerial reconnaissance of the villa and was promptly shot down by British fighters. Unscathed, he returned disguised as a rating on an E-boat, only to

Outer prison wall breached by RAF bombs. (*Imperial War Museum*)

find that Mussolini had been moved. Finally, in early September he was located at the Hotel Albergo-Rifugio on the Gran Sasso, a mountain in the Abruzzi range, from which he was rescued by glider assault. A full description of this classical operation appears in Charles Foley's *Commando Extraordinary*. The success of this rescue can be ascribed to Skorzeny's persistence and his personal control of both the vital intelligence-gathering phase and the operation's final execution, which ensured that the rescuers could respond to rapidly changing events and withstand changes of fortune.

The second operation had its origins in the Italian surrender on 8 September, as the Allies completed their invasion of Sicily and launched sea-borne attacks on the foot of Italy. For the next four days thousands of Allied prisoners were free, many for the first time since their capture in the campaigns in the Western Desert. Some senior British officers, believing that the camps would soon be liberated by the Allied armies, gave orders expressly forbidding escape on pain of court martial. Many soldiers, 80,000 according to Winston Churchill, left anyway, trekking south towards the friendly lines. Behind them, the camp commandants were proved wrong and the German Army seized control of the country and shipped the Allied prisoners back to Germany. Suddenly, the POWs, drifting south supported by hospitable Italians, found themselves on the run and faced with fending for themselves. Pursued by German patrols and aircraft, they fled into the mountains. When the news of their plight reached England, British politicians ordered the Army to mount a rescue operation.

By late September, this had been hastily cobbled together. Small groups of men from the Parachute Regiment, and attached Italian-speaking intelligence staff, were equipped with radios and parachuted into the Apennines on the Adriatic coast from Pescarra to Ancona. Their job was to visit farmhouses and other possible hiding places and organise the POWs into groups for evacuation. They were to be joined by SAS patrols who, while widening the net, also acted as guides to lead groups of ex-prisoners down to the coast for evacuation by the navy. The parachutists dropped blind onto rough-and-ready mountain DZs. The darkness and difficult terrain resulted in many groups losing contact almost as soon as they left the aircraft. Over the next two months, individually or in groups, the parachutists gathered ex-prisoners together and set off for the coast, though the rescues were numbered in hundreds rather than thousands. One group of 500 came to grief after two POWs attempted to break into a farmhouse, thereby alerting a German patrol; in the event only 40 of them escaped onto the boats. This operation has been heralded as a failure but, given the preparation required, the area to be covered, the fact that many POWs were demoralised and suspicious of their rescuers and the difficulties in conducting large groups through hostile territory (a significant factor affecting the escape of parachutists from Arnhem), any measure of success should be seen positively.

The Philippines saw the two largest rescue operations of the war, with Richard Sikakida's efforts at Muntinglupa only just surpassed by the 6th Ranger Battalion's rescue of 513 American POWs at Cabanatuan. In January 1945, the Americans landed at Linayen Gulf on Luzon, immediately isolating a Japanese army corps which attempted to delay the American advance as it withdrew into strongholds in the Zambales mountains. This was the beginning of the end for the Japanese in the Philippines and the Allies greatly feared that some Japanese commanders would respond by giving orders to kill American POWs. When intelligence discovered a POW camp at Cabanatuan, a reinforced company of the 6th Rangers was sent to rescue them.

Speed was essential and the company set out on Sunday, 28 January, infiltrating Japanese lines to contact a large guerrilla force at Lobang, before moving all night to arrive at Balingcari early the following morning. Keeping up the momentum of the operation, Colonel Mucci immediately dispatched

Alamo Scouts (one of the forerunners of the modern LRRP teams) to reconnoitre the prison. The Scouts rejoined the main force at Plateros that evening to relay the bad news that the camp garrison was around 500-strong and, further, that a Japanese division was moving through the town of Cabu, close to the camp. The Scouts provided a sketch-map of the prison and there, on the jungle floor, an extraordinarily detailed and careful operational plan was worked out.

The next evening, after allowing time for the Japanese division to move out of the area, the Rangers moved close to the camp. To the north lay a Japanese garrison of 800 men in the town of Cabu and to the south was the sizeable town of Cabanatuan, with 9,000 inhabitants. Two blocking forces of guerrillas effectively isolated the camp from these potential sources of Japanese reinforcements by laying ambushes on the road either side of the camp and, at the last moment, completed the camp's isolation by cutting the telephone wires. At 19.45 hours, Ranger units attacked the camp under the cover of bazooka anti-tank fire, directed towards targets of opportunity. As the guard-towers and pill-boxes were eliminated, assault platoons broke through the main gate, destroyed the camp's radios and made contact with the POWs. As Colonel Mucci had foreseen, Japanese guards poured out of their barracks and rushed towards the compound in a convoy of trucks and tanks, only to be liquidated by bazooka and small-arms fire. Other pockets of Japanese, in the camp's many buildings, were pinned down by support fire and, where necessary, mopped up piecemeal by groups of Rangers. After only 30 minutes, the prisoners were being conducted down a cleared lane to freedom. Gratefully, the two blocking guerrilla units withdrew to join the main force; one is reported to have held off between 800–2,000 Japanese attempting to force their way through from Cabu.

The most astonishing aspect of this operation was the escape back to American lines. American ex-prisoners too sick to walk were carried by the Rangers until local *caraboa* carts could be rounded up to transport them. En route, the most severely ill were treated by the guerrillas' and Rangers' doctors. Early the next morning, as the force completed the 25 mile trek back to friendly lines, the mile-and-a-half column, made up of 51 carts, was protected by flanking and rearguard units of guerrillas and Rangers. When they met up with units of the American Sixth Army, a fleet of ambulances was provided to evacuate the rescued prisoners. This heroic operation cost the lives of only 26 Rangers and guerrillas and undoubtedly succeeded because of the size of the combined Special Forces rescue force, the dispersed nature of the fighting and their close proximity to American forces sweeping across Luzon.

VIETNAM

It is one of the quirks of history that a captain commanding one of the Ranger companies at Cabanatuan later found fame when he was asked to command the most famous rescue operation in Vietnam. His name was 'Bull' Simons and his commission was the rescue of American POWs from a North Vietnamese prison camp on the Red River, on the outskirts of a city called Son Tay, near Hanoi.

In the spring of 1970, representatives of the United States and North and South Vietnam met in Paris in an attempt to hammer out a peace settlement. As had been expected, the North Vietnamese used American POWs as a bargaining counter. They had used the same ploy after the French withdrawal in 1954, with POWs and personnel listed as 'Missing in Action' (MIA) surfacing years later to be used as an inducement for French aid. In April 1970, an opportunity presented itself to remove some of these bargaining counters. An Air Force Technical Sergeant employed at the USAF's 1127th Field Activities Group, Virginia, while examining air reconnaissance photographs of suspected POW camps, identified what appeared to be a Search and Rescue (SAR) message spelt out using the prisoners' laundered uniforms. The tattered rags, washed and left on the ground to dry, appeared to contain a message to the effect that 55 prisoners were held in the camp and that six desperately required evacuation. Further photographs taken by SR-71 Blackbird reconnaissance aircraft, unmanned 'Buffalo Hunter' drones, satellites and information reputedly from prisoner interrogations and South Vietnamese Special Forces LRRP teams confirmed this analysis. Almost immediately, Air Force staff started working on a plan to rescue them.

Alas, the immense size and complexity of America's bureaucratic intelligence and military communities effectively strangled the operation from the outset. By August, Technical Sergeant Norval Clineball and Colonel George J. Iles had submitted their ideas in the form of a report to Air Force staff at Plans and Operations in the Pentagon. The matter was then referred to Brigadier General Donald D. Blackburn, the Assistant for Counter-insurgency and Special Activities. Assent for the operation was solicited from the Chairman of the Joint Chiefs of Staff (in fact, twice, as the first incumbent retired), after which Operation IVORY COAST was circulated to the CIA and the military's Defence Intelligence Agency (DIA) for their recommendations. The President's Adviser on National Security Affairs, Dr Henry Kissinger, supported the plan but ordered the operation delayed until November. Meanwhile, Colonel Arthur 'Bull' Simons and his team of 92 assault troops from Army Special Forces personnel stationed at Fort Bragg, had conducted over 170 night assault rehearsals on a model of the Son Tay compound built by the CIA at a cost of $60,000. By day, the 'camp' was dismantled to avoid the attentions of Soviet reconnaissance satellites.

The rescue mission was finally launched from Udorn on the Thailand/Laos

Opposite: An essential feature of the commando rescue is the requirement to break into the prison to release the captives. (*PMA Pictures*)

border on the night of 20 November 1970. The plan called for a single HH-3E helicopter to be crash-landed inside the compound, while the rest of the assault team and rescued prisoners would be carried by five HH-53 helicopters. The helicopters were supported by two C-130 aircraft, acting as tankers and flare-ships.

As the rescue force crossed the North Vietnamese border, 116 support aircraft took off from seven bases in Thailand and three carriers in the Gulf of Tonkin. Their missions included locking-out the surface-to-air (SAM) sites in the Son Tay area, saturating the Chinese/North Vietnamese radar defences, conducting a fake distracting raid on the port of Haiphong and trawling for patrolling Mig fighters.

In the final analysis, the rescue was a tactical success. After an initial error in attacking a sapper school 400yds beyond the prison, Simons recovered the initiative and successfully seized the prison complex. The outcome is well known. Four months earlier, in July, the North Vietnamese had moved the prisoners to Dan Hoi prison, seven-and-a-half miles away, partly because an unusually heavy rainy season had caused the local rivers to burst their banks and the camp's water supply was contaminated and also because they had decided to divide the prisoners on the basis of religious denomination. Sadly, this change had actually been noted in recent intelligence indicators. A highly-placed Vietnamese official working for the DIA had passed a coded message to an agency contact to the effect that Son Tay prison had been closed, and, in addition, reconnaissance photographs taken immediately prior to the rescue attempt had shown no signs of any occupants.

Son Tay provided a lesson that was well learnt. Dr Edward N. Luttwak, a Senior Fellow at the Center for Strategic and International Studies, Georgetown University, had this to say at the 1983 Symposium on *The Role of Special Operations in US Strategy for the 1980s*:

> When a bureaucratised and engineering-orientated military establishment attempts commando operations, it is always unlucky. I will give you two examples: first Son Tay. The action starts with the information that was received on 9 May, 1970: American POWs in Ap Loy and Son Tay. Had this information gone to a commando organisation – consisting of, say, 30 to 40 officers who have spent 5 or 6 years doing only commando work – their own self-contained planning group would have said, 'Right. This is where they are. What's the most prosaic vehicle that will get us there?' Then they would have gone in to take the POWs out.

Son Tay was undoubtedly a stepping stone on the road to the creation of USSOCOM – still a relatively large bureaucratic structure but nevertheless a self-contained commando organisation.

It is satisfying to note that Colonel 'Bull' Simons was to have his day, shortly before dying of a heart attack in 1979. In the previous year, two executives from the Texas-based company, Electronic Data Systems Corporation, were imprisoned in revolutionary Iran on trumpted-up charges. Ross Perot, millionaire Chairman of EDS, appealed for his friend's help. In a meticulously-planned operation, Simons assembled a small team, which flew to Tehran and patiently negotiated their temporary release, then escape, across the Turkish border.

Not all rescue operations were plagued by bureaucracy and small commando units did conduct successful rescues in Vietnam. During the war, there were approximately 119 rescue operations, of which 20 successfully brought back a total of 368 prisoners. Most were carried out under the auspices of a MACVSOG intelligence programme, designed to rescue American POWs. In this, BRIGHT LIGHT was unsuccessful, in that no Americans were freed, all the released prisoners being Vietnamese. Communist forces kept their US prisoners in remote camps or constantly on the move. South Vietnamese ARVN POWs were luckier. Combined SOG and South Vietnamese forces launched a successful raid 40 miles inside Laos to rescue soldiers and civilians held in a camp at Lem Son. Another six of the most successful rescues were conducted by the US Navy's SEALs, freeing 152 POWs in some of the most dangerous and fraught operations of the war. Additionally, many other BRIGHT LIGHT missions were conducted by various LRRP teams to rescue downed pilots and other reconnaissance team personnel who found themselves evading capture.

In May 1972, BRIGHT LIGHT intelligence received a report that American POWs, in a camp close to Hanoi, would attempt to escape under cover of a US air raid and make their way down the Red River in a stolen sampan to the Gulf of Tonkin. The operation to recover them was codenamed THUNDERHEAD and called for a 22-day surveillance of 50 miles of coastline by Search and Rescue helicopters. However, surveillance north of the Red River was screened by a North Vietnamese occupied island and plans were made to insert a SEAL team onto the island to help with surveillance and recovery.

On 3 June, an SOF submarine, USS *Grayback*, took up position on the bottom of the Red River estuary, carrying SEAL Team One, under the command of Lieutenant Spence Dry, and 14 divers from UDT 13. On their first attempt to land on the island, a mixed SEAL/UDT team under the command of Spence Dry attempted to negotiate their SEAL delivery vehicle (SDV) through the fearful underwater currents produced by the river at low tide. When the batteries finally expired, the team was forced to surface and radio for helicopter extraction. A second team attempted the insertion next morning but, because near total radio silence was in operation, they had no knowledge of the previous team's problems. They too lost their SDV and were forced to make a free ascent to the surface.

Meanwhile, the first team were being carried back to the submarine by SAR helicopter, intending to jump 30ft into the water and swim down, entering the submarine through the 'lock-out' chamber. The helicopter was guided to the sub by an infrared beam transmitted through the periscope but weather conditions and darkness prevented the pilot from seeing the horizon. The team were dropped from 100ft with the result that Spence Dry was killed on impact and a UDT operator severely injured. On Friday 9 of June, the USS *Harold E. Holt*, relieving the patrol vessel USS *Eversole* and unaware of the submarine's presence, detected the *Grayback* snorkelling close to the surface and fired at it. The submarine escaped unscathed but the SEAL mission was abandoned – as was the whole operation since the POWs failed to appear.

While it is tempting to ascribe the failure of all American special missions to problems in command and control, the timing and location of the SEAL insertion was dictated by the operation. The real problem was the river currents.

During the Vietnam War, the routine rescue of downed pilots and occasionally Special Forces teams, from behind enemy lines, fell to the USAF's Air Rescue Service (later the Aerospace Rescue and Recovery Service), supplemented by the CIA-controlled Air America in Laos. This Service was a special force in its own right. Quite apart from the highly-trained aircrew, each aircraft carried a parachute and SCUBA trained 'pararescuemen' who could be dropped onto the ground to render immediate aid to injured personnel and facilitate their evacuation.

By 1967, there were 50 USAF aircraft and helicopters in South-East Asia dedicated to wartime SAR missions and designed to rescue 'evaders', most of whom were pilots. Analysts later calculated that a survivor's chances of rescue were good if the rescue aircraft reached him within 15 minutes. If a pilot had not been picked up in 30 minutes, his chances of rescue were rapidly diminishing. Not surprisingly, it was found that 47 per cent of all unsuccessful rescues resulted from the slow speed of the helicopters. Nevertheless, the Service spared no effort to rescue pilots, often at great sacrifice to themselves.

The Service was forced to rationalise its philosophy after the now famous rescue of Lieutenant Colonel Iceal E. Hambleton. While pinpointing North Vietnamese surface-to-air missile sites on 2 April 1972, a missile was launched, which destroyed his Douglas EB-66 twin-engine jet electronic warfare plane, *Bat 21*. Hambleton, an electronic warfare specialist and an expert on the American ballistic missile system, was blown clear of the plane but landed amidst a heavy concentration of Communist troops around the Song Mieu Giang River. Heavy ground fire resulted in the loss of two US Army UH-1 choppers which attempted an impromptu rescue and a no-fire artillery zone was declared around the flyer.

Over the next 11 days, up to 90 sorties a day were used to keep enemy troops away, with a further loss of two OV-10 observation aircraft and a Jolly Green Giant (HH-53) helicopter that attempted a further rescue. Throughout this period, Hambleton remained in radio contact with circling US aircraft which enabled a rescue plan to be cobbled together. Technology had failed and it was left to commandos to effect the rescue. Hambleton's rescuers were drawn from the Strategic Technical Directorate Assistance Team (STDAT)

The Search and Recovery (SAR) units of the US Air Force are a special unit in their own right. (*PMA Pictures*)

158. STDAT had been activated in April 1972 to replace MACVSOG. After rescuing one of the missing OV-10 crewmen, SEAL Lieutenant Thomas Norris, together with Vietnamese SEAL, Nguyen Van Kiet, paddled up the river on the night of 12 April. Dressed as peasants, the men unobtrusively reached the RV and made contact with Hambleton. Behind them, NVA patrols began to block their escape route and the party had to stop frequently, to call for air-strikes on NVA forces along the bank.

Unfortunately, the enemy used the no-fire zone to their advantage, inflicting heavy losses on the 3rd ARVN which were unable to use counter-artillery fire or request tactical air strikes in the area. Subsequently, many SAR aircrew believed that they had discovered their limits and that, against opposition such as was encountered on the *Bat 21* mission, 'the traditional SAR task force was useless'.

OPERATION EAGLE CLAW

On 4 November 1979, some 500 Iranian Revolutionary Guards and students broke into the United States Embassy in Tehran and seized 63 members of the Embassy staff. After an abortive attempt to trade them for the exiled Shah, the hostages became pawns in a complicated nexus of international and internal politics. Eventually, humiliation and political embarrassment drove the Americans to attempt a rescue operation. On the evening of 24 April 1980, C-130s carrying an American rescue force approached a staging area in the Dasht-e-Karir salt desert, 265nm from Tehran, a remote site that would become known throughout the world by its codename: DESERT ONE. As the first aircraft approached, 'pathfinder' radio beacons, planted a month earlier by a CIA reconnaissance aircraft, were switched on, illuminating the LZ. The first troops off the aircraft were Rangers on motor-cycles and jeeps, tasked with blocking a nearby road. Meanwhile, 100 soldiers from the American hostage rescue unit, Delta Force, waited for the eight US Navy RH-53D 'Sea Stallion' helicopters that were to carry them to a second remote staging area DESERT TWO, close to Tehran.

At this point the plan became complicated. The CIA had no HUMINT sources inside Iran, having previously relied on members of the Shah's own secret police, Savak, now running for their lives, and the staff of the CIA Tehran Station, now amongst the hostages. To fill this gap, three Delta operators and an Iranian exile were infiltrated into the city under 'cover' provided by the CIA. Their first task was to conduct 'close reconnaissance' of the Embassy compound, providing details of hostage locations and guard positions and strengths – information not easily obtained from the reconnaissance photographs taken by satellites or high-flying SR-71 reconnaissance aircraft. Their second task was to rendezvous with the rescue team at last light on the second day and conduct Colonel Beckwith and some of his staff on a reconnaissance of the route and target, using six hired Mercedes trucks driven by former supporters of the ex-Shah who were recruited for the operation.

On the third night of the operation, the rescue force was to be collected by the undercover team and driven to the Embassy. A four-man sniper team was detailed to eliminate guards overlooking the east wall, before the 75 Delta Force operators scaled the wall using padded aluminium ladders. Once inside, some were detailed to disperse to individual targets, while others were to clear the compound of obstructions erected by the Iranians to prevent surprise landings.

Meanwhile, a smaller 13-man team was tasked with rescuing three other American diplomats, held in the Foreign Ministry, by using suction cups to scale the outside of the building and break into the third floor. With Delta stretched to the limit, this job was allotted to the 10th Special Forces Group, who had conducted their own training in Germany and had joined the rescue force in Frankfurt three days before the planned attack.

The last phase of the rescue was to involve helicopters picking up the hostages and rescuers and flying them to a disused airfield at Manzariyeh, 35 miles to the south of Tehran. The airfield was to be captured by a large force of Rangers arriving in C-141 Starlifters, while two AC-130 Spectre gunships and fighters from the aircraft carriers USS *Coral Sea* and USS *Nimitz*, covered the withdrawal. Each man was equipped with an escape and evasion kit and Iranian currency. If the rescue failed, the personnel were briefed to escape overland to the Turkish border.

Like Son Tay, the outcome of EAGLE CLAW is well known. The Ranger's road-block netted a surprisingly large number of night-time travellers but a petrol tanker attempted to break through and was hit by an anti-tank rocket. The large explosion and resulting fire-ball endangered the security of the operation and, to make matters worse, the tanker crew escaped in a car that was travelling behind. Meanwhile, the eight helicopters en-route for DESERT ONE found themselves in savage dust storms (*haboobs*) which resulted in one crash landing and another being forced to turn back. This reduced the helicopter force to the bare minimum necessary for the operation. Then it was reported that another helicopter had developed a hydraulic leak, forcing Beckwith to abort the operation. As the surviving helicopters attempted to refuel in the chaos of the large, confused landing zone, one collided with a parked C-130 transport packed with troops and aviation fuel. The instantaneous explosion and resulting fire killed the C-130's five USAF aircrew and the three marines crewing the helicopter. The retreat came close to panic. All the remaining personnel and wounded were loaded onto other C-130 transports and flown back to Masirah, leaving behind helicopters with their engines still running, codes, plans and even details of agents operating in Iran.

In his testimony to Congress, Beckwith described the operation as an '*ad hoc* affair'. It was certainly that, involving all three services and a total of 21 different agencies, using 51 different radio frequencies and more than 150 code words and call signs. In addition, the operation employed 17 different LZs and airfields and the different components of the operation never trained together. More importantly, Delta was trained as a counter-terrorist force (see Chapter 12) for hostage rescue operations, behind friendly lines, and assuming the full co-operation of a willing and hospitable host government. Indeed, such was the scale of the opposition in revolutionary Iran, that it could be argued that Delta should have been the mere spearhead of a large quick reaction force. Had events at DESERT ONE been different, the complex operation might still have turned sour in Tehran, with an even greater loss of life.

ENTEBBE AND THE GAMBIA

On Sunday 27 June 1976, when terrorists seized the 258 passengers and crew of *Air France* flight 139 en route from Tel Aviv to Paris, they were blissfully unaware that they were setting the scene for one of history's great combat rescue operations. Indeed, the terrorist chiefs who had planned the hijack, Dr Wadi Hadad, head of operations of the Palestinian Popular Front for the Liberation of Palestine (PFLP) and his Venezuelan accomplice, Ilich Pamirez Sanchez, also known as Carlos or 'the Jackal', thought it was they who had the monopoly on surprise. Nobody was amazed when the hijacked aircraft was flown to Libya but when, after refuelling at Benghazi, it turned away from the usual Middle Eastern circuit of friendly Arab countries and headed south, the chances of a relatively uncomplicated hostage rescue mission began to diminish. The aircraft's final destination was Entebbe airport, in Uganda. There, the four terrorists from the West German *Baader Meinhof* terrorist group and the PFLP were met by another five of the PFLP's senior operators and Uganda's unstable President, Idi Amin, who greeted the hijack team warmly.

Over the course of the next week, all but 103 Jewish hostages were released. Once again Israel stood alone but, predictably, an Israeli rescue plan was far advanced. The key organisations in the Israeli project were Mossad and Israel's equally aggressive recce-commando unit, *Sayaret Matkal*. Together they examined the options and decided upon an air-assault.

Airforce chief Benny Peled was given the difficult task of getting the force to Entebbe, 3,125 miles from Israel's most southerly airforce base at the tip of the Sinai peninsula. Peled chose four Hercules C-130 transports and two Boeing 707s, one to serve as an airborne hospital and the other as a circling airborne electronic warfare centre and command post for Peled and his staff. The Hercules were to make the trip non-stop, refuelling en route and then flying to Nairobi airport in Kenya to meet up with the Boeing designated as a hospital. For part of the journey, the fleet of aircraft would be covered by Israeli Phantoms.

Kenya was Mossad's responsibility. On 30 June, El Al flight LY 535 landed at Nairobi with an undercover team of some 50 Mossad officers on board, sufficient, when the time came, to seize Nairobi airport by force if necessary. This proved unnecessary. Quartered at the house of an Israeli merchant, they were visited by the heads of Nairobi's police force and Kenya's General Service Unit: President Kenyatta would affect not to notice if Israeli aircraft refuelled at Nairobi.

Other Mossad teams infiltrated Uganda across Lake Victoria and on a regular flight from London. Mossad operators reputedly fired the first shots in the rescue as the first Israeli Hercules came in to land at Entebbe. Presumably, their task was to serve as a reception/pathfinder team for the main force, possibly deploying emergency landing lights and warning the flying command post of any last minute increase in the number of Ugandan troops.

The actual rescue of the hostages in the terminal building was left to *Sayaret Matkal* under the command of Lieutenant Colonel Yonatan ('Yoni') Netanyahu. The unit built a scale model of the airport and practised leaving the aircraft and reaching the terminal building in under two minutes. They also devised a 'Trojan horse' in the form of a black Mercedes similar to that used by Idi Amin. It was planned that the flying command post would announce the 'imminent arrival of the Ugandan President' and the Mercedes would lead the line of Land Rovers in the dash to the terminal building, thus confusing the Ugandan soldiers for a few vital minutes.

However, *Sayaret Matkal* were not sufficient in themselves. Uganda's army had been well trained in the past by Israeli instructors and were well equipped with small arms and light support weapons. Half were based less than 21 miles from the airport. They were supported by a number of Soviet built T-54 tanks and Czech OT-64 armoured personnel carriers, also based near the airport. Additionally, the Ugandan Air Force was equipped with over 50 combat planes including 30 Mig-9s and Mig-17s, 21 of which were actually based at Entebbe, itself ringed by infantry and tanks.

To counter these threats, volunteers were drawn from the 35th Parachute Brigade and élite Golani Infantry Brigade, many of them reservists. One group was tasked with guarding the aircraft and providing any necessary covering fire. This group also contained 33 doctors and combat-medics. The second was given the mission of destroying the Migs and radar installation, taking care to collect vital Soviet-built components for later intelligence analysis. Group three was given the vital job of securing the approach roads to block Ugandan reinforcements. The entire force of just over 100 men was under the command of Brigadier General Dan Shomron.

Fortune does indeed favour the brave. Operation THUNDERBOLT went into effect at 15.30 hours on Saturday, 3 July. The C-130s flew in a dispersed pattern over the Red Sea within normal commercial airlanes but later descended to two hundred feet to escape the attention of groups of Arab radar ships. Behind came the two Boeing 707s repainted in El Al colours. After overflying Ethiopia and crossing Kenyan airspace, the rescue force arrived over Entebbe at 00.01 hours on Sunday morning. The rest is history.

The ground units held a 'dress rehearsal', just before emplaning, in which the entire 'assault and rescue' took 55 minutes; on the actual mission, the aircraft were back in the air in just 53 minutes. All seven terrorists and an unknown number of Ugandan soldiers were killed at a cost of just one soldier killed and three wounded. Two hostages were killed, one by terrorists and one by accident. A further hospitalised hostage, Mrs Dora Bloch, was later murdered by Ugandan security police. Nevertheless, Israel had cause to mourn. The soldier killed by the last sporadic shots from the control tower was 'Yoni' Netanyahu. An Israeli in the tradition of the soldier poets, Netanyahu had been severely wounded in the Six Day War and left Israel to read philosophy at Harvard. He returned to help plan and execute one of the greatest commando operations of all time.

The Israelis had followed the recipe for successful combat rescue missions provided by Otto Skorzeny in his rescue of Mussolini: operations planned and executed by a small team of commandos with a simple command and control structure that is immediately responsive to operational changes. Ideally, they

Otto Skorzeny. (*Imperial War Museum*)

should also be responsible for reconnaissance and tactical intelligence-gathering, minimising the reaction time.

The British SAS have a tradition of learning from the mistakes and experiences of others. When the family of the President of Gambia, Sir Dawda Jawara, were kidnapped by rebels, while he was attending the London wedding of Prince Charles and Lady Diana Spencer, the British Foreign Office moved swiftly. The French were informed and they called upon Gambia's neighbour, Senegal, to dispatch French-trained paratroops to retake the capital, Banjul, from the Marxist revolutionaries. America was concerned about Libyan-backed insurgency in the region and offered the services of Delta Force. But when the US State Department blocked the initiative, the Foreign

Office telephoned 22 SAS Headquarters at Hereford. By then Banjul's airport was in the hands of Senegalese troops, which would provide access for a small rescue team. The Regiment dispatched three men.

The mission was entrusted to Major Ian Crooke, second-in-command of the Regiment. He selected two subordinates and, together with bags packed with weapons, explosives and a satellite communication system, boarded a flight to Paris – much to the alarm of the French Customs. On arrival at Banjul, the team were able to slip past the rebel lines and make their way to the British Embassy. There they learnt that the rebels were holding the President's family and other hostages at the village of Bakau, seven miles east of the capital and had threatened to start killing them, unless the Senegalese troops withdrew. However, a more recent report suggested that the President's wife had been moved to the Medical Research Centre, after one of her children had developed a fever. The team arrived at the hospital, quietly eliminated the guards on the gate and, with the help of a British doctor, spirited mother and child back to the British Embassy. The team then re-crossed the lines and, assembling a force of Senegalese paratroops with counter-terrorist training, launched an assault that led to the collapse of the rebellion four days later.

10

Raids, Sabotage and Assassination

*I saw the Commander-in-Chief [Field Marshal Montgomery] yes-
terday and told him that I would be speaking to you today ... It
is considered that the operations you have carried out have had
more effect in hastening the disintegration of the German Seventh
and Fifth Armies than any other single effort in the Army. Considering the numbers involved, you have done a job of work
which has had a most telling effect on the enemy ...*

Radio broadcast by Lieutenant General F.A.M. Browning to
SAS troops behind the lines in Normandy, 8 September 1944.

*The intention would be to create the same situation as existed in
Normandy in 1944. We would control the air so they would be
unable to move anything anywhere.*

MOD spokesman's comment to *The Sunday Times*,
on the proposed Allied invasion of Kuwait.

There is little disagreement over the value of Special Forces in low-intensity
conflicts, but what of the more intense wars, where conventional forces firmly
command the centre stage? Ideally, their activities should be aimed at dam-
aging the enemy, arming and training partisan groups and collecting intelligence; in short, this means using raids, ambushes, sabotage and assassination.

On Good Friday, 24 March 1945, part of the Norwegian Special Operations Group (OSS) parachuted into Norway. In the bleak winter of the sixth
year of the war, Germany was in chaos but the army was still capable of
maintaining a spirited defence of the Fatherland. To this end, German troops
were leaving the northern front and travelling home at a rate of a battalion a
day, using the Northland Railway, and it was this that the OSS saboteurs had

orders to cut (Operation RYPE). Most of the soldiers were Americans of Norwegian extraction who had served with the OSS in France. The party was led by 24-year-old Major William Colby, later destined to become director of the CIA.

Winter still held the Norwegian mountains in its icy grip and the insertion was dogged by disaster. Three of the aircraft on the first lift were forced to turn back and a fourth dropped its parachutists in neutral Sweden. While the party awaited reinforcements they used their camouflaged parachutes as tents and put their survival skills to good use in the forests around the DZ. The reinforcements never arrived, their black-painted Liberators crashing somewhere in Norway, and Colby, with 36 men, was left to complete the operational tasks.

The main target was the Grana Bridge, almost a 100 miles away. It was reached after a six-day ordeal of skiing and climbing, during which each man carried a 50lb ski-Bergen and took turns in pulling a pulk (sledge) loaded with 60lb of explosives. Finding the Grana Bridge heavily defended, the OSS destroyed the smaller 5-metre Tangen Bridge before heading for Sweden. With his men safely across the border, Colby and two others audaciously turned back to hit the railway a second time. On 23 April the saboteurs laid 240 separate charges on the tracks and were able to prevent all but one further battalion from reaching Germany. A month later, the fighting was over and Colby travelled down the line as a passenger, disappointed to discover that, after so much effort and cost in lives, the line had been repaired so quickly.

STRATEGIC TARGETS

Lines of Communication

The transient effect of raids and sabotage has led some writers and military thinkers to dismiss the successes of small units behind the lines as marginal. Attacks on the enemy's lines of communication are easily repaired, unless harnessed to support a conventional operation such as an invasion or offensive. In their absence, there is no lasting effect, as witness the prolonged American operations to block the 'Ho Chi Minh Trail', a massive effort involving not only Special Forces but the might of American air power and conventional ground operations.

Small-, and not-so-small-unit operations in Normandy provide the last real 'combat-laboratory' for sabotage activities in support of an invasion. In Northern France, Allied bombing made movement by rail almost impossible. In the south, SOE and the Resistance attempted to do the same. Superficially, some of these attempts were disastrous. The formidable *Das Reich* 2nd SS Panzer Division was refitting in Southern France when the first Allied assault troops splashed ashore in Normandy. When ordered to move to Normandy on 7 June, the unit's vehicles were forced onto the roads. In their path were

The destruction of a German column north of Kerien by the French Resistance.
(*Imperial War Museum*)

large groups of *maquisards* and local resistance circuits, which SOE officers, Jedburgh teams and parties of SAS attempted to direct and control.

The 15,000-strong 2nd SS Panzer Division remained unscathed, losing approximately 35 men killed in action, but it lost something more valuable – time. It took *Das Reich* seven days to travel 150 miles and a further week to re-group before going into action. During those two weeks, the Allied forces moved inland from the beach-heads to consolidate their invasion of France. On each of those 14 days, the German Army lost approximately 2–3,000 men and desperately needed replacements. Other units were delayed or simply disappeared and eight low-grade German divisions were diverted from the fighting in an attempt to suppress Resistance activities. Irregular activities, Allied air power and the invasion itself all contributed to the panic and chaos behind the German lines.

Other small irregular groups had better luck. Combined, the operations of the 1st and 2nd SAS Regiments accounted for more than 3,220 troops killed, wounded or captured. Road traffic was attacked by parties in jeeps, each sporting three twin Vickers machine-guns. The jeeps, parachuted to the teams by the RAF, often exerted a powerful effect on those who saw them. Since vehicles simply did not fall from the sky, the SAS parties were thought to be forward elements of Allied units which had broken through the front line. Two jeeps from the KIPLING party (Auxerre area of Central France) drove into Les Ormes with almost reckless abandon and interrupted the execution of 20 French hostages. In the resulting fire-fight, 60 SS troops were killed for the loss of one SAS soldier. All but two hostages escaped and the effect of this on the French civilian population can only be imagined. In total, SAS ambushes and jeep patrols accounted for more than 154 trucks, 14 horse-drawn transports, three armoured cars and five staff cars.

The 1st and 2nd SAS Regiments also severed at least 65 railway lines, derailing more than 30 trains and destroying at least 40 railway trucks. Many SAS parties were sufficiently experienced to know that they were simply playing for time. The lines would soon be repaired by heavily guarded work-parties operating from armoured trains. In order to maximise the destruction and delay the reopening of the line, trains were derailed in tunnels, rails on opposite sides were cut at different points on the track, or the party simply returned again to sabotage the line at a different point (HOUNDSWORTH cut the Dijon-Paris line 22 times).

In addition, the British and Belgian SAS, supporting MI9, rescued approximately 366 Allied aircrew, while SAS and Phantom teams pinpointed a range of targets for RAF air strikes. The 1st SAS contribution included General Rommel's headquarters, 12 ammunition dumps, 11 petrol trains, two airfields and one flying-bomb launch-site, one SS barracks and a military radio-station. To the overall balance sheet must be added the many successes of the Resistance, operating with or without Jedburgh and SOE support.

Interestingly, when the KIPLING team deployed to the HOUNDSWORTH area, they discovered that the RAF had dropped an artillery piece. This was successfully used to defend their base at Chalaux against an attack by 200 Germans, demonstrating that, properly armed, irregular forces are not totally vulnerable to counter-attack. The experiences of larger forces of resistance fighters and French paratroops in Brittany tend to support this assumption. On the flank of the invasion, approximately 20,000 FFI partisans, 423 soldiers from the 3rd and 4th French Parachute Battalions and assorted Jedburgh and SAS parties were able to paralyse 70,000 German troops. Roads, railways and telephone lines were constantly cut and the German forces virtually confined to the ports and towns.

The Germans naturally felt moved to attack the partisan's countryside bases. In the course of one such battle, a German force, supported by mortars and artillery, suffered 600 casualties. The Resistance incurred less than a 100 casualties and at the end of the 36-hour engagement, most of the *maquis* and FFI were able to slip away. In August 1944, the second phase began and the Resistance were able to seize bridges and strong-points ahead of the advancing American armour.

What of future conflicts where troops behind enemy lines are likely to encounter forces more formidable than *Das Reich*? While many small parties

Railway lines cut by Special Forces parties are soon repaired. At best, these sabotage operations are aimed at delaying the re-opening of the line for as long as possible. (*Private Collection*)

of Special Forces will undoubtedly strike carefully-selected strategic targets, recent American thinking has also centred on what could be called the Brittany model. Such a war is likely to be fast and furious and thus unlikely to enjoy the support of well-trained and organised Resistance forces. This role has been adopted by the light infantry brigade protected by a 'heavy' armoured partner.

In his paper, *Deep Behind Enemy Lines*, Colonel Wolf D. Kutter, Commander of the US 1st Brigade, 10th Mountain Division (Light Infantry) explained the new philosophy and outlined recent exercises. The infantry will either infiltrate the lines or remain with their buried caches of supplies in 'stay-behind' positions. Operating 20–80km behind the front-line and under the protection of friendly artillery and air-strikes, the infantry will target the enemy's combat support units, service units and lines of communication. During the enemy offensive, the light infantry will pinpoint targets such as fuel depots and artillery command centres for friendly artillery strikes. Should the enemy retreat, the targets will be switched to enemy attack-helicopters, reserve formations and lines of communication.

During the second phase of operations, the light infantry disperse to raid and ambush enemy forces, thus creating a 'zone of disruption'. As the enemy front line starts to buckle, the light infantry link up with amoured units to take the offensive and plunge even deeper into enemy territory, isolating enemy units in the front-line – so-called deep battle. In the event of an unexpected reversal, the light infantry re-cross the lines using clandestine medical evacuation routes and exfiltration RVs. Today, disruption behind the lines is firmly under the control of the commanding general: chaos is orchestrated.

Airfields

Air superiority is of crucial importance in the modern conflict. In July 1940, mixed groups of German bombers and fighter-bombers, protected by fighters, attacked radar installations and airfields in Britain. During the next four months, the Battle of Britain, the Germans lost 1,733 aircraft and the RAF 915, approximately a 2:1 kill ratio which forced Germany to shelve its invasion plans.

A year later in the Western Desert, David Stirling formed the core of his Special Air Service Regiment from the LAYFORCE army commandos. Among their first targets were airfields. It was reasoned that if small groups of men could slip undetected through the sandy wilderness, a somewhat better kill ratio might be achieved by destroying the German air force on the ground. The Germans had 350 aircraft in Africa to support their offensive, together with 300 transports and 250 bombers operating from Mediterranean bases. In a now famous series of raids, the SAS destroyed around 243 aircraft together with assorted workshops and hangars. Then, as the Special Boat Service, part of the Regiment joined other maritime raiders and demonstrated that German airfields in the Mediterranean could be attacked from the sea.

In 1982, 22 SAS prepared to repeat these classical raids in the Falklands.

Damaged and abandoned, these Pucara aircraft remain as a memorial to the SAS raid at Pebble Island. (*Private Collection*)

During the run-up to the invasion, it was feared that the airbase on Pebble Island and its Pucara ground-attack aircraft were a threat to British helicopters flying outside the air defence umbrella over the beachhead. On 10 May, a reconnaissance patrol from D Squadron's Boat Troop landed by canoe and set up a surveillance hide close to the airfield. The airfield appeared well guarded and harboured 11 Pucara and five other assorted trainers and transports. A raid was mounted by the Squadron four nights later. With the SAS were Naval Gunfire Support Forward Observers (NGSFO), commando and parachute-trained personnel who served alongside the SAS and SBS throughout the Falkland's campaign. After landing by helicopter at an RV chosen by the reconnaissance patrol, two Troops deployed to protect the LZ and cover the approaches to the settlements. A third, Mountain Troop, crept close to the airfield and started to attack the aircraft with 66mm rockets and small arms fire. Then, as naval gunfire began to fall around the Argentine trenches, the SAS moved forward to systematically destroy the remaining aircraft with explosive charges and rockets. The well-planned raid succeeded, sustaining only two casualties.

Britain also planned another more highly secret operation, to strike at airfields inside Argentina. Its target was the Super Etendard aircraft and their Exocet missiles that were inflicting considerable damage to the British fleet. An air-strike might have been more effective but such an overt strike at targets inside South America might have escalated the conflict to embroil Venezuela and Peru.

Some weeks after the raid on Pebble Island, a Sea King helicopter dropped two SAS reconnaissance patrols on the sparsely-inhabited grass-lands, close to the Rio Gallegos airfield, on the southern tip of Argentina. The Argentine air force constantly moved their valuable aircraft to protect them against surprise attack. It was the reconnaissance parties' task to confirm other sources of intelligence that placed the aircraft at Rio Gallegos. According to a *Sunday Times Insight* report, within hours a full SAS squadron in two Hercules C-130 transports took off from Ascension Island to begin the 5,000 mile journey to Argentina. Their aim was an 'Entebbe-style' assault that would wipe out the aircraft and missile stocks, using grenade-launchers and anti-aircraft missiles, before escaping across the border into neutral Chile. At some time during that long night, a coded message from Northwood cancelled the mission. The helicopter carrying the LRRP had been ordered to ditch at sea but bad weather had forced a landing on a beach inside Chile; the secrecy desperately required for a surprise attack was compromised. Left to their own devices, the eight-man reconnaissance party turned south and slipped across the Chilean border.

The Military-Industrial Infrastructure

The industrialisation of war has produced a range of new legitimate strategic targets in the factory, research laboratory, supply depot and civilian transportation systems. Destroying the enemy's military-economic complex became particularly acute during 1939–45, as Germany, already a world leader in engineering and applied science, began to use the industries of the occupied countries to support its war effort.

While many targets were left to Allied air-power, SOE was specifically directed to 'Set Europe Ablaze' by attacking the industrial infrastructure in the occupied countries with everything at its disposal. Sabotaging the German war effort was achieved with varying degrees of subtlety. A direct appeal to the patriotism of the factory owner sometimes resulted in a cut in production. If that failed, the factory could be threatened with an RAF bombing raid or the owner persuaded to co-operate while SOE's saboteurs did the job themselves.

Occasionally, active intervention came from outside in the form of a commando raid. In excess of 50 sea-borne commando operations were launched against north-west Europe. In the Mediterranean and North Africa, the commandos, American Rangers and other forces are credited with more than 62 operations, while the SAS and LRDG carried out another 20-plus deep penetration raids in the desert. From November 1943, the SAS, LRDG and elements of the Commandos conducted another 381 operations as Raiding Forces Middle East, landing on more than 70 islands in the Aegean and eastern Mediterranean.

Many were pinprick raids designed to gather intelligence on the German defences but some were specifically directed against industrial/economic targets. For the most part, the targets were determined by the ease with which they could be safely reached without detection. The rugged, relatively sparsely populated Norwegian coastline provided the opportunity for attacks against the herring factories, docks and telephone exchange at Vaagso (Operation ARCHERY, 27 December 1941), the hydro-electric plant at Giomfjord, (MUSKETOON, 20 September 1942) and the iron pyrites mine and processing plant at Lillebo (CARTOON, 23 January 1943). In March 1942, one of the most important sea-borne raids denied the German battleship, *Tirpitz*, the dry-dock facilities at St Nazaire on the Loire estuary. Operation CHARIOT culminated in the explosives-laden destroyer, *Campbelltown*, being rammed into the dock gates.

Some targets of economic importance were difficult to bomb and inaccessible to sea-borne raiding parties. During the early stages of the war, it was thought desirable to cripple the Italian campaign in the African desert by a raid to sever the water supply to the ports of Taranto, Brindisi and Bari. The object of the raid was the Acquedetto Pugliese, a system of aqueducts that carried water from the River Sele across the Apennines. This task was given to elements of No 2 (Army) Commando who had re-trained as parachutists and were destined to form part of the nucleus of the Parachute Regiment. In the interim, they were given the deliberately deceptive title of the 11 Special Air Service Battalion.

Operation COLOSSUS was carried out on the night of 10–11 February 1941 by a force of five officers and 30 other ranks. After landing 'blind', enough explosives were recovered to blow up the main viaduct and a smaller bridge across the River Ginestra. Unfortunately, all of the party were captured before reaching their rendezvous with a submarine. Local reservoirs supplied sufficient water to cover the period of repairs.

Air-Defence Systems

A more successful parachute raid was conducted in February 1942. A new type of German *Wurzburg* target-tracking radar installation appeared along the northern French coast. This device was believed to be partly responsible for the unsustainable losses being experienced by RAF Bomber Command. On the night of 27–28 February, 'C' Company of the 2nd Parachute Battalion and an RAF radar technician parachuted onto the French coast at Bruneval (Operation BITING) and stole the novel electronic components, before being evacuated by sea. Deciphering the principles of the device, British physicists were able to devise a means of blinding the new radar sites by the simple expedient of dropping tin-foil in front of the bomber formations.

In 1969, the Israelis brilliantly repeated the British success at Bruneval. The Egyptians were being bolstered by Soviet aid as the 'War of Attrition' between the two countries reached its climax. This aid package included new radar devices previously unseen in the West. One variant, the Barlock GCI, was seized in September 1969 by an armoured task force that landed by sea on the Egyptian coast at Ras Zaafrana. The second, the P-12 SPOONREST-A, represented a greater threat to the Israeli Air Force because it was mobile and designed to detect low-flying aircraft, a strategy that the Israelis were using to great effect against the Soviet-supported Egyptian Air Force. In a carefully planned operation in December 1969, an entire device was hijacked from its fortified coastal site at Ras Gharib by *Sayaret Matkal* and a crack *Nahal* parachute unit. Landing by helicopter at a distant LZ, the paratroops captured the site after a gruelling march. The installation was then examined, intact, by radar technicians before being dismantled and flown to Israel, slung beneath a Sikorsky CH-530 helicopter.

Special Weapons

If the optimal use of Special Forces is against strategic targets, it is no surprise that these troops have had a long involvement with special weapons: both came of age at the same time. During the Second World War, German scientists designed and produced delivery vehicles that were capable of carrying warheads to the enemy's civilian population. The V-1 and V-2 missiles were targeted against Britain but the proposed V-4 rocket (the V-3 was a long-range gun) would have been the world's first inter-continental missile, capable of hitting America's east coast.

Hitler's programme was delayed by internecine squabbles between the Luftwaffe, which developed the V-1, and the Army, which was responsible for

The German radar tracking station at Bruneval in Northern France. (*Imperial War Museum*)

the V-2. In March 1944, the confusion intensified when the German SS, in an attempt to gain control of the whole programme, arrested several key scientists. Several elements of Allied intelligence did their best to delay things even further. A source deep within the German High Command provided the British SIS with a comprehensive account of German science in 1939 (the 'Oslo Report'). A year later, an agent within German Military Intelligence identified Peenemunde, on the Baltic coast, as the experimental test area for the *Vergeltung* (Revenge) weapons. After confirmation from photographic reconnaissance and the surreptitious recordings of conversations between German POWs, RAF Bomber Command launched a massive strike on the night of 17 August 1943. Five hundred and ninety six bombers hit Peenemunde in three waves, dropping 77,530 bombs and killing 120–170 members of the regular German staff and 500–600 foreign workers. Although, hailed as 'the raid that won the war', historian David Irving and Professor R. V. Jones have both estimated that the raid delayed the German weapons programme for no more than two months.

In the months before the 1944 Normandy invasion, the RAF and British intelligence switched their attentions to the V-weapon launch sites on the coasts of Belgium and France. Before the onslaught, Allied intelligence lacked one piece of vital information: the exact size and nature of the war-heads. Intelligence agents and the Resistance helped solve that problem. When a V-2 fired from Peenemunde landed in Sweden, useful components found their way to British Intelligence. Another came down intact in a Polish forest, where it was hidden, dismantled and secretly transported to England. It was calculated to contain around one ton of explosive but this also left the possibility of special war-heads. The storm broke too late – only after the D-Day landings – but was terrible enough. During the period of the V-1 and V-2 attacks, more than 29,400 houses in London were completely destroyed and another 250,000 damaged.

The most frightening warhead, or bomb, was a nuclear munition. As the Germans had achieved nuclear fission in 1938, they only needed to produce sufficient weapons-grade material and solve the essentially technical problem of turning it into a workable bomb. The most obvious element of the German nuclear weapons programme was the German-owned Norsk Hydro Company's Heavy Water Plant at Vermork, in the Norwegian province of Telemark. The production of heavy water was a vital part of one process to produce a nuclear weapon and required a lot of electricity, which was in short supply in Germany at that time.

The Vermork plant, hidden deep in a steep valley, was difficult to bomb from the air at night, the major tactic employed by the RAF at this time. During the winter of 1942–43, the problem was assigned a high priority and turned over to the commando-planners in Headquarters Combined Operations. In order to carry sufficient explosives and trained engineers deep into Norway, the planners decided to land a party by glider. Volunteers for Operation FRESHMAN were drawn from Royal Engineer units within 1 Airborne Division. After the operation, the paratroops were briefed to 'escape and evade' across the mountains into neutral Sweden.

The chosen glider LZ was the high Hardanger Plateau, north of Vermork. This had to be located at night, under winter conditions, and with a release-point calculated to take account of the fierce air-currents for which the Hardanger was noted. This problem was partly solved by recruiting four Norwegian patriots to act as pathfinders, clearing and illuminating a landing-strip, setting out EUREKA radio homing-beacons and finally guiding the commandos to the Heavy Water Plant in the valley below. This team was parachuted onto the Plateau on the night of 18 October 1942. They immediately needed all their indigenous survival skills to cope with the appalling weather conditions that were frustrating their efforts to clear a landing-strip.

Over the next month the weather worsened, and promised to deteriorate even further during the next full moon period. The mission was deemed vital and, on the night of 19 November 1942, two gliders and their Halifax 'tugs' set off across the North Sea. As they approached the Norwegian coast, ice began to form on the aircraft which lost height rapidly. Worse followed as the REBECCA radio-receivers became unservicable, which meant the aircraft had no way of picking up the signals from the EUREKA beacons on the LZ. With little hope of pulling the gliders back across the North Sea, the pilots pressed on, attempting to relate their air-navigation maps to the moon-lit snowscape. The first glider parted company with its 'tug' and crashed into the mountains overlooking Lysefjord when the iced tow-rope parted. Eight of the 17 men in the glider were killed. The survivors fell into the hands of the Gestapo and were either shot or killed by lethal injection. The second glider crash-landed in the mountains north-east of Helleland. The Halifax 'tug' managed to pull clear, only to crash into the next range of mountains to the south. The second party of survivors were also captured and shot.

There had been a significant number of commando raids in Norway and when Operation FRESHMAN reached its abortive end the Germans were apparently still unaware of its target. This left the field open for SOE to try another option (Operation GUNNERSIDE), and they set about training a small group of saboteurs. Meanwhile, the advance party on the Plateau survived on oats and moss; it was five weeks before one of the partisans managed to shoot a reindeer after a difficult and long stalk. On 17 February 1943, the demolition party parachuted onto a distant DZ to draw attention away from Vermork and were forced to endure several days' march through blizzard conditions. GUNNERSIDE was successful and was probably the most important strategic operation of the war. The saboteurs had been trained on mock-ups of the plant's most vulnerable component: the 18 electrolytic concentration cells. On the night of Wednesday 24 February, a three-man demolition team entered the factory and laid their charges of plastic explosive around the cells. The small explosion – unnoticed by the guards – completely destroyed the electrolysis unit.

Another fierce storm closed on the mountains and covered the demolition party's tracks. But a bar of British chocolate, given to a reindeer hunter, inadvertently betrayed them and some 10,000 German troops started to search the plateau. Most of the team slipped away to join various Milorg Resistance groups. One of the advance party, Claus Helberg, was almost caught by a German ski patrol but outdistanced all but one of them, whom he ambushed and shot.

As with many such raids, the operation only bought that nevertheless precious commodity – time. Within 16 weeks the factory was back in production. On 20 November 1944, the USAAF attempted a daylight bombing raid, but with little success. On 20 February 1945, Knut Haukelid, the second-in-command of the demolition team, returned to the area and sank a ferry carrying 50kg of heavy water across Lake Tinnsjo. Germany was again denied a sizeable quantity of heavy water, although the sinking claimed the lives of 14 civilians. With the war almost over, Hitler had lost the opportunity to develop an atomic weapon.

Some historians have argued that the operations against the heavy water

The acquisition of targets for airforce 'sniping raids' is an important hidden contribution of parties fighting behind the lines. This photograph shows rocket-firing Beaufighters of the Balkan Airforce attacking a German barracks near Trieste in Yugoslavia. The target was identified by partisans of the Yugoslav National Liberation Army. (*Imperial War Museum*)

plant were unnecessary as the German atomic weapons programme had taken a wrong turn early in the war; however it is easy to be wise after the event. Allied intelligence analysis was based on the belief that the Germans had discovered the 'secret' of the atomic bomb. Indeed, OSS operational teams began planning to kidnap the great German physicist, Werner Heisenberg, in the belief that the German atomic bomb programme would collapse without him. In fact, Germany was at the same stage as some Third World countries today, in searching for technical solutions to concentrate sufficient Uranium 235 to produce a bomb.

In his book *Heller als Tausend Sonnen*, Robert Jungk claims that a workable solution to the problem of uranium concentration was mooted by the élite scientific research unit attached to the German Post Office and sent to the German High Command. However, to Hitler, a postman was merely someone who delivered the mail and he joked to his generals: 'Look here gentlemen!

You are all racking your brains to discover how we are going to win this war, and lo and behold, here comes our postmaster, of all people, with a solution to the problem!' Had somebody informed Hitler that Albert Einstein had done his best work while in a similar post, as a Scientific Officer in the Berne Patent Office, events might have taken a very different course. Jungk's amusing and yet chilling tale appears, translated, in Volkman's and Baggett's book, *Secret Intelligence*.

Worries about German special weapons did not stop at the atomic bomb. In late 1943, OSS Intelligence reported to the Joint Chiefs of Staff that there were strong indications that Germany had developed biological weapons, based on the highly lethal Botulinus toxin. Early in 1944 the American Army was galvanised into action to produce 235,000 self-inoculating doses of the anti-dote to the toxin and Allied troops were to carry their syringes on to the Normandy beaches on 6 June 1944. It was thought that the Germans in-tended to deploy the toxin in the warhead of the V-1 rocket. When, in 1944, the first flying bomb crossed the English Channel to explode with a big bang, demonstrating that they were only filled with high explosive, the General Staffs all heaved an immense sigh of relief.

In the decade after the end of the Second World War, Israel found itself confronting hostile neighbours engaged in developing their own missile pro-grammes. With the help of German rocket scientists, Egypt test-fired four missiles in July 1962, reputedly with operational ranges between 175–350 miles. When Israeli Intelligence learnt that the Egyptian missiles were to carry warheads containing cobalt and strontium waste – a 'poor man's atomic bomb' – Mossad teams targeted the ex-Nazis in Cairo. At least one senior scientist disappeared, several staff at one of the rocket factories were killed by parcel bombs and an attempt was made to shoot a key German electronics expert.

By the late 1970s Israel had developed its own atomic arsenal but now found itself facing a more serious threat than the Egyptian missiles. It began when Military Intelligence sent the head of Mossad a file containing details of Iraqi efforts to obtain a nuclear arsenal. France was preparing to supply 10lb of enriched uranium for a 700-megawatt commercial reactor but the Iraqis were also looking to other European countries to supply enrichment tech-nology – high speed centrifuges that would convert the 10lb of uranium into four atomic weapons.

Mossad acted immediately. One of the Iraqi scientists overseeing the project in France, was lured into the classical 'honey-trap' and blackmailed into revealing details of the Osirak nuclear complex in Baghdad. He also identified an Egyptian physicist who, he claimed, was overseeing the project on Iraq's behalf – a man who was reputed to have told French scientists: 'We are making a change in the face of Arab world history'. When a French offer to replace the uranium with a cheaper source of fuel that could not be refined into weapons was refused, the Israeli operation started to move.

An Israeli special operations team entered France, and on 5 April 1979, five saboteurs and a nuclear physicist concealed themselves in a container truck and managed to penetrate the security around the French plant holding the Iraqi nuclear cores. The Israeli physicist identified the exact points on the core where plastic explosive would do the most damage. The explosion destroyed the fruits of a three-year project. A month later, the Egyptian physicist was assassinated and with him a French prostitute, who had unknowingly been used by the Israelis.

The Israeli Special Services had bought their country some time. Two years later, the breathing space finally expired. In the late afternoon of Sunday 7 June, 1981, waves of Israeli F-15 and F-16 aircraft took off from Beersheba airbase for the 650-mile flight to Baghdad. As they crossed into Jordanian airspace, they were spotted by Jordan's King Hussein, out for a Sunday afternoon jaunt in his light aircraft. As he attempted to give the alarm, his communications were blocked by a 707 electronic warfare plane circling high above Israel. Then an Israeli intelligence officer, speaking Arabic with a Jordanian-Bedouin accent, and using the correct codes and call-signs, acknowledged the King's message, promising to alert the Iraqis. It is reported to have taken Hussein three days to discover the subterfuge.

The aircraft pressed on, flying below Iraqi radar and refuelling from a Boeing 707 disguised as an Aer Lingus airliner. Ninety minutes after take-off, the aircraft dropped their bombs and laser-guided weapons on the Osirak nuclear plant. Prior to the attack, an Israeli pathfinder team had laid beacons around the installation. To make absolutely sure, Mossad had recruited a French technician to take another homing device into the plant. Still inside when the aircraft dropped their munitions, he was the only casualty of the raid.

Modern day Special Forces units are still intimately involved with special weapons. The present day strategic nuclear balance rests upon Mutual Assured Destruction. If one side felt able to launch a first strike that would knock out most of the enemy missile silos, this assurance would break down, increasing the likelihood of nuclear weapons being used in a future general war. Consequently, missile silos are hardened to survive a first-strike and Intercontinental Ballistic Missiles (ICBMs) are constantly moved about to prevent accurate targeting.

Congressional opponents of the new American rail M-X missile system have argued that it would be particularly vulnerable to attack by Spetsnaz forces. The system will deploy 50 ICBMs, on 25 trains disguised as commercial freight. Dispersed over 180,000 miles of track, the missile trains would move intermittently between tunnels, culverts or reinforced covert sites.

Spetsnaz forces would not have to attack the heavily-guarded trains. It would be sufficient to pinpoint them for Soviet missile strikes, and attack vital tunnels, switch-points and junctions to prevent their movement and dispersal for a few vital hours. Such a politically high-risk mission could best be achieved during the transition to war, and as such, would require advanced covert two-way radio communications with the planners in Moscow. An extensive operation of this kind would also require the co-operation of 'frozen' operatives and other GRU agents. These would perform reconnaissance tasks and provide safe-houses, equipment caches, transport and the necessary operational intelligence.

What is the likelihood of this scenario? In assessing the threat for the readers of *Armed Forces Journal International*, policy analyst Marc Berkowitz points out that Spetsnaz forces were expanded in the mid-1950s in response to NATO's programme of deploying Intermediate-range Nuclear Forces. Indeed, even before Pershing II and the ground-launched cruise missiles were in place in Germany, Spetsnaz troops were already training on full-scale models of the missile bases, at their training camps in Eastern Europe and the western USSR.

The Enemy Fleet

Just as aircraft can be destroyed on the ground, enemy shipping can be destroyed while in harbour. The first recorded use of so-called human torpedoes took place in the Northern Adriatic on the night of 31 October–1 November 1918. Two Italians, Rossetti and Paolucci, negotiated their way through the Pola defences on an S-1 craft of their own design and placed mines against the hulls of the Austrian flagship *Viribus Unitis* and the liner *Wien*. The ease with which capital ships could be destroyed cheaply, and with virtually no risk to life, had a profound effect on Italian naval thinking.

Despite his prevarications, it is now clear that Mussolini realised, as early as 1935, that his fleet would be no match for the Royal Navy in any future war in the Mediterranean. Accordingly, and mindful of the success of the S-1 craft, he ordered the creation of a dedicated mini-submarine squadron with a view to attacking the British capital ships in their home bases.

The mini-submarines with which the squadron was equipped were without peer. Capable of carrying a 300kg detachable warhead, they were equipped to operate at depths in excess of 30 metres, making them invisible to the most sensitive acoustic detectors of the time. On 19 September 1941, the squadron proved its worth. In one night it sank two tankers and a 10,900-ton cargo vessel sheltering within the outer defences of Gibraltar harbour. Three months later, on 21 December, six brave men from the squadron scored Italy's greatest naval victory of the war when they breached the Alexandria harbour defences, sunk a destroyer and tanker and crippled the 30,000 ton battleships HMS *Valiant* and *Queen Elizabeth*. The Royal Navy was left temporarily impotent east of Malta. A year later, at the height of their power, the entire might of the Axis air forces were never able to better this feat.

Humiliated and furious, Churchill demanded revenge. Within three months Britain had introduced its own manned torpedoes to the theatre. These Chariots, invariably known as 'Jeeps' after a rodent-like creature in the Popeye cartoons, achieved some notable successes in the Mediterranean, sinking the 8,500-ton Italian transport *Viminale* and the new cruiser *Ulpio Traiano* at Palermo in January 1943. In June 1944, Italian crews, now allies, joined with the British charioteers to launch a successful attack on the German-controlled Italian cruisers *Bolzano* and *Gorizia* sheltering in La Spezia harbour.

The British X-craft and XE-craft were even more successful. Relatively independent, well armed and adaptable, they were employed on a number of raids against both German and Japanese capital ships. In the most notable feat the 42,000 ton battleship *Tirpitz* was crippled. On 11–12 September 1943 six 'X-craft', manned by reserve crews and towed by two conventional submarines, set off for Norway from Loch Cairnbawm in Northern Scotland. The mission began badly when the tows parted on two of the craft (X-8 and X-9.) Two of the surviving craft (X-6 and X-7) successfully penetrated Soroy Sound, negotiated a German minefield, sailed submerged up Alten Fjord and into the head of the Kaa Fjord where *Tirpitz* lay at anchor. Penetrating the outer boom and anti-torpedo nets, they released four two-ton 'side-cargoes' – delayed action mines – beneath their huge target. At 08.12 on 22 September 1943 the charges detonated, crippling the German Navy's last remaining operational capital ship. Six men from the two four-man crews survived to be taken prisoner. Both successful commanding officers, Cameron and Place, were awarded the Victoria Cross.

These wartime operations provided many lessons. It was obvious that midget submarines could be built quickly, cheaply and, above all, secretly. It was grudgingly accepted that, although their crews would require months rather than weeks of intensive specialist training, once competent, they could prove a match for any static anti-submarine or anti-torpedo defences. It was also realised that attacks did not have to be mounted from the security of a home base as the submersibles could be carried to the edge of the operational zone within the protective hulls of larger ships.

It was also realised that mini-submarines were admirably suited to reconnaissance operations and for secretly landing agents and special forces parties. The Soviet Union has experimented widely in the use of mini-submersibles and there is good evidence that extensive reconnaissance incursions have been undertaken by Naval Spetsnaz midget submarine crews along the Brazilian, Japanese and Scandinavian coastlines.

Violations of Swedish neutrality by submarines escalated throughout the 1980s. Detected incursions rose from ten in 1981 to between 40 and 50 in 1982. In October 1982, six or more submarines penetrated the Swedish naval base at Musko. Of these, at least one was a manned, bottom-crawling mini-submarine. Marks left on the seabed indicated that one of these had tracks and a single propeller while another had a reinforced keel and twin propellers. There were also indications of a rendezvous between the tracked mini-submarine and a mother ship. In 1984, the Swedish naval base at Karlskrona harbour was violated by three large submarines, several midget submarines, divers and small motorised swimmer delivery vehicles. These vessels apparently took part in an exercise that lasted 30 days.

The design of the small tracked craft is unknown but may have been based upon the German *Seeteufel* (Sea Devil), the blueprints of which fell into Soviet hands at the end of the war. Uniquely capable of operating submerged or on land, the *Seeteufel* could carry torpedoes or mines and was armed with machine guns, rockets or flame-throwers. It is also likely that these ships were manned by elements of the Midget Submarine Group comprising part of the Naval Spetsnaz brigade attached to the Double Red Banner Baltic Fleet. The Baltic Fleet's independent Intelligence Service is headed by a Rear Admiral with responsibilities both to the fleet commander and to the Fifth Directorate of the GRU. He is in charge of recruitment and operations relating to Spetsnaz units under his control and would be able to arrange, relatively easily, the covert carriage of mini-submarines inside the hull or on the deck of a merchant ship, from their home base to their operational area. It is nonetheless possible that certain incursions into Swedish waters have been undertaken by submarines from other commands. It is worthy of note that a *Whiskey*-II-class submarine that ran aground near a sensitive Swedish naval installation in 1981, was commanded by an officer serving in the Northern Fleet.

SPETSNAZ COUPS D'ETAT

Dr Kirsten Amundsen, a notable and well-published expert on Scandinavian-Soviet affairs, claims that the submarine incursions are simply a well-

Yugoslav mini-submarine or 'dry' swimmer delivery vehicle. Mini-submersibles are not only a means of sabotaging enemy shipping but also provide a covert means of landing and recovering agents and other clandestine operators. (*Guy Taylor Research*)

publicised tip of a clandestine iceberg. She argues that Soviet mini-submersibles would carry Spetsnaz sabotage teams tasked with attacking Swedish command and control centres in the vanguard of an invasion. To this end, movements of the country's fighter pilots have been closely reconnoitred to facilitate their assassination by KGB and GRU operatives, landing from the sea or transported in sealed TIR trucks, during the transition to war. Although her views have been dismissed by the Swedish Government, this must be seen in the context of its longstanding policy of diplomatic non-aggression towards its powerful neighbour in the East. Indeed, Dr Amundsen's views are strongly supported by a number of senior officers in Sweden's armed forces.

It is possible, however, that whereas Amundsen's views are correct in principle they are exaggerated in certain specifics. The discovery of caches of food, even of charts and radios, on a deserted beach may indicate espionage or Naval Spetsnaz reconnaissance activities rather than some greater threat. Only a tiny professional cadre of Soviet intelligence and military Special Purpose troops are trained for assassination. In the event of an East-West clash, the size of the clandestine pool targeting key countries such as Britain is estimated to be relatively small (50–100). While these 'illegals' might arrive by a variety of means, it is generally believed that they would primarily undertake sabotage raids against lightly-defended key installations.

The political thaw in Europe has greatly reduced this potential threat. A successful invasion of Scandinavia, whether or not preceded by an attack on Sweden, would have required the co-operation of the East German navy together with the Polish 7th Lujycka Naval Assault Division in the South and the 45th and 54th motor rifle divisions, supported by the 63rd 'Kirkenes' Naval Infantry Brigade, with its ancillary Spetsnaz units, to the North. Clearly neither Germany nor Poland would now commit troops to such a venture, whilst the Soviets in the area are at present heavily involved in the maintenance of internal order. Many of the élite troops photographed on the streets of the Baltic republics during the recent crisis, and erroneously described by the press as paratroopers, were in fact naval infantry.

Nevertheless, Special Operations are greatly simplified for the invader, whose troops can 'insert' on commercial flights, during the transition to war, and await recovery in safe-houses, rather than risk the perils of extraction. A German Special Operation provided Hitler with a thin excuse to invade Poland. A small party of SS troops entered the German radio station at Gleiwitz and pretended that it had been seized by Poles. After killing a German policeman, the party left several murdered concentration-camp inmates dressed in Polish uniforms.

During the invasion of Russia (Operation BARBAROSSA), the Special Unit Brandenburg crossed Soviet lines wearing Red Army greatcoats and equipped with weapons and transport captured by the Finns during the Winter War. Taking full advantage of the inevitable chaos, the Brandenburgers, many of whom were Russian exiles fluent in the language, simply bluffed their way through the disintegrating forward positions until they reached their objectives. Once in position they neutralised the guard force, de-activated any demolitions and held on desperately until the arrival of the forward elements of the main army. The bridges, tunnels, airfields and road junctions secured by the Brandenburgers on the first days of the Eastern campaign were crucial to the German advance.

Traditionally, the Soviet doctrine of unconventional warfare has been concerned with the 'liberation' of foreign countries. Today, Spetsnaz forms an important part of the Soviet Union's unconventional warfare capability. It operates within the 2nd Department of the GRU, also responsible for reconnaissance (*voiskovaya razvedka*), agent-derived intelligence (*agentur-naya razvedka*), information-processing and radio interception. Its troops do not therefore normally assume intelligence or reconnaissance roles, although they can be tasked to do so in exceptional circumstances.

In war, Spetsnaz has several diverse roles. Of prime importance is the destruction of enemy command and control. Professional troops, attached at independent company strength to each army, may be tasked with the hunting down and assassination of political and military leaders, possibly in conjunction with KGB operatives. Each independent company, consisting of 115 men, including nine officers and 11 warrant officers, is trained to operate as a single group or may divide into smaller groups up to a total of 15. Each has its own communications platoon upon which its groups rely for information and orders.

Other Spetsnaz units are trained to neutralise the enemy's nuclear delivery means either targeting them for missile or air attack or destroying them by direct action. Thereafter airfields, naval bases and air defence installations would be targeted, particularly in support of an early airborne or heliborne landing requiring localised, short-term air superiority.

Having completed their primary missions the majority of Spetsnaz units would be extracted for retasking or would face 'escape and evasion' until relieved by their own advancing forces. Whilst behind enemy lines they would not lie dormant but continue to seek targets of opportunity such as lightly-defended power stations, oil and gas storage centres, pipelines and power lines.

Spetsnaz forces were used to devastating effect during the suppression of the 'Prague Spring' in 1968. Determined to mask their intentions towards Czech-oslovakia for as long as possible, and being well versed in the art of deception (*maskirovka*), the Soviets pointedly left the majority of their most experienced troops within GSFG (Group of Soviet Forces Germany) in barracks immediately prior to the invasion. The Czechs had no reason to feel suspicious, therefore, when a civilian Aeroflot aircraft landed unscheduled at Prague's Ruzyne Airport at approximately 20.30 hours on 20 August, taxied to the end of the runway and parked. An hour later a second Aeroflot An-24 landed and its passengers cleared customs in the normal way before departing for the city centre.

At approximately 02.00 hours the 'passengers' returned, now fully armed, to take over the control tower, airport communications and customs, and foreign departure areas. At about the same time one, possibly two, further unannounced An-12 aircraft landed and at once disgorged teams of uniformed Spetsnaz who immediately linked up with their 'civilian' colleagues. A series of transports, containing more Spetsnaz supported by members of the 103rd Guards Airborne Division, then landed in quick succession, reportedly guided by the initial An-24 still sitting anonymously at the end of the runway. Within two hours of the first uniformed Spetsnaz troops landing, the airport and its surroundings were secured and troops were advancing on the capital. The presidential palace, the radio and television studios and transmitters, the bridges over the Vltava, the post office, major telephone exchanges and railway stations were all secured whilst the bulk of the population slept. Next morning the citizens of Prague awoke to find their elected leadership under arrest and their city occupied.

The role of Spetsnaz was no less crucial during the initial invasion of Afghanistan in 1979. The majority of Soviet troops involved in the initial overthrow of the Afghan government were *in situ* prior to the event, having been invited into the country by its unsuspecting President, under the Soviet-Afghan Treaty of Friendship, in an attempt to assist him in the maintenance of order. During 8–10 December, and some 14 days before the invasion, an airborne regiment of more than 1,500 men with tanks and artillery was deployed to Bagram, a key town to the North of Kabul, to secure the Salang Highway with its critical tunnel. At some time between the 10–24 December a battalion from the regiment was moved to Kabul International Airport, only three kilometres from the city centre. Simultaneously, large quantities of Afghan armoured and transport vehicles were recalled to workshops by Soviet 'advisers', ostensibly for servicing before a big push against the rebels. Crucially, President Amin was persuaded by the Soviet military command to retreat to his palace complex at Darulaman, some seven miles south-west of Kabul, which was deemed to be more secure.

Between 24–27 December Soviet airborne troops, supported by Spetsnaz, landed at, and secured, Kabul airport together with the air force bases at Bagram, Shindand and Kandahar. Once the bases were captured, the remaining two regiments of the 105th Guards Airborne Division landed at Bagram and Kabul and began to prepare for offensive action.

On the next night the still unsuspecting Afghan government, gathered en masse at the Kabul Intercontinental Hotel, were arrested. At approximately 19.00 hours, Spetsnaz teams demolished the central military communications centre and seized the still functioning Ministry of the Interior, the Kabul radio station and several other key points. By dawn next morning the city was firmly in Soviet hands.

The crux of the attack was the assault on Darulaman, where Amin remained under the protection of a loyal armoured regiment supported by eight T-55 tanks. The attack was led by Spetsnaz forces with KGB assistance, supported by two or three airborne battalions equipped with BMD armoured personnel carriers. Amin was killed, as was his family, his security guards and entourage. For their part, the Soviets reportedly sustained 25 dead and 225 wounded. The dead included KGB Colonel Bayerenov, killed in crossfire by his own troops.

By the time that Moscow Radio broadcast a report stating that Soviet troops had moved in large numbers into Afghanistan at the request of its government to help restore order, the leaders of that government were dead, killed by their 'protectors', and the radio station, together with all other means of communication, were firmly in Soviet hands. Once again the path to Soviet victory had been paved by the painstaking use of *maskirovka* backed up, when necessary, by brutal but devastatingly effective localised force.

ASSASSINATION AND KIDNAP

The value of assassination and kidnap is strongly dependent upon the importance of the person being removed and the ease with which he can be replaced. In June 1942, SOE-trained Czech agents assassinated Reinhard Heydrich. The loss of the *Reichprotektor* of Bohemia and Moravia had little permanent effect but moved Hitler to retaliate by obliterating the Czech village of Lidice. Two other SOE operatives kidnapped the German commander of Crete in April 1944; but that officer was so unpopular that the operation is said to have provided a significant boost to the morale of the island's garrison.

However, key personnel may be irreplaceable within a short time. Laycock's abortive attempt to eliminate General Ewin Rommel at his headquarters in North Africa might have changed the course of the war in the desert. The attempt failed and most of the commandos were lost, probably needlessly, as Allied military intelligence was aware that Rommel was, in fact, in Rome. The SAS also targeted Rommel's headquarters in France for air-strikes. Rommel was finally severely wounded in an Allied air raid and this can also probably be credited to Special Operations personnel. In May 1944, No 10 Inter-Allied Commando was tasked with exploring the proposed invasion beaches in Normandy. Survivors of one of these TARBRUSH operations were foolishly, interviewed by Rommel at a Chateau near La Petite Roche Guyon. One of the commandos spotted a road sign and managed to pass this information back to Allied Intelligence, from his POW camp in Germany. The Allied fighter-bombers are reputed to have caught Rommel's car on the road outside the Chateau.

In the Far East, American signals intelligence broke the Japanese naval codes and General Isoroku Yamamoto was lured into an ambush, his transport being shot down by American fighters over Bougainville on 18 April 1943. His loss was regarded as a major blow to Japanese morale.

Otto Skorzeny's special force spearheaded Germany's 1944 counter-offensive in the Ardennes, dressed as American soldiers. Under interrogation, captured German commandos reputedly told of an operation to assassinate

Allied Supreme Commander, General Eisenhower, but this may have been an attempt to mislead Allied Intelligence as the primary aim of Operation GREIF was to capture the Meuse bridges. Nevertheless, the disinformation worked like a charm; General Eisenhower was confined to his headquarters during the crucial period of the battle, while General Bradley, snared by the resulting chaos on the roads, bitterly commented upon the spectacle of 'half a million GIs ... playing cat and mouse with each other every time they met'.

Rumours of assassination and kidnap may have a considerable effect on a country immediately prior to invasion. Government ministers and senior military personnel may be difficult to replace at short notice. Other public figures are irreplaceable. If the 1981 assassination attempt on Pope John Paul II had succeeded, it is likely that his successor would have been an Italian with no more than a passing interest in Poland.

Part Three

The Changing Face of Warfare

Modern warfare carries the attendant risk that chemical, biological or nuclear weapons will be deployed. A conflict which saw these munitions used on a large scale might indeed be a war to end all wars. Under the shadow of the Cold War a more limited form of warfare developed, embodied in a host of terms such as covert action, special activities, special operations and direct action missions, they embraced commando raids, combat-rescue missions, paramilitary operations, counter-terrorism, war by proxy, intervention and peace-keeping missions and even assassination and kidnapping.

The final part of this book deals with three manifestations of this new style of limited warfare that have provided new roles for the Special Forces and a range of other military and paramilitary personnel: secret deniable operations, conducted by Special Operations Forces or surrogates, counter-terrorism and quick reaction force operations.

11

War by Proxy – Deniable Operations

Special Activities: US operations, planned and executed so that the role of the United States Government is not apparent or acknowledged publicly, are solely a CIA responsibility in peacetime. Covert activities must be approved by the President.
Covert operations: Activities that conceal the identity of sponsors or participants or facilitate plausible denial of their involvement.
Proxy operations: A form of limited warfare in which a competitor seeks to avoid direct confrontation with opponents, yet accomplish security objectives at reduced cost and risk, by relying on *de facto* or *de jure* surrogates.
Direct Action Mission: An overt, covert or clandestine land attack by armed individuals or small groups to damage or destroy inanimate targets or slay or seize a person or persons.

From *Green Berets, Seals & Spetsnaz: US & Soviet Military Operations* by John M. Collins

Deniable operations have various aims but all are directed towards avoiding open conflict or escalating existing conflicts. Covert activities are not new. Historically, they were born out of the desire to avoid the often dreadful penalties of open warfare. Some early conflicts were wars of annihilation; defeated armies were slaughtered and their civilians often fared little better. During the war between Athens and Sparta, it was understood that, if a besieged city fell, its men would be killed and their women and children sold into slavery. The total destruction of Magdeburg and its civilian population in May 1631 has been described by one historian as the 'Hiroshima of the Thirty Years War'. Today, the 'Sword of Damocles' is the weapons of mass destruction.

A covert operation thwarted by the Royal Navy. The frigate HMS AJAX intercepted seven sampans off the coast of Kuala Selangor. The boats were carrying 22 Indonesian military saboteurs, commanded by a sergeant. (*Imperial War Museum*)

COVERT ACTION: A SUBSTITUTE FOR OPEN CONFLICT

Members of the American intelligence community explored the historical roots of covert action in *Intelligence Requirements for the 1980s: Covert Action*, a symposium sponsored jointly by the Defence University and the National Strategy Information Center. One of the speakers, Theodore G. Shackley, speaking on paramilitary covert action, explained how he saw the modern options for world powers like America:

> Before Congress, William Colby, then Director of the Central Intelligence Agency, accurately summed up the [post-Vietnam] dilemma in which the nation had locked itself; the nation had two options short of nuclear confrontation in coping with inter-

national crises. We could send in the Marines. We could do nothing.

Senior intelligence officers, who had experience in irregular warfare operations, insisted the United States should also consider *the third option, the use of insurgency and counterinsurgency techniques and covert action to achieve policy goals* [Shackley's italics]. In our view, paramilitary skills would give the United States an additional arrow in its national defence quiver.

Within the field of covert action there is a spectrum of plausible deniability. During the war in Laos, the CIA fought Communist infiltration with its secret army of Hmong tribesmen. On the world stage, America could truthfully deny US military involvement in the fighting but it was not expected to fool the North Vietnamese. At the other end of the spectrum, direct action operations, like the sinking of the Greenpeace ship *Rainbow Warrior*, are clearly intended to hide their authorship. If the French operation had employed outside forces, the gap between the act and the sponsors would have widened and the French denials would have appeared more credible. Who, then, are these shadowy pawns on the international chess board?

SPECIAL OPERATIONAL FORCES

Traditionally, the foreign intelligence services handle direct action operations in peacetime. The CIA has disbanded its Covert Action Branch but admits to maintaining civilian special operations forces. John Collins' handbook informs us that they:

> mingle with selected military personnel on loan from US armed services. Total numbers are classified, but are certainly small, because they conduct covert special activities individually or rely extensively on foreign resources (such as tribes in Laos and Vietnam) . . .

The KGB is also reputed to have disbanded its infamous Department V, responsible for 'Wet Affairs' (assassinations), but the First Chief Directorate continues to maintain Directorate T (Active Measures) and Directorate A (Disinformation and Covert Action). Additionally, the KGB deploys its own special purpose forces for deniable covert operations within Directorate S (Illegals), Department Eight of the First Chief Directorate. This Department is responsible for economic and political sabotage operations designed to dislocate government and create panic among the civilian population.

Civilian SOF, often ex-soldiers, are used on more politically-sensitive operations than their military counterparts. In Borneo, the SAS were restricted to operations just across the border, while MI6 led surrogate forces on deeper incursions. After the Soviet invasion of Afghanistan, military Spetsnaz operated inside the country, leaving some observers to speculate that attacks on guerrilla bases in Pakistan were the work of KGB special purpose troops. However, when the operation calls for highly-specialised training in insertion techniques, a unique variety of skills and operational support, military special forces offer the most obvious pool of talent.

One nation not only deploys the most highly-trained cadre of special purpose forces but can be said to have written a dubious chapter in the textbook on covert action. At the end of the Korean War, the Communist North continued the conflict with a series of deadly covert operations against the Republic of Korea (ROK). The operations were directed by the North Korean intelligence community: then the Public Security Bureau and the foreign intelligence service or Korean Worker's Party Liaison Department (KWPLD). Its operatives were drawn from the massive special purpose forces, currently 12–15 per cent of the 700,000-strong North Korean army.

In January 1968, a 31-man team from the 124th Army Unit started training for an undisclosed operation. A local provincial headquarters building served as the high-priority target and the team practised assaulting it by both day and night. On the final practice assault, the immediate area was held by 500 members of the Worker's Peasant Red Guard. The exercise was successful and 30 of the peasants impersonating the enemy, were hospitalised with injuries. Insertion training was restricted to long runs across the mountains. Carrying 60lbs of sand, the men were expected to cover the 40-mile course in a staggering six and a half hours!

After eight days of training, Lieutenant General Kim Chung Tae gave the team its orders: 'Your mission is to go to Seoul and cut off the head of [President] Chung Hee Park. You are to kill any others you find in the residence.' It was believed that the death of the President would bring South Korea to revolution. The men would wear South Korean army uniforms covered by dark overalls. Deniability was ensured by another order: team members were to kill themselves rather than be captured.

On the night of 17 January, the team was led across the mine fields and security fences of the Demilitarised Zone by guides, before disappearing into an isolated forest on the Republican side of the border. Splitting into small groups and moving by night, the team reached the northern outskirts of Seoul at dawn three days later. Removing their overalls, the men moved towards a rendezvous close to the President's official residence, the Blue House.

The raid almost succeeded but, at the last moment, a group of woodcutters alerted security forces to the incursion. The team, posing as an ROK counter-intelligence unit, were engaged by security police and, in the resulting manhunt, 28 North Koreans were killed or killed themselves. As a result of the raid, 68 ROK soldiers and civilians were killed and another 66 wounded. (In 1974, another attempt was made on the President's life, causing the death of his wife. In August 1982, Canadian police uncovered a third attempt to kill him during a visit to that country.)

In October 1968, another North Korean force landed along an isolated and rugged stretch of the Republic's eastern coast. Their task was to preach revolution to the local people. Unimpressed, the peasants informed the security forces and most of the 100-man force were captured or killed. In 1978, North Korean long-range reconnaissance personnel kidnapped two ROK film stars, Shin San Ok and his wife Choi Un Hui, who, like other kidnapped foreigners, have been used to train North Korean SOF in the customs and culture of their target countries. In the early 1980s, North Korean combat swimmers again began landing on the east coast and the many isolated islands in the Yellow Sea. Their aim was to establish guerrilla bands within the ROK and collect military and political intelligence.

By 1983, the North Koreans were ready to make another attempt on the life of President Park's successor, General Chun Doo-Hwan. On 17 September, a three-man North Korean team entered Rangoon, Burma, aboard the freighter *Tong Gon Ae Guk Ho*. Drawn from a reconnaissance brigade, it comprised a commander and two demolition specialists, all very highly trained and fluent in Russian, Chinese and English.

On 22 September, the team left the ship with other crew members and were met by a woman agent of the North Korean Intelligence Service, KWPLD. The home of a counsellor from the North Korean Embassy provided a welcome safe-house to cache weapons and explosives. Two days later, the team received its orders. On 9 October, the President was due to lay a wreath at the 'Martyr's Mausoleum', and the saboteurs were to ensure that he would die there. On 7 October, after conducting a thorough reconnaissance of the Mausoleum, the team gained entry and laid their charges.

On the day of the State visit, the saboteurs made their error. Mistaking the South Korean Ambassador's motorcade for that of the President, they detonated the explosives. As Burmese security forces began a massive man-hunt, the team moved towards the extraction RV with the North Korean freighter. The next day, the team commander, Major Zin Mo, was seen swimming a river and was promptly captured. Two days later, the two other saboteurs were located on a river bank. In the resulting fire-fight, Captain Kim Chi-o was killed and Captain Kang Min-chul captured as he attempted to kill himself.

A more recent direct-action operation employing North Korean SOF was considered too sensitive for military special forces. Instead, a small team of men and women was drawn from the KWPLD. Their target was Korean Airlines flight KAL 858 which was destroyed by a bomb on 29 November 1987, while en-route from Abu Dhabi to Seoul. Using forged passports believed to be issued by the North Korean resident's association in Japan, a man and a woman placed a bomb aboard the aircraft concealed in their luggage. The fact that neither boarded the flight, quickly brought the couple to the attention of the investigators during the subsequent manhunt. Intercepted on their way back to North Korea, the woman attempted suicide as capture appeared imminent. Subsequent interrogation revealed both were members of a North Korean Intelligence section; the Research Department for External Intelligence, and could speak Chinese and Japanese, suggesting extensive training.

MERCENARIES

The use of highly-motivated ex-military personnel further obscures the sponsorship of covert activities. In September 1962, the Yemeni government was toppled by an Egyptian-backed coup, further destabilising a volatile region. To the south-east, the Oman had already suffered an insurgency, while Yemen's southern neighbour, Aden, was a British Protectorate which the British hoped to leave, after establishing self-government. Behind these events there lay a larger chess game. American intelligence analysts believed that the Soviet Union was using proxy nations such as Egypt to acquire bases close to the oil fields of the Middle East, which were vital to the Western Alliance.

Britain attempted to counter the coup by proxy. As thousands of Egyptian troops entered the country, a mercenary force, composed of French, Belgian and ex-British SAS personnel and backed by influential British SOE and SAS veterans, was hurriedly created to assist the Royalist forces now fighting a guerrilla war. Infiltrating into Yemen from safe-houses in Aden, the mercenaries split into three-man modules (commander, radio-operator and medic) reminiscent of the Second World War 'Jedburgh Teams'. Supplies of arms and ammunition were dropped to the teams by Rhodesian Air Services and the Shah's Iranian Air Force. The guerrilla war lasted for eight years but the outcome was never in doubt. The Royalists insisted on using conventional tactics and the Egyptians used every weapon in their arsenal, including chemical warfare, against them.

Other countries have used mercenaries to influence the outcome of conflicts. In Vietnam, the Americans used the Chinese Nungs in sensitive MACVSOG operations. During the Nigerian civil war, France supplied Biafra with mercenaries and aid from Gabon, an ex-French colony also protected by a French mercenary force. On the other side, the Nigerian air force had the assistance of East German piloted Mig-19s and *Ilyushin* bombers flown by Egyptian pilots.

However, the use of real soldiers-of-fortune in covert operations has naturally been restricted and the intelligence services have quickly scotched any attempts at free-lancing. In 1971, the British SIS and the Italian intelligence service exposed an operation by ex-SAS soldiers to release 150 political prisoners held in Colonel Gaddafi's Tripoli prison – the so-called 'Hilton Assignment'. The SIS and the British Foreign and Commonwealth Office again intervened when ex-SAS soldiers were recruited to topple the government in the African state of Togo.

PARAMILITARY AND OTHER FORCES

Partisans, guerrillas, terrorists and other more sinister forces are the non-aligned pawns on the global chess board. To pursue their own aims they seek support in the form of arms and funds. In providing this support, the sponsor seeks to control and direct their activities. These forces are often referred to as 'mercenaries' but this label, applied by the sponsors, only serves to obscure the true relationship. This is underlined by the story of the Ukrainian partisans who were employed as proxies simultaneously by both sides during the Second World War.

The Ukrainian homelands stretch from southern Russia to Poland and Czechoslovakia. After the First World War and the upheavals in the Soviet Union, the Ukraine found itself divided up between the Soviet Union and Poland. In 1929, the Organisation of Ukrainian Nationalists (OUN) was founded, at a conference in Vienna. Cells from this organisation spread throughout Eastern Europe, establishing informal links with most intelligence services. In 1930, the Ukrainian Military Organisation (UMO) was set up to take terrorism and guerrilla warfare to the Poles and Soviets. At the outbreak of the Second World War some nationalists allied themselves with Nazi Germany, joining the SS *Galizien* Division. Others formed the Ukrainian Insurgent Army (UIA) and here a strange story unfolds as related through German archival material by the authors, Tomas Rezac and Valentin Tsurkan, in their book *Wanted*.

The UIA fought the Red Army and Soviet partisan forces, sometimes acting as scouts or guerrillas for the German Army. Soviet propaganda labelled them as German mercenaries but a report written in 1944 by SS Brigadefuhrer Brenner suggests otherwise. 'In encounters with German units, UIA detachments identify themselves by a special sign, holding the left hand with spread fingers before the face. *They are not to be fired on unless fire is opened from the other side.*' (Author's italics) Other reports by senior SS officers made it clear that the Germans sought to bring the UIA under their control. The UIA thought otherwise: 'Collaboration with the German command [should be seen as] a tactical step and by no means as real co-operation'. The Germans offered arms but the UIA were already well supplied with weapons. Who was the other sponsor?

Documents suggested that German military intelligence believed that the UIA received captured German weapons from the British SIS by way of the Polish Underground (*Armia Krajowa*). 'In order not to arouse the Soviet's suspicions about collaboration, the British dropped from planes only weapons captured from the Germans.' Rezac and Tsurkan claim that as the Second World War ended, UIA members were told by Western Intelligence agencies that 'they were the first freedom fighters in the Third World War, which might begin at any time'.

Ultimately, the UIA were killed as the Communist security police located their underground shelters; but for whom were they fighting? These so-called mercenaries fought for the romantic ideal of liberating the Ukraine from the Soviet Union and to that end, as a French intelligence report (later leaked to the French press) makes clear 'they declare their readiness to collaborate with any movement directed against Communism.' In essence, most paramilitaries fight for themselves as was illustrated by the Montagnard revolts in Vietnam.

The United States and the Soviet Union have both supported proxy forces to launch or defeat insurgencies. The Soviet Union has supported over 30 insurgencies in Africa, South America and the Middle East. When direct confrontation with Western security forces appeared likely, Soviet allies, such as East Germany and Cuba, were themselves used as proxies. The same pattern has been used for covert operations. East Germany and Libya have supplied arms and information for terrorist attacks in Europe. The North Koreans provided training facilities for Japanese Red Army operations to disrupt the 1988 Olympics. The attempted assassination of Pope John Paul II is reputed to have had a Bulgarian-KGB connection. KGB defector, Victor Ivanovich Sheymov, has claimed that he saw the cable from KGB chief, Yuri Andropov, ordering the Pope's assassination. If true, the recruitment of a terrorist with ultra-right connections was an unrivalled piece of ingenuity.

America used Cuban exiles to launch their abortive invasion of Cuba. Tribesmen in Tibet, Vietnam, Burma and Laos have been used as para-militaries and covert operators, the two latter forces continuing to fight after their sponsor withdrew from the conflict. Burmese insurgents now rely on the sale of opium to finance their operations. More recently, fearing Soviet influence on Daniel Ortega's regime in Nicaragua, the Americans have supported the 15,000 ex-Somoza followers of the *Fueza Democratica Nicaraguense*, better known as the 'Contras'.

More modest about its achievements, Britain created the first paramilitaries in Kenya and used other such forces for civilian irregular defence in Malaya, Cyprus and the Oman. In Borneo, tribesmen were used in deep penetration covert activities.

What of more dangerous liaisons with criminal groups? Conspiracy theories surrounding the assassination of American President John Kennedy, placed the CIA in league with organised crime. These accusations stemmed from reports that the CIA had previously offered mafia chiefs John Rosselli, Santos Trafficante and Sam Giancana, $150,000 to kill Fidel Castro. Alfred McCoy's *The Politics of Heroin in Southeast Asia*, further alleges CIA involvement with the heroin trade. Indeed, opium provided an excellent means of financing under-funded and highly secret covert operations in South-East Asia. The French special services used this form of revenue in Laos and it seems clear that the American proxies engaged in the opium trade. However, the CIA has consistently denied any systematic involvement by field officers or its secret air force, Air America, claiming that such allegations were based on side-deals between the proxies and Thai and Laotian officers.

To discover the real dangers of links between criminal syndicates with the capability for direct action and intelligence, we must turn to the Far East. It is

Covert operations in Borneo. Iban paramilitaries bring in an Indonesian infiltrator, probably Indonesian Special Forces. (*Imperial War Museum*)

here that we find adept, cynical and perennial organisations with a very
distinct political bias. The Japanese *yakuza* are unlike any Western crime
syndicate. They trace their origins to the *bakuto*, or traditional gamblers, and
the *tetiya* street pedlars. Since the Second World War, some of the 2,500
yakuza 'families' have maintained strong links with ultra-nationalist movements, funding and organising political campaigns and even resorting to
political violence and assassination.

During the Lockheed scandal it was alleged that the CIA used the company
as a means to channel funds to Japanese of the far-Right and possibly the
yakuza. But the *yakuza* owes loyalty only to itself and in 1973 they involved
Japanese and American officials in a breath-taking last minute rescue. The
sponsor of this operation was the South Korean foreign intelligence service,
known variously as the KCIA or the Korean Intelligence and Security Service.
The proxies were reputed to be one of the most powerful Korean *yakuza*
families in Japan. Its task was to help assassinate a popular South Korean
politician, Kim Dae Jung, whose only crime was to stand against President
Park in the 1971 presidential elections.

On 8 August 1973, Kim was snatched from the Grand Palace Hotel in
Tokyo. Beaten, drugged, and with his face covered with masking-tape, he was

taken to the coast and transferred to a small boat. Some way off the coast, Kim was transferred to a larger ship, where the crew attached weights to his hands and feet, to ensure that his body should never be found. Suddenly, an aircraft appeared overhead and Kim's abductors panicked; the weights were removed and his bonds loosened. The next day, he was landed in South Korea and dropped, still blindfolded, close to his home.

In Tokyo, police discovered the finger-prints of the KCIA Tokyo station chief at the kidnapping site. Apparently the *yakuza* family had leased the entire hotel floor where Kim was attacked. The Tokyo police have never released their report into the affair but Pharis Harvey, a researcher preparing a report for the US House Subcommittee on International Organisations of the Committee on International Relations ['Activities of the Korean Central Intelligence Agency in the United States', March 17, 1976] concluded '. . . KCIA and the Korean *yakuza* were certainly intermingled, so it was never certain what was an official KCIA initiative and what was from a mobster organisation'.

Any account of freelance paramilitaries would be incomplete without mention of another Japanese organisation – the *ninja*. Amidst the fascination and hysteria accompanying books, films and now cartoons on this subject, it has been suggested that some *ninjutsu* (the art of stealth) schools in Japan continue to ply their trade on behalf of the intelligence services and organised crime.

Together with the fighting arts, *ninjutsu* was introduced to Japan in 522 AD. At first it was the preserve of the mountain priests, mystical warriors known as *Yamabushi*. During Japan's Heian Period (794–1192), when the great Japanese families fought for power, *ninjutsu* was taught at schools run by lower-class families or clans such as the Hattori's. The seeds of this clandestine art, aimed at intelligence-gathering, raids and assassination were nourished by Japan's caste system and its ferocious style of warfare. Candidates were often taught from childhood and by their early 'teens they were at home in the forests and were masters of camouflage and concealment. The *ninja* was trained in unarmed combat and was also taught to use many everyday objects as weapons. He was also skilled in folk medicine and probably used herbal drugs to heighten awareness. *Ninjutsu* peaked during the Kamakura period (1192–1333) when there were at least 50 schools in the Koga province alone. Subsequently, many of the schools disappeared as a result of Japan's strict laws controlling the martial arts.

Even relatively late in Japan's history, these freelance operators may have served the state as nascent special forces. It is reputed that *ninja* combat swimmers boarded Commodore Perry's ship on its diplomatic mission to Japan in 1854, to ascertain his intentions. In 1895, *ninja*-trained operatives of the 'Dark Ocean Society' murdered the Korean Queen as a prelude to invasion by Japan. During the Second World War, *ninja* were reputedly used to infiltrate American lines during the battles for the Pacific Islands and *ninja*-commandos are said to have planned to kill General Douglas

MacArthur. It has been claimed that the CIA recruited some of these men after the war.

Today there is one official *Ninjutsu* school in Japan: the *Togakure Ryu*. This highly respected organisation draws many of its recruits from the professions and is seen as providing a spiritual way of life, while maintaining a fragment of Japanese tradition and culture. Commenting on the existence of illegal, so-called 'black' schools, an informed source within the Japanese police said:

> These are just wild stories. We have seen no evidence of these schools or their involvement with criminal organisations such as the *yakuza*. Apart from one respected organisation, *ninjutsu* is extinct.

12

Counter-Terrorism

... Horror has a face and you must make a friend of horror. Horror and moral terror are your friends and if they are not, they are enemies to be feared – they are truly enemies.
From Francis Ford Coppola's film, *Apocalypse Now*.

Terror ... that means of persuasion and influence.
Lenin

The deaths of the Israeli athletes at the 1972 Munich Olympics impressed upon the West the need for highly-trained personnel to respond to terrorist incidents. As many terrorist groups were attempting to blackmail governments by seizing hostages, these units were primarily tasked as Hostage Rescue Units (HRUs).

DEFENSIVE COUNTER-TERRORISM

The counter-terrorist must be more highly trained and committed than his enemy. From the outset, the HRU is severely disadvantaged. Its operators are forced to storm heavily-defended buildings and vehicles and combat a prepared enemy in order to release the hostages. In theory, the initial training in hostage rescue – fighting in built-up areas (FIBUA) – is the most formidable task an ordinary combat soldier will be asked to undertake. The hostages and their captors are enclosed in some sort of box (vehicle or building). Regardless of its nature, the outer wall must be breached, allowing the assault team to gain entry with sufficient surprise and speed to effect a rescue. Firstly, a group of snipers or marksmen must cordon off the building to prevent the terrorists escaping or being suddenly reinforced. Then the entry group and assault team assemble prior to the actual assault. Once the outer wall has been breached, the assault team move in pairs towards the groups of hostages and terrorists, already located by sophisticated surveillance devices. The actual rescue places great demands on the individual HRU members' close quarter-battle (CQB) skills, requiring them to distinguish terrorist and hostage with split-second accuracy.

In theory, the starting point for training in hostage rescue is the most formidable task an ordinary combat soldier will be asked to undertake: fighting in built-up areas (FIBUA). (*PMA Pictures*)

An advertisement for the ideal counter-terrorist would seek a highly-motivated, resourceful and intelligent individual who has been trained in assault techniques, communications, ordnance disposal, unarmed-combat and marksmanship, reconnaissance and surveillance, combat medicine, hostage management, close personal protection and insertion techniques. Consequently, many countries turned to their Special Forces to supply these units. Other countries, notably West Germany and France, decided to use police officers, while the Soviet Union formed its HRU from its trusted KGB.

MILITARY HOSTAGE RESCUE TEAMS

The British 22 SAS Regiment became involved with international terrorism in 1969, when it interested the Ministry of Defence in the idea of forming training teams to protect friendly overseas heads of state. Under the umbrella of 'Special Projects', 22 SAS maintains a Counter-Revolutionary Warfare (CRW) Wing, VIP protection teams, surveillance and HRU capabilities. SAS Sabre Squadrons, with all their prior experience and training, rotate in turn through CRW duties to sharpen their CQB skills. While exercising on mock-ups of aircraft and other potential terrorist targets, CQB training is conducted in the 'Killing House'. Sophisticated technology now ensures the safety of the 'Special Projects' teams training in the 'House'. Film of the 'terrorists' and their 'hostages' in one room is simultaneously transmitted to a second room and projected onto the wall. During the six-week 'Killing House' refresher course, each soldier is reputed to fire 1,500 rounds at the life-size projected images.

The British SAS has led the world in designing and using counter-terrorist technology. The Regiment is reputed to work with a computerised data-base of public buildings and other high-risk targets known as SPIES. Relevant information can be down-loaded onto a portable computer to allow the field commander instant access to plans that reveal such tactical information as blind spots and arcs of fire. The SAS also designed the stun grenade, which detonates with a loud bang and brilliant light, and a range of light aluminium ladders and climbing equipment for HRU incidents. Their dedicated signals support unit, 246 Signals Squadron (SAS), maintains a satellite-communication system capable of providing worldwide links with SAS headquarters in Hereford. In May 1980, after their successful storming of the Iranian Embassy in London, to rescue hostages, Britain's SAS achieved international fame. Although spectacular, this operation is dwarfed by the Regiment's enduring contribution to security force operations in Northern Ireland.

In 1987, the SAS broke new ground when they successfully rescued a prison warder held at knife point in Peterhead jail. A range of new technology is now available for these delicate operations: a thermal lance that cuts through the bars on prison windows in seconds, a high-powered cannon that can breach walls with water-filled shells and a range of new gases to disable the inmates.

The US 1st Special Forces Operational Detachment (Delta Force), activated in November 1977, was the creation of a Special Forces officer, Charles Beckwith. Unlike the other highly-specialised elements of America's Special Forces, Delta's structure, selection and philosophy were heavily influenced by the British SAS. Like the SAS, Delta has its own CQB house with pop-up friend or foe targets, 'immediate engagement scenarios', night-shooting and assault rooms. Delta has an establishment of 400 personnel, of which about half are combat-operators organised into two squadrons. While most of Delta is based at Fort Bragg, in the US, a small forward detachment of 20 men is based in West Germany.

In the aftermath of the abortive rescue of the American hostages in Iran, a joint US counter-terrorist force was established, composed of SEAL Team Six, Delta, Helicopter Task Force 160 and USAF special operations assets. Although based at the US naval base at Norfolk, Virginia, SEAL Team Six is tasked by Joint Special Operations Command (JSOC). Currently, it is training SEAL Team Five in counter-terrorist operations. The US Army has also decided to involve all combat units up to battalion level in counter-terrorism/counter-insurgency training. The Joint Readiness Training Centre is based at Little Rock, Arkansas and is staffed by 500 SOF instructors under Delta Force supervision.

Top counter-terrorist units are also deployed by Israel. Unit 101 was formed in 1953 to conduct unconventional warfare, in particular cross-border reprisal raids into Jordan. Israeli victory in the Six-Day War of 1967 resulted in a new wave of terrorism, prompting the establishment of *Sayaret Matkal* or General Staff Reconnaissance Unit 269. *Sayaret Matkal* had a strength of approximately 200 personnel and was tasked by the Chief of Israeli Intelligence. Many members of the unit had already received extensive military training with the naval combat-swimmers and paratroops. The usual SF-skills were supplemented with the necessary training for covert Middle Eastern operations, particularly desert training and languages, including the many dialects of Arabic. *Sayaret Matkal* was responsible for a long string of successful military operations and counter-terrorist strikes in support of Mossad.

However, the unit suffered a political disaster on 15 May 1974, when the Popular Democratic Front for the Liberation of Palestine (PDFLP) killed five civilians and seized the school in Ma'alot. In the resulting rescue, 22 children were killed and another 60 were injured. A government inquiry revealed that *Sayaret Matkal* had lost the element of surprise and had also assaulted the wrong floor of the building, using phosphorus grenades that blinded terrorist and counter-terrorist alike. In the resulting public outcry, two new units were formed, replacing *Sayaret Matkal* for internal counter-terrorist operations. The new HRU (*Yamam*) is deployed by the border police and supported by an army battalion of technical specialists known as *Shal-dag* (a bird that snaps fish out of the water). *Sayaret Matkal* has been retained for military and foreign operations.

POLICE HOSTAGE RESCUE UNITS

West Germany's *Grenzschutzgruppe-9* (GSG-9) has drawn most of its recruits from the *Bundesgrenzschutz* (Federal border police). An initial interview selects candidates who can demonstrate a high proficiency in police work. Selectors also look for academic qualifications, social graces and self-confidence, as GSG-9 officers are expected to act as bodyguards for senior diplomats and politicians and undertake advanced training in German law, languages and intelligence duties. Primary selection is based upon written examinations in advanced police procedure and tough HRU-training scenarios that involve a high degree of physical fitness and markmanship. All combat-teams (*Specialein-satztrupp*) spend three half-days and one additional evening per week on the firing range, expending more than a million rounds per year. While preparing to rescue hostages from cars, trains, aircraft, boats and buildings, exercise scenarios also involve the pursuit of 'terrorists' along the German autobahns.

Combat teams are organised into companies called Strike Teams. Strike Team Two is composed of combat-swimmers, specialised in maritime operations, who pay particular attention to the German oil rigs in the North Sea and Baltic and their country's large fleet of tankers. Strike Team Three members are trained in High Altitude Low Opening (HALO) parachuting, which they employ as a means of silently infiltrating a terrorist-held area. The other Strike Teams are trained in surveillance and close personal protection duties and operate in support of the federal police and SWAT-type units in each of the German states. GSG-9's most famous operation was the rescue of hostages from the the Lufthansa Boeing 737 at Mogadishu. A consistent string of successes, such as a subsequent operation that placed a terrorist arms cache under surveillance, helped break the German Red Army Faction.

In November 1973, the French Government decided to create a counter-terrorist unit from the *Gendarmerie Nationale*, a 60,000-strong paramilitary police force under the control of the Ministry of Defence. Unlike other police or intelligence units, the *Groupment d'Intervention de la Gendarmerie Nationale* (GIGN) is a low-profile force which handles politically-sensitive hostage rescues, prison-riots and the transport of dangerous criminals.

Candidates have to complete basic parachute and diving courses before selection for the unit. GIGN places a lot of emphasis on fitness and stamina-training and officers face a punishing routine of cross-country runs, callisthenics, weight-training and full-contact karate. On average, the GIGN officer fires 9,000 rounds with his revolver and 3,000 rounds from his rifle on the range each year. With the revolver, the operator is expected to hit a moving target at a range of 25 metres or more, in two seconds. Faced with

Opposite: Climbing and abseiling techniques are equally important in combat assault and HRU operations. (*Special Forces HQ; Australian DOD*)

multiple targets, he must hit a 'vital' spot on six targets at 25 metres, within five seconds.

The unit's greatest success was at Djibouti in February 1976, when GIGN and the 2nd REP rescued French school-children from a terrorist-held bus. GIGN was asked to intervene at Clairvaux prison in January 1978, when two inmates seized a deputy warden and two prison officers. The siege ended, like Djibouti, with precision sniper fire. Like other crack counter-terrorist teams, GIGN has 'hardened' the security of French embassies in high-risk countries such as the Lebanon. When French diplomats were held hostage at the French Embassy in Salvador, the news that a GIGN team had arrived in the country convinced the terrorists that it was time to surrender. In total, the unit has rescued more than 250 hostages.

Surprisingly, the most frequently hijacked airline in the world is the Soviet national carrier, Aeroflot. On 8 March 1988, an 11-member family jazz band hijacked a Tu-154 en route for Leningrad from Irkutsk. Concealing shot-guns amongst their musical instruments, the Ovechkins seized the plane and demanded to be flown to London. Instead the pilot landed at Leningrad, pretending that it was a refuelling stop in Finland. This superficial ruse was exposed when the hijackers saw Soviet militiamen and troops on the runway. After two hours of fruitless negotiations, a Ministry of Internal Affairs (MVD) assault-team attempted a hasty rescue. In the resulting fire-fight, nine people were killed and another 19 wounded. As a final gesture the hijackers detonated an explosive device that turned the rear of the aircraft into an inferno.

The wave of adverse publicity that followed this operation enabled the KGB to take control of hostage-rescue operations. The resulting 'special group' of the KGB was commanded by Colonel R. Ishmiyarov and divided into two departments, dealing respectively with analysis and operations, supported by additional communications specialists and negotiators. The unit's transport and recruits are provided by the KGB's Border Guards Directorate. Thus, in principle, the new KGB unit most closely resembles GSG-9. Although directly under the command of the deputy chairman of the KGB, operational control is managed by the 'Urgent Action Crisis Headquarters' in Moscow, staffed by officials of the KGB, MVD, Foreign Ministry and Ministry of Civil Aviation.

The new unit came to the West's attention in December 1988, when four hijackers seized a school bus in Ordzhonikidze. In what appeared to be a text-book operation, the terrorists exchanged the children for weapons, money and a Il-76T airliner, which they forced to fly to Israel. The KGB followed behind, with orders to recover the plane, its crew and the terrorists, while minimising the political impact of the incident. Two days later, after the Israelis had persuaded the hijackers to surrender, the Soviet HRU was photographed hustling their captives aboard their Tu-154 pursuit aircraft. More recently, a five-man rescue team overpowered a 22-year old loner who threatened to blow up a flight from Astrakhan to Baku, while a combined KGB-MVD force released four female staff held by prisoners at a penal colony in the Soviet Far East.

INTELLIGENCE SUPPORT FOR COUNTER-TERRORIST OPERATIONS

In his book *The Cult of Counterterrorism*, Neil C. Livingstone, an academic and authority on international terrorism, provided a fascinating account of Colonel Oliver North's role in the capture of the *Achille Lauro* hijackers. The story, as related by Livingstone, is also an excellent example of the need for accurate intelligence when mounting counter-terrorist operations.

The Italian cruise ship, *Achille Lauro*, with 507 passengers and crew, was seized by four members of the Palestine Liberation Front on 7 October 1985. The next day, they emphasised their demands by shooting one of the passengers, a 69-year old handicapped American named Leon Klinghoffer, and dumping his body into the sea. Thirty hours later, a rescue force of Delta and SEAL Team Six operators arrived at the British base at Akrotiri in Cyprus. The team planned to take off during the night of Wednesday 9 October and make a HAHO parachute descent over the Mediterranean, gliding down onto the ship to take the terrorists by surprise. But, on Tuesday, US intelligence was forced to admit that it had lost track of the ship.

Then head of the special White House counter-terrorist force, Colonel North established contact with Major General Simhoni at the Israeli Embassy in Washington. Within minutes, North had his information: the ship was in Syrian waters. But on Wednesday, the day of the planned operation, the ship was lost a second time. Again, the Israelis came up with its location. Meanwhile, the *Achille Lauro* returned to Port Said, where the terrorists surrendered to Egyptian authorities as part of a deal between Italy, Egypt and the PLO. When the Americans requested extradition, the Egyptians claimed that the terrorists had already left the country.

At this point, North decided to use his contacts with Israeli intelligence to pursue the terrorists. Israeli SigInt installations in the Negev desert intercepted telephone calls in Egypt which confirmed that the terrorists were still in that country. They were also able to discover the identification numbers and call-sign of the Egyptian airliner scheduled to take them to Tunisia. Once off the ground, Israeli and American flying command posts shadowed the Egyptian aircraft, blocking its communications and fooling the pilot into believing that he had been refused permission to land at Tunis. The airliner was finally conducted to Sigonella Air Base in Cyprus by American fighters operating from the aircraft carrier, USS *Saratoga*. After several tense minutes on the tarmac, as American and Egyptian commandos and Italian *Carabinieri* confronted each other, the terrorists were taken into Italian custody.

The success of this operation was mainly due to signals intelligence. However, a highly secret American army unit had been on hand to provide the American rescue force with any necessary HumInt. Originally called the Foreign Operating Group, the Intelligence Support Activity (ISA), was formed in the aftermath of the abortive Iranian rescue. Charged with providing detailed global tactical intelligence assistance for American special operations, the ISA conducts reconnaissance, identifies and prepares drop-zones and provides transport and guides for foreign operations. The 120-man force is divided into an operations squadron and deep penetration unit employing communications and intelligence specialists, deep penetration agents and a small team of commandos. Most of its personnel are recruited from US Special Forces. In theory, the ISA is responsible to Army Intelligence and Security Command (INSCOM) but is mainly tasked by the Defence Intelligence Agency and the Army's Assistant Chief of Staff for Intelligence (ACSI).

While the ISA was involved in the successful operation that freed eight American hostages captured by Sudanese rebels, it was reportedly able to pinpoint the location of American hostages held in the Lebanon. During 1983–84, the Iranian Revolutionary Guards took over the *Hezbollah* (Party of God) and America suffered a number of reversals in the Lebanon, including the bombing of the US Embassy and US Marine barracks and the abduction and murder of CIA Station Chief, William Buckley. The following year, American concern became acute as more of its citizens were kidnapped. Finally, Delta Force was tasked with mounting a rescue and ISA undercover operatives went in ahead to gather intelligence.

Working with the Christian Militia and other contacts in Lebanon, the ISA was able to pinpoint most of the hostages in a small village called Britel in the Bekaa Valley. Others were apparently being held at Bir el Aabed in Moslem West Beirut and the Sheik Abdalah barracks in the heights around northern Bekaa. The job of routine surveillance was then passed to the Overhead Reconnaissance Office and its US Key-Hole-11 spy satellites, which were repositioned to watch these prisons controlled by the Revolutionary Guards. The intelligence proved accurate and a combined force of 50–60 Delta and SEAL Team Six operators prepared to move to safe-houses in East Beirut provided by the Christian Lebanese forces. The commandos were to split into three groups. The first two teams would hit the Bekaa and Bir el Aabed simultaneously, while the third would remain in reserve. US ships and heli-copters would provide a swift extraction, with Israel agreeing to provide a quick-exit in the event of a mishap. At the last moment, the rescue was aborted, possibly as a result of the US Government's arms-for-hostages negotiations with Iran.

SECURITY AND COUNTER-INTELLIGENCE

On the basis that prevention is better than cure, protecting potential high-risk terrorist targets is far more cost-effective than finding ways of recovering them once they are in terrorist hands. As various special units are tasked with breaching such defences in wartime, it is not surprising that this task initially fell to regiments such as the SAS. Once the defences have been tested and hardened, routine security must, of necessity, fall to other larger less specialised bodies.

In Britain, the 22nd SAS Regiment pioneered these tasks, both overseas and

US Delta Force operators arrive by helicopter to begin a hostage rescue exercise. (*PMA Pictures*)

at home. The Regiment was asked to test the security around prisons and military bases, while providing close personal protection for politicians and the Royal Family during periods of heightened threat. Overseas, SAS teams trained bodyguards for friendly heads of state. This responsibility is now shared with other national counter-terrorist forces such as Delta, GSG-9, GIGN and commercial firms employing ex-soldiers. Currently, the Royal Military Police provides teams to protect Britain's embassies and their diplomats, while domestic duties are the preserve of the Metropolitan Police and the Special Branch. 'C' Branch of the Security Service (DI5) is responsible for providing intelligence and co-ordinating domestic counter-terrorist operations. The SAS continue to provide protection for high-risk targets such as defectors and certain senior defence personnel.

Some threats and targets are assigned the highest priorities. The Royal Marine's Comacchio Group is tasked with defending Britain's nuclear arsenal and oil rigs, while the Special Boat Service handles maritime terrorist incidents. The defence of military bases, particularly against attacks by Soviet Spetsnaz commandos, is the job of the Intelligence Corps' security companies.

In America, the FBI maintains a domestic HRU. Known as the Hostage Response Team, the 50-strong force is reputed to be among the best in the world. The Bureau also maintains small counter-terrorist teams in each State.

Other counter-terrorist intervention teams are maintained by the Secret Service's (Treasury Department) Executive Protection Division, National Park Police and US Marshal's Service. Preventing the theft of nuclear weapons or weapons-grade fuel is the job of the Energy Department's Nuclear Emergency Search Team (NEST). American overseas army and air force bases are defended by the Military Police and Security Police respectively. The latter are reputed to have been highly trained in counter-terrorism by Germany's GSG-9.

Other more specialised units were formed to protect American bases against Spetsnaz and Soviet intelligence. The security measures taken by US naval installations against potential terrorist and foreign intelligence penetration are tested by the US Navy's Security and Co-ordination Team; known informally by its codename RED CELL, this unit is part of SEAL Team Six.

A small team of US Army counter-HUMINT specialists were formed in 1982, with the codename YELLOW FRUIT. A small part of the overall Offensive Counter-Intelligence Operation (OFCO) directed against Soviet forces, the unit's operational cover name was Business Security International. Part of its task, while attached to Intelligence and Security Command's (INSCOM's) Technical Surveillance Countermeasures Team, was to challenge the physical and electronic security of US Army bases and defence industry facilities. Later, it was combined with a Quick Reaction Team to produce a unit that could immediately respond to threats against US Army bases anywhere in the world. Unfortunately secrecy and mismanagement of the covert finances led to allegations of fraud and YELLOW FRUIT's demise. A new unit, designated Technical Analysis Team (TAT), has been formed in their stead and is currently responsible for countering all military insurgency threats, including that of Spetsnaz.

Responses to terrorism vary with the perception of the threat. The passive counter-measures outlined above can, to a degree, protect against the threat of terrorist attack or make an efficient response to terrorist incidents when they occur. Active counter-terrorism seeks to take a more aggressive approach by eliminating terrorist groups and cutting their source of funds and supporting infrastructure.

COUNTERING NARCO-TERRORISM

Earlier insurgencies were defeated by cutting off the guerrillas' source of recruits and supplies and wooing the local populace with civil aid projects and social reform, before organising them into militia for their own defence. Today's terrorist is financed by organised crime and drugs. This support is harder to overcome and efforts to do so are currently in the balance.

More than 80 per cent of Lebanon's Bekaa Valley is used to grow opium and hashish under the control of the *Hezbollah*. Not only does the trade provide money to buy arms but it is seen as a means of weakening the West through drug addiction. Currently, 30 per cent of Lebanon's gross national product is derived from drugs traffic.

The coca plant, the natural source of cocaine, is one of the main cash crops of peasant farmers in Columbia, Peru and Bolivia. In Columbia, the traffic is controlled by two crime syndicates: the *Medellin* and *Carli* cartels. These gangsters are at the centre of a whirlpool of corruption, kidnap, murder and terror that threatens to topple democracy in Columbia. Internal terrorists such as the Communist *Fuerzas Armadas Revolucionarias Colombianes* (FARC), the Maoist People's Liberation Army (EPL) and the Castroist M19 levy a 10 per cent tax on peasants growing coca and have good relations with the traffickers. The urban-based M19 carries out killings and reprisals on the drug barons' behalf. In June 1987, Colombian guerrillas acted as proxies for the gangsters when they crossed the border and attacked Venezuelan National Guardsmen engaged in destroying drug plantations.

In Peru, the drug barons are protected by the Maoist 'Shining Path' movement. Peru grows 50 per cent of the world's cocaine, much of it in the Huallaga Valley. From there the drugs are transported by light aircraft to distribution centres in Mexico and the Caribbean. The terrorists are reported to defend the traffickers for a 15 per cent cut of the proceeds and aircraft landing fees of $15,000.

When Jose Blandon, a former aide to Panamanian dictator, General Noriega, testified before a US Senate sub-committee on 10 February 1988, a shocked America learnt that Fidel Castro and Manuel Noriega were working together to promote 'drug-financed guerrilla movements throughout Latin America'. The *Medellin* cartel chief, Pablo Escobar Gaviria, was reputed to be supported by Castro, who provided cartel ships with a naval base on the islet of Piedra, off the northern coast of Cuba. From there speed boats took cocaine, hashish and methaqualone to distribution networks in Florida. A former intelligence officer of the Cuban DGI has told a US Senate hearing that thousands of Cuban agents are distributing drugs with the aim of increasing addiction, violent crime and corruption in North America. Thus drugs and organised crime are not only a means of funding terrorism; they are proving to be weapons in their own right.

Under Operation SNOWCAP, US agencies, such as the Drug Enforcement Agency (DEA), the Pentagon and the CIA are spearheading efforts to counter narco-terrorism in South America. Spy satellites are being used to identify drug plantations, air-strips and processing sites, while helicopters carry police units on fast search and destroy missions. A crop substitution programme aims at introducing other cash crops into the economy. American and British Special Forces are a more recent addition.

US Special Forces are training the Peruvian police in a range of SF-patrol skills that culminate in helicopter raids on drug factories in the Huallaga Valley. Defence analysts have recently criticised these Vietnam-style tactics, claiming that the Huallaga will become another 'Ho Chi Minh Trail'. Peasants bound up in the drugs economy provide an early-warning system for the

The Special Forces have returned to the jungle to help combat narco-terrorism.
British and American troops are training élite South American police units in
the techniques of long range patrolling and surveillance. (*Special Forces HQ;
Australian DOD*)

terrorists and gangsters. How long, it is asked, before the LZs are staked out and police units vanish as a result of ambush? The Huallaga is truly 'behind the lines'. In response, the Pentagon has given permission for the instructors to accompany their students on operations.

Instructors from Britain's 22 SAS are confronting this very problem in Columbia. Both the SAS and their Elite Force police commando students are putting emphasis on LRRP tactics similar to the CLARET patrols in Borneo. If used at all, helicopters have become a means of inserting long-range patrols and strike forces close to drug areas. From a remote LZ, the patrols enter contested areas by foot. Gone are the rifle slings from the students' Israeli automatic weapons; the Elite Force have adopted the 'Belfast Cradle', with weapons crooked in the forearms, allowing a quick response to surprise contacts. Their patrols are deploying lead scouts and flankers and learning to travel long distances in the gruelling heat, pausing only for short water-breaks. Behind them a helicopter-borne reaction force remains on standby to follow up contacts.

Overall, security force operations in South America have shown a measure of success. A senior Shining Path leader, Osman Morote Barrionuevo, was captured in June 1988. A year later, 1,026 Shining Path terrorists were killed in actions with the security forces. In return, the Shining Path killed 293 police and soldiers and 1,016 civilians, including 123 mayors, assassinated as part of the terror campaign. Colombian drugs chief, Pablo Escobar Gaviria, and Fabio Ochoa, another active member of the Medellin family, have surrendered to the Colombian authorities – who believe that a promise not to extradite drug traffickers to the US holds the key to future mass surrenders.

DIRECT ACTION MISSIONS

One reported instance of covert operations concerns three Soviet diplomats kidnapped in the Lebanon in September 1985. A fourth Russian, Arkady Kathov, was brutally shot during the course of the abduction. Within days a KGB team arrived in Beirut, identified the kidnappers and paid a Druze militia group to abduct four of the leader's family. The terrorist chief was engaged in clandestine activities in Europe, when a messenger arrived bearing four ears and a note demanding the release of his Soviet captives. Within hours the diplomats were free.

Prize-winning journalist, Bob Woodward, related an American direct action in his controversial book, *Veil: The Secret Wars of the CIA*. After the loss of CIA agents and US Marines in successive bombing incidents in Beirut, the CIA decided to act against the terrorists. Israeli intelligence implicated the Syrians and Iranian-backed Sheikh Fadlallah, leader of the *Hezbollah*. To distance the CIA from the reprisal operation, Saudi Intelligence was paid to recruit an assassin. The Saudis came up with an Englishman who had served with 22 SAS before leaving to become a contract soldier. This man organised the operation and Lebanese Intelligence provided hired proxies to carry it out. On 8 March 1985, a car-bomb exploded 50 yards from Fadlallah's high-rise apartment, devastating most of the street and killing 80 people and wounding another 200, mostly local residents. As part of an after-action deception operation, the CIA ensured that Fadlallah's people learnt of the identities of the Lebanese mercenaries.

For a country to countenance the use of direct action missions in the war against terrorism, both the government and its citizens must perceive the same threat. This has little to do with the doctrines of civilised government. All nations retain the right to fight the 'just war' and all wars result in deaths, including those of innocent civilians. Israel sees Middle Eastern terrorism, much of it state-sponsored, as part of a total war: a war for survival.

After the deaths of the Israeli Olympic athletes in Munich in 1972, Mossad went after the terrorists. When the mission required highly-trained commandos, the intelligence service turned to *Sayaret Matkal*. When a person was identified by Mossad as being guilty of spilling Israeli blood, his name was passed to the Prime Minister's Office, which in turn forwarded it to a secret judicial committee. The committee, sitting as a military court, tried the accused in their absence. When the court rendered a guilty verdict, Mossad was ordered to bring the accused to Israel for trial or, if this proved too dangerous, to assassinate them. Condemned terrorists were placed on an execution list, approved and signed by the Israeli Prime Minister.

In April 1973, 30 *Sayaret Matkal* operators landed on a beach near Beirut to be met by eight Mossad agents with rented Avis trucks. The commandos and intelligence officers split into three groups. One group shot and killed Black September leader, Abu Youssef, and his right-hand man, Kemel Adwan; the second destroyed the headquarters of the People's Front for the Liberation of Palestine, while the third blew up a Black September bomb-factory. On their way back to the beach and the Zodiac assault craft, the Israelis found themselves closely pursued by armed terrorists. Israel was forced to acknowledge authorship of the raid by sending in support helicopters. Cannon fire and iron spikes designed to puncture car tyres enabled the team to make good their escape.

Throughout the 1980s, in pursuit of an élite PLO commando unit known as Force 17, Israel demonstrated the lengths to which it would go in hunting down terrorists. After the Israeli invasion of Lebanon and the PLO's subsequent expulsion from Beirut, the terrorist organisation established a new headquarters near Tunis. From Tunisia, Force 17 launched several sea-borne raids against Israel, using Larnaca harbour on Cyprus as a staging post. After two terrorist boats were intercepted by the Israeli Navy in April 1985, Force 17 decided that Mossad agents in Cyprus were maintaining surveillance on their operations. On 18 September, the Jewish feast of *Yom Kippur*, a three-man hit squad – one of whom was a Englishman – boarded a yacht in Larnaca harbour and murdered three Israeli tourists.

Israeli intelligence was running a spy, Jonathan Jay Pollard, inside the

Washington US Naval Intelligence Office. Pollard had passed his Israeli controller satellite photographs identifying the PLO headquarters and vital details of the Tunisian air defences. A week after the Larnaca massacre, eight Israeli F-16s used Pollard's intelligence to attack the PLO headquarters at Hammam beach just outside Tunis. The raid killed 60 people, including the Force 17 commander, Mohammed Natour. All the Israeli aircraft returned intact but Pollard's subsequent accidental exposure and trial in the United States, sparked a huge diplomatic row which threatened to destroy the close relationship between Israel and the United States.

A year later, a European Israeli operation against Force 17 resulted in another serious diplomatic row. In Britain, an Arab Mossad officer, Ismael Sowan, became so close to Major Abdul-Rahim Mustapha, a Force 17 European-cell leader, that Sowan was caught by the British police harbouring a cache of terrorist weapons and explosives. Britain reputedly threatened to remove Mossad from the list of friendly intelligence services with whom Britain co-operates and shares intelligence.

COUNTER-TERROR

Most terror groups pursue a dual campaign, combining bombings and murder with political and diplomatic initiatives. The 'political wing' is kept rigorously apart from the gunmen but it pursues the same aims through the democratic process and the media, though usually gaining little support. But there are other supporters of terrorism. During the peak of the Red Army Faction atrocities in Germany, the police estimated that the 200 activists were supported by 400 sympathisers who acted as couriers and provided logistical support such as safe-houses. The German police aptly listed this latter group as 'criminals without crime'.

As part of the 'other war' in Vietnam, the Americans found themselves faced with a Viet-Cong support infrastructure, consisting of tax collectors, propaganda cadres and officials of an alternative administration living in the shadows. Under the umbrella of Civil Operations and Revolutionary Development Support (CORDS), civil militia and intelligence units were created to protect the hamlets from guerrilla incursions. This was seen as preferable to the forcible relocation of the population or the creation of free-fire zones. With them came CIA 'Counter-Terror' or Provincial Reconnaissance Teams, whose task was to destroy the Viet-Cong infrastructure in hamlets listed by the Hamlet Evaluation System (HES) as being under their control. The programme was named after a Vietnamese mythical bird which could fly anywhere and was given the compromise English translation: Phoenix.

The Phoenix programme drew its recruits from Vietnamese and American Special Forces and indigenous personnel. In addition, the ARVN Regional Forces and Popular Forces ran a similar sort of programme. William Colby was later to state, in 1971, that 28,000 VC had been captured in the whole of

South Vietnam under the programme, while another 20,000 had been killed and 17,000 had defected. The programme was an outstanding military success. The destruction of the infrastructure defeated the Viet-Cong's war for the hamlets and forced General Giap to conclude, in January 1970, that Hanoi could win only after the Americans had left and then 'only through regular war in which the main forces fight in a concentrated manner'.

Phoenix was partly responsible for its own demise. The programme was indiscriminate. Names came from denunciations, were revealed in interrogations or picked up at checkpoints or from defectors. The Saigon government used the programme to extort money from the frightened populace, while troops in the provinces misused it by turning over anyone who was seen to obstruct their operations. In his book, *Once a Warrior King*, counter-revolutionary warfare officer, David Donovan, remarked how easy it would have been to have removed a particularly obnoxious and anti-social priest by calling in the local counter-terror team. To his great credit, Donovan resisted the temptation. America's revulsion was similar to that of the French during the Algerian war.

Predictably, the IRA has claimed that a similar programme was operated by British forces in Northern Ireland. After a shooting incident involving undercover forces in June 1972, the Northern Ireland Civil Rights Association claimed that this was one of many attacks on non-military republicans. Later, these accusations were expanded into claims of a general 'shoot to kill' policy. The conspiracy theories were partly fed by the British Government's traditional taciturn approach to information management. Author Martin Dillon has explored these areas in depth in his books, *Political Murder in Northern Ireland* and *The Dirty War*. In his massive, thorough and masterly account of undercover operations in the province, Dillon prefaced *The Dirty War* with these remarks:

> Much of the evidence in print or by word of mouth pointed to the involvement of British intelligence groupings in political murder and the manipulation of Loyalist paramilitaries for counter-terror. My conclusions may not please people in both communities or some of the Left in Britain but I believe it has to be said that the vast majority of the conspiracy theories in this regard are inaccurate and in some instances are the deliberate creation of black propaganda for the purpose of discrediting the security forces. In a few instances I uncovered evidence which pointed to the involvement of members of the security forces in terrorism but the overwhelming evidence indicated that such involvement was personal and not part of a stated policy.

Counter-Terror operations against non-military terrorist personnel alienate public opinion and drive a stake into the heart of hard-won, counter-insurgency doctrines. Currently, the Peruvian army is hindering US efforts in the drugs war. Quite apart from a reluctance to take part in operations against the traffickers, the United Nations holds military counter-terror teams responsible for the 'disappearance' of 10,000 Peruvians in a 'human rights abuse unequalled in the world today'. In a show of contempt, the military twice attempted to murder the head of the government commission investigating the 'disappeared'. Army terror, coca cultivation and the terrorist's strict social order are winning recruits for the Shining Path. The war in Peru may well be lost for the want of discrimination.

The face of state-sponsored terrorism. Two Indonesian-trained insurgents lie wounded on the floor of a Wessex helicopter. Their party was tracked and finally eliminated by British security forces near Sibu in Sarawak. (*Imperial War Museum*)

13

The Quick Reaction Force

Last Friday, Noriega declared his military dictatorship to be in a state of war with the United States and publicly threatened the lives of Americans in Panama. The very next day, forces under his command shot and killed an unarmed American serviceman, wounded another, arrested and brutally beat a third American serviceman and then brutally interrogated his wife, threatening her with sexual abuse. That was enough.

President Bush's speech to the American people on the events
that led to Operation JUST CAUSE, 21 December 1989.

In the Belgian Congo, now Zaire, just before 08.00 on 24 November 1964, four years after Independence, rebel forces at the Lumumba monument in Stanleyville fired the first ragged volley of shots at groups of European hostages. Other execution squads of Simba rebels were combing the streets of the city, searching for any Europeans still in hiding. When the bullets ran out, men, women and children were speared or hacked to death.

For two hours the rebels had heard the sound of gunfire from the direction of the airport. It was well known that the Congolese Government had dispatched a rescue force led by mercenaries but the rebels' Intelligence placed the main column many hours away. They considered that they still had plenty of time to finish butchering their captives before withdrawing. In the event, they had less than four minutes.

Twenty minutes earlier, reconnaissance elements of the 11th Belgian Para-Commando Company had reached the outskirts of the city. Around the monument were 250 hostages. Two children, five women and 15 men were already dead; army medics were to report another 40 wounded, five mortally, when the sudden appearance of the parachutists put an end to the massacre. Operation *DRAGON ROUGE* (Red Dragon) caught the rebels by surprise – and Europe marvelled at the first rapid projection of military power to secure a limited objective.

THE COMING OF THE DRAGON

Operation RED DRAGON was bedevilled by many of the same political and logistical problems that currently complicate the use of the modern rapid deployment force. Nearly 2,000 foreign nationals were being held in Stanleyville as political pawns. The Americans and Belgians who were backing the Congolese Government were told to end their support or the hostages would be butchered. However, even the President of the rebel 'Popular Republic', Christophe Gbenye, lacked total control of the 'Popular Army of Liberation', particularly the dreaded Simbas. They threatened to grill the hostages alive and eat them if the rebel terms were not accepted. The threat had already been endorsed by their particularly hideous record of murder, rape, torture and cannibalism. Then, after 101 days of intense negotiation and military concessions, time ran out. As part of a new government offensive, a mercenary-led column advanced on Stanleyville.

Belgium was ill prepared for a rapid, long-distance intervention. An earlier operation to rescue some of its countrymen had resulted in the United Nations supervising the Belgian Army's own departure. Now the only army unit capable of launching a rescue in the allotted time-scale was the Para-Commando Regiment, an airborne training unit that prepared young conscripts for service in the reserves. Nevertheless, the 1st and 2nd battalions eagerly produced 545 experienced officers and men and the United States provided the necessary transport.

On 14 November, the paratroops, under the command of Colonel Laurent, together with armoured jeeps and tricycles, were lifted in 12 US C-130 transports to the British base at Ascension Island. There the paratroops waited while negotiations proceeded. On 20 November, the element of surprise was lost. Stories about a joint US-Belgian rescue appeared in the press, forcing the Belgian Government to make a final decision. Under the cover of a joint 'long range airborne exercise', the paratroops flew the second 2,400-mile leg to a base in Katanga. Early on the morning of 24 November, the 111th day of captivity for the hostages, the C-130 transports took off for Stanleyville.

At 06.00hrs the plan began to unfold above the Stanleyville Golf Club as 320 men from the 1st Battalion and Regimental HQ leapt into the slipstream. For the rescue to have any chance of success, the paras needed to capture the adjoining airfield and clear the runway of obstacles so that the two aircraft carrying their vehicles could land. Within 30 minutes the eight armoured jeeps should be ready for the dash to the city. Suddenly, the operation encountered an unforeseen problem: one of the aircraft had been forced to turn back. For the next hour the paras would be forced to operate with only half of their vehicles. At 07.00 hrs, as five more C-130s landed with supplies and a rein-forcing company, lead elements of Colonel Laurent's force were responding to information that the hostages were being held at the Victoria Hotel.

RED DRAGON was no ordinary combat-rescue operation. For the next five hours the lightly-armed parachutists fought to clear and hold Stanleyville. When Congolese forces arrived at midday, Laurent took the decision to extend the operation to encompass groups of isolated settlers at Paulis, Bunia and Watsa (Operations BLACK, GREEN and WHITE DRAGONs). Overall, the operation released 375 hostages and secured the evacuation of 2,000 foreign nationals for the loss of one paratroop killed and seven wounded.

OPERATION LEOPARD

While the conventional paratroop assault was clearly proving unsuitable for the technological battlefield, another rescue in Africa was to underscore its potential for rapid deployment operations. In May 1978, Zaire again saw fighting which involved around 2,300 foreign workers and technicians living in the new town of Kolwezi. The rebel soldiers of the Congolese National Liberation Front (FNLC) held a grudge against foreigners. A year earlier, FNLC forces, backed by Cuban advisers, had launched an invasion of Shaba Province from bases in Angola. This was soundly defeated by President Mobutu's Zairean Army led by French and Moroccan instructors. Now, the rebels wanted revenge. What started as the summary executions of 'French and Moroccan mercenaries' degenerated into bloody murder and rape, engulfing black and white alike.

Four days later, President Mobutu launched an international appeal for assistance. Once again the majority of the captives were Belgian ex-patriots but, while offering assistance, the Belgian Government declined to commit fighting troops. It was left to France to provide another model for speedy intervention. On the evening of 17 May, Lieutenant Colonel Erulin gave the legionnaire parachutists of the 2nd REP orders to prepare to move. At 08.00hrs on the following morning, 650 men of four rifle companies plus the regimental headquarters, reconnaissance and mortar platoons, started to em-plane. The men would jump light with just 40 rounds of ammunition. Vehi-cles, support-weapons and further ammunition would follow later. This would be the Legion's first operational parachute descent since Dien Bien Phu – almost 24 years previously.

A mere day-and-a-half after the regiment had received the movement order, the French paras prepared to jump over Kolwezi. After two sleepless nights, using American parachutes unsuitable for their equipment containers and literally crammed into strange C-130 aircraft, the French jumpmasters struggled to arrange the first wave into sticks. At the first appearance of parachutes above the town, some rebels ran for the Angolan border. Blocking forces prevented others from retreating with their hostages, while the 1st and 2nd Companies moved towards the Jean XXIII School and hospital. Throughout that day the paras fought to clear the town of rebels, coming under continual harassing fire. As night fell the town echoed with gunfire as the FNLC counter-attacked using automatic weapons and rocket-propelled grenades.

At first light, more parachutes appeared in the sky as the reconnaissance and mortar platoons arrived. An hour later most of the town was in French hands and companies of paras were clearing the old gendarmerie barracks and the labyrinthine Manika housing estate. By 20 May, resistance was reduced to sporadic sniper fire, which the paras followed up with uncommon zeal, having by then discovered the remains of several mass killings. Other Europeans survived, hiding in cavities between walls or under piles of rotting corpses.

At the beginning of June the legionnaires returned to Corsica. French intervention was credited with saving 2,000 lives while 413 rebels had been killed or captured. The Legion had suffered five killed and another 25 wounded.

THE QUICK REACTION FORCE

One of the lessons of the African operations was that a rapid deployment force should have its own support, either parachute-trained or capable of air-

The central element of America's rapid deployment force is the élite 82nd Airborne. (*PMA Pictures*)

landing on airfields seized by the parachute element. Once complete, the force should be capable of defending itself until the mission is accomplished, or relieved by heavier battle groups. This was the case in Saudi Arabia where, during DESERT SHIELD, the central element of America's rapid deployment force, the 82nd Airborne, provided a political 'trip-wire' to deter an Iraqi invasion.

The first 82nd Airborne unit to arrive in an area is the Initial Ready Company. If an airfield is available, it is seized and secured, allowing the second wave to be air-landed. If none is available, or if the runways are blocked or heavily defended, a dropping zone is secured. The Company is quickly reinforced by the Divisional Ready Force, provided with an artillery battery, engineer platoon, water-duties platoon and bulldozer teams. This larger force crushes enemy opposition and seizes the initial operational objectives, while ensuring that the landing-zone is ready for the rest of the brigade. Finally, the Division Ready Brigade arrives, in the form of three infantry battalions and further support units. Additional logistical 'packages' are available to be added to the Divisional Ready Force or the Division Ready Brigade. These include airfield construction units, anti-aircraft systems, civil affairs units and helicopters that can be transported inside aircraft.

THE PATHFINDERS

One essential element of this limited invasion has still to be mentioned. These are the first troops on the ground, performing one of the oldest special forces tasks in the world: pathfinding. Modern pathfinders appeared during the Second World War, to clear and hold the invasion beaches and dropping-zones. Today, pathfinding is still an important prelude to rapid deployment force operations. Dropping-zone acquisition and management by HALO-inserted airborne pathfinders has become a precise art. Radio and laser beacons carried by the pathfinder teams draw the approaching aircraft to the DZ like moths to a flame. Other lights or markers identify the release point, where the pilot will switch the jump indicator light from red to green. The required length of the DZ is calculated as a function of the ground speed of the aircraft, multiplied by the time needed to release the parachutists, who jump at a rate of approximately one per second. More lights or marker panels can be used to indicate the line of approach, wind speed and direction. The pathfinder team can fine-tune events by employing UHF radio transmissions to shepherd the planes into an aerial control point and thence onto the release point, flying over the DZ and out onto a return flight path.

Candidates for Britain's Mountain and Arctic Warfare Cadre undergo a more traditional pathfinder course orientated towards the mountains and forests of the Northern Front. America's SEAL Teams and Britain's Special Boat Service provide maritime pathfinder teams. Proposed beaches for landings are carefully surveyed, noting the type of sand, tidal ranges, incline of the beach, enemy strong-points, connecting roads and the presence of underwater

The Pathfinder Platoon is the spearhead of British airborne rapid deployment operations. (*PMA Pictures*)

obstacles, data required to assess whether landing craft carrying an operational commando brigade can be landed successfully.

Beach reconnaissance is a vital part of the peacetime work of the swimmer/canoeists. Data from all beach surveys carried out by the British SBS is fed into a computer database aboard the Landing Platform Docks (LPDs), HMS *Fearless* and HMS *Intrepid*. Once a particular beach has been chosen for the landing, the computer can print out hundreds of copies of up-to-date maps of the immediate area in a matter of hours.

Immediately prior to the invasion, the swimmers will neutralise any light enemy defences before setting explosive charges on underwater obstacles and then guiding the landing craft into the cleared corridors. Naval Gunfire Support Forward Observers (NGSFOs) with the team can also direct naval gunfire onto well defended or 'hardened' targets, such as artillery emplacements. Cliff assaults, to remove defensive positions overlooking the beaches, may be led by the experienced climbers of the Mountain and Arctic Warfare Cadre, acting as pathfinders for their commando comrades.

OPERATION URGENT FURY

America's 1983 invasion of Grenada was to be the first test of its modern rapid deployment forces. However, Operation URGENT FURY was more of a hasty invasion than a quick-reaction force mission. Its stated aim was the rescue of 1,000 US citizens, mostly students on the True Blue Medical Campus. Its major target became the 2,000 militia supporting an unpopular revolutionary government and 784 Cubans providing military and civil aid.

American planners by-passed the Joint Deployment Agency set up in 1979 to co-ordinate the rapid deployment forces, the job of planning and managing the operation being given instead to the Commander-in-Chief Atlantic (CINCLANT) planning group. A Marine Amphibious Group and a carrier force en route for the Mediterranean was re-routed to the waters off Grenada. The Marines were given the task of capturing the north of the island. The south was given to the Rangers. Their job was to seize Salines airfield, before handing over to the 82nd Airborne.

Just after dusk on 23 October, and a full 36-hours before the main assault, four air force combat control team members parachuted into the sea 30km off the south-west tip of Grenada. Their task was to place radio beacons close to the Salines airfield. The Air Force had insisted on using their air traffic control specialists as pathfinders. With them went a 12-man team of SEALs, highly trained in covert insertion. Within minutes, a quarter of the men were dead. One historian has claimed that the SEALs were using a low altitude parachute extraction system (LAPES), deploying the parachute early so that men, boats and equipment were pulled out of the aircraft at a mere 250ft above the sea. It is more likely that the boat and equipment were deployed by LAPES at 250ft, before the C-130 rose briefly to 1,000ft to allow the team a normal static-line descent. Water jumps are tricky. The parachutist is required to press the quick release early, hang from harness and drop into the water so that he is not enveloped and drowned by the canopy. A significant number of men have been killed during daylight jumps when they have misjudged their height above the waves. The Grenada pathfinders jumped at night, in 25-knot winds, above a wave-tossed sea.

Australian Commandos prepare to make a static-line parachute jump into the sea, as their equipment laden boat is pulled out of the back of the aircraft. The Grenada pathfinders jumped at night, in 25-knot winds, above a wave-tossed sea. (*Special Forces HQ; Australian DOD*)

The survivors continued their insertion onto the coastline but, after stopping to avoid collision with a fishing boat, their boat was swamped and the engine refused to restart. A back-up team attempted the insertion the next night and, only hours before the invasion, suffered the same fate. Some hours after the second SEAL attempt, a 35-man Ranger pathfinder group left an AC-130 Spectre high above Salines. It, too, ran into difficulties.

Consequently, despite the fact that the leading MC-130 Combat Talons in the first wave of aircraft were equipped with advanced navigation systems, two pathfinder teams were crippled, the element of surprise lost and H-hour delayed to accommodate the second attempt to place the beacons.

The first element of 'A' Company 1/75th Rangers jumped in daylight. The runway was still blocked and there was no sign of the pathfinders. When the balance of the first wave of 1/75th Rangers (06.45hrs) and lead elements of the 2/75th (07.07hrs) appeared over Salines, both were forced to parachute. Still under fire from the eastern end of the runway, the Rangers began to clear the terminal building and high ground to the west. By 10.00hrs the airport was in American hands and, in the early afternoon, the first of six battalions of the 82nd Airborne were air-landed aboard Starlifters. In mid-afternoon a last futile enemy counter-attack by three BTR-60 armoured personnel carriers (APCs) was smashed by the Rangers and a circling Spectre.

The Marines had better luck, quickly capturing Pearls airport and advancing inland. Resistance was slight and a second landing late on the first day at Grand Mal enveloped 80 per cent of the island. By the second day, the Army and Marines had linked up and evacuated most of the students. More importantly, the Marine's rapid advance had retrieved a series of disastrous special operations. SEAL Team Six successfully captured the Beausejour transmitting station but was forced to withdraw in the face of a counter-attack led by an APC. The SEALs also successfully rescued the Governor General, Sir Paul Scoon, but again found themselves defenceless against armoured vehicles. Two Cobra gunships that went to their rescue were shot down. The rescue party was eventually relieved by advancing American troops. Finally, a force composed of Rangers and Delta operatives, assigned to capture the Richmond Hill Prison, found themselves under anti-aircraft fire from Fort Fredrick. The assault was beaten off and one of the five Black Hawk helicopters was brought down. All these missions were launched in daylight after the invasion had begun. Some observers considered URGENT FURY to be nothing less than a military disaster.

OPERATION JUST CAUSE

The American operation to bring Panama's dictator, Manuel Noriega, to a Miami Federal District Court to answer charges of corruption and drug trafficking began just after midnight on 20 December 1989. Its aim was to seize Noriega and disarm his supporters, leaving the country in the hands of a democratically-elected government. The plan called for five reinforced quick-reaction force strikes to paralyse opposition. Task Force BAYONET would seize Noriega's HQ and secure American bases around Panama City, while to the west SEMPER FIDELIS would block reinforcements at the Bridge of the America's, while Task Force PACIFIC blocked eastern routes into the city. On Panama's Atlantic coastline, Task Force ATLANTIC would secure Gamboa

Prison, Maddam Dam and Sierra Tigre power plant, neutralise opposition and reinforce US bases around Colon. Meanwhile, Task Force RED would capture Omar-Torrijos International Airport at Tocumen.

Long before H-Hour at 01.00hrs, American Cable News Network (CNN) speculated on the movement of Starlifter transports leaving Fort Bragg. Nevertheless, 1,400 miles later and a few minutes after midnight on 20 October, nine special operations teams went into action. Some of the attacks were carried out by AC-130H Spectre gunships from the 16th Special Operations Squadron, striking at élite Panama Defence Forces (PDF) targets such as the Comandancia fortress in Panama City, which served as Noriega's military headquarters, and the Puma Battalion barracks located close to Torrijos International Airport.

Simultaneously, SOF ground forces began to close the net around Noriega. All were high-risk missions. At Paitilla Airfield near Panama City, four members of a SEAL demolitions team were killed in a fire-fight with armoured vehicles. Pushing on to their target, the team destroyed Noriega's Lear Jet, closing a potential escape route. Spearheading Task Force RED, three Ranger battalions made low-level jumps (150m) over Torrijos Airport and the military airfield at Rio Hato. At Torrijos Airport, the 1st Battalion and a company from the 3/75 Rangers ran into spirited resistance from the the PDF 2nd Rifle Company. Three counter-attacking Commando V150 armoured vehicles were destroyed; two by circling USAF AC-130H gunships and the third by the Rangers.

The 2/75 Rangers and two companies of the 3rd Battalion had the hardest task at Rio Hato. Their job was to seize the airfield and block the adjoining Pan American Highway before neutralising two military compounds, an NCO academy, and Noriega's beach house. Less than an hour after jumping, the 150-strong Bravo Company (2/75) began a one-hour trek through heavy jungle to reach the compounds. Expecting to be faced with more than 340 men from two well-armed PDF companies, the assault was supported by mortars, gunships and two F-117 Stealth fighters which dropped 2,000lb bombs to stun the defenders. It still took two hours to clear each compound and a further four hours operation to sweep neighbouring villages for military personnel.

With the runways cleared at Torrijos Airport, the first of the second assault wave arrived in the form of Task Force PACIFIC. It was left to lead elements of the 82nd Airborne, equipped with air-portable M551 Sheridan tanks, to secure the airport, although much of the fighting actually involved pursuing groups of PDF soldiers through the passenger lounges with small-arms and stun-grenades. The rest of the Task Force, arriving in 20 C-141B Starlifter transports, blocked access across the Pacora River to prevent PDF units reinforcing Panama City from the east. On the other side of the city, Task Force SEMPER FIDELIS, composed of US Marines and a light mechanised infantry company, closed access from the west by seizing the Bridge of the America's.

The largest area of operations was allotted to Task Force ATLANTIC.

Across the Panamanian Atlantic seaboard, elements of the 82nd Airborne and 7th Light Infantry captured a series of military and economic targets such as the Madden Dam and the Sierra Tigre power plant, before securing US bases in the Colon area. Within the Atlantic area of operations, the US counter-terrorist force, Delta, launched a successful assault on Gamboa prison. It is reputed that the mission's primary aim was to secure the release of an agent who had organised a CIA intelligence network in Panama.

The hub of Operation JUST CAUSE and the scene of the worst fighting was Panama City. The initial assault was led by the light infantry and tanks of Task Force BAYONET. Resistance at the Comandancia was quickly crushed and BAYONET reinforced American troops already in the Canal Zone for an attack on PDF units at Fort Amador. Other troops surrounded foreign embassies in the hunt for Noriega, while civilian hostages were released from the Marriott Hotel. An estimated 2,000 members of Noriega's Dignity Battalions, together with other PDF elements, responded by launching guerrilla strikes on US forces. The US Embassy and Southern Command Head-quarters were attacked and an assassination attempt was made on the newly-installed Panamanian Vice President. The military situation was further complicated by the presence of armed mobs looting the city, intense sniper fire and 7,000 refugees at Balboa Stadium. The initial assault force of 7,000 grew to 12,000 over the next week.

Operation JUST CAUSE finally ended when Manuel Noriega left the Vatican ambassador's residence and surrendered to American custody. Despite 'No Notice' training exercises such as GOLDEN PHEASANT, conducted in Honduras in 1988 and designed to streamline American operations in the aftermath of Grenada, JUST CAUSE was still dogged by problems. Ice on the wings of aircraft at Fort Bragg forced the 82nd Airborne to operate with only 50 per cent of its assets; 28 C-141s carrying 84 of the Division's heavy-drop platforms – including Sheridan tanks – were parachuted into a bog, where they remained for two days; and sticks of parachutists were dropped into tall elephant grass some way from the DZs and spent hours searching for the assembly RVs. More importantly, while the operation was associated with a low number of fatalities (23 Americans, 200 Panamanian combatants, and 202 civilian deaths), it proved to be a diplomatic disaster. Noriega succeeded in mounting a spirited legal defence, there has been no reduction in the volume of drugs entering the USA and stability in Panama appears to be dependent on a continuing American military presence.

MULTINATIONAL RAPID REACTION FORCES

The NATO Alliance deploys a multinational mobile emergency reserve of brigade strength: the Allied Command Europe (ACE) Mobile Force. In the wake of the Gulf War and the liberalisation of Eastern Europe, this has been joined by a 70,000-strong multinational strategic reserve or Rapid Reaction

Territorial defence and civil emergencies in the Canadian arctic call for many of the human resources and skills developed by the Special Service Force. (*Special Service Force HQ, Canadian DOD*)

Corps (RRC). Britain's contribution to this second European force will include a German-based armoured division, a UK-based strategic reserve force of one armoured brigade and Britain's airborne and commando brigades and one brigade of heliborne infantry (24th Airmobile Brigade). Further assets may include German and American ground forces and airmobile and attack helicopter units from Belgium, Germany and the Netherlands.

Military representatives from the United States, Great Britain, France, the Netherlands, Italy and Spain have also met to discuss the continuing security problem posed by Iraq and proposals to create a Rapid Reaction Force to be based in eastern Turkey. The 3,000–5,000 strong force will consist mostly of paratroops, supported by combat aircraft and transport and attack helicopters. Additional air-cover may be provided by American aircraft carriers in the eastern Mediterranean and F-15, F-111 and F-117 strike-aircraft based in Saudi Arabia. The multinational force would be empowered to prevent Iraqi forces from entering the demilitarised zone created to protect the Kurds or its aircraft from operating in Kurdistan beyond the 36th Parallel.

LET US DARE: AN INTERNAL QUICK-REACTION FORCE

The quick-reaction force concept is still evolving. What started as rescue operations in the Third World, by small forces of paratroops, has formed the vanguard of international police operations. Today, the 'quick-reaction' elements merely seize a bridge-head for the heavier conventional elements; but

what of tomorrow? One senior officer believes that future international operations may not be possible as the developing countries build up powerful armies
with large armoured and air-defence components. However, one variant of
the concept is likely to endure.

Faced with defending its large landmass and long broken Arctic border,
Canada has applied the rapid-deployment force concept to internal defence.
Canadian units outside those based in Europe are grouped into the Mobile
Command. The Command has a three-fold brief to support NATO, prepare
for international peace-keeping operations and maintain a territorial defence
force. Much of the responsibility for the latter role rests with the 'immediate
reaction' Special Service Force (SSF).

Based at Petawawa, Ontario, the SSF maintains a 3,000-strong highly
mobile, self-contained army. The 700-strong Canadian Airborne Regiment
and the 1st Battalion Royal Canadian Regiment provide the unit's infantry.
These are supported by the light armoured Royal Canadian Dragoons (direct
fire-support and reconnaissance); 2nd Regiment Royal Canadian Horse Artillery (105mm howitzers and 81mm mortars); 2 Combat Engineer Regiment; 2
Service Battalion (logistics and supply); 2 Field Ambulance; 2 Military Police
Platoon and the 427 Tactical Helicopter Squadron. Command and control
are provided by the 200 troops of the SSF HQ and Signals Squadron.

While continuing to train for conventional conflicts and UN intervention
operations, the force performs a wide range of internal duties. At home in the
Canadian wilderness, the soldiers of the SSF are tasked with providing aid
during major air disasters. The loss of an airliner over the hostile Arctic would
call for much of the human resources and skills developed by specialised
troops. Not surprisingly, some of the Canadian paras have chosen to join the
Search and Rescue organisation as skilled para-medics who jump into the
wilderness to recover the survivors of light-aircraft crashes. Other tasks include maintaining a presence in the Canadian north by mounting long-range
surveillance patrols and preparing to support US forces in defending continental North America. An important additional role is providing support for
security and counter-terrorist operations and armed intervention at federal
penitentiaries. The motto of the SSF is borne on a shoulder patch and is
appropriate for such a multi-purpose force. It bears a single word; the French
intentional verb 'OSONS' – Let Us Dare.

Postscript

The Gulf War

*We put special forces deep into enemy territory. They went out
on strategic reconnaissance for us and they let us know what was
going on out there. They were the eyes that were out there, and it
is very important that I do not forget those folks.*

General Norman Schwarzkopf's press briefing on
Operation DESERT STORM, Riyadh, 27 February 1991

Numbering around 5,000, a mere fraction of the total Allied force, US and
British Special Forces undertook a number of vital tasks intended to hasten the
end of the Gulf War. The participants included two components of UK Special
Forces Group – 22 SAS (reinforced by selected personnel from 21 and 23 SAS)
and the SBS; the 5th US Army Special Forces Group; US Delta Force and three
American Navy SEAL teams. These were supported by RAF special duties
flights and elements of the USAF's 20th, 8th, 16th and 21st Special Operations
Squadrons. General Schwarzkopf is reported to have requested two Ranger
battalions but was told by the Pentagon that these were being held in reserve;
only one Ranger company was sent to the Gulf.

Special operations behind-the-lines in both Kuwait and Iraq were supported
by a mixture of the latest technology and traditional guile. Satellites were used
for both navigation and covert communications. Teams inserting across the
long Saudi-Iraqi border by Light Strike Vehicle/'Pink Panther' (SAS) or
Chenowth Fast Attack Vehicle (US teams) had this equipment built into their
transport. Other teams, inserted into Kuwait and Southern Iraq by MH-53J
Pave Low helicopters or by HALO/HAHO parachute descents, carried their
SATNAV/SATCOM equipment in their rucksacks. One report claims that
two Special Forces bases were established in southern Iraq; these may have
been similar to the forward operating bases – such as Jalo Oasis – used by the

Second World War LRDG and SAS parties. Guile was used to penetrate Iraqi bases and towns. Parties disguised as Bedouins, equipped with Iraqi identification papers and speaking fluent Arabic, may even have infiltrated Baghdad. One story tells of an operator hawking vegetables and fruit to senior Iraqi officers before leaving a radio beacon to 'acquire' the camp for an Allied air-strike.

While more details will undoubtedly emerge in the future, it is worth noting that the Iraqis also used irregular forces in random operations. Pave Low helicopters (20th SOS) returning from attacking targets inside Iraq had two SA-7 SAMs fired at them from **inside** Saudi Arabia. Both helicopters dropped flares to decoy the heat-seeking missiles. It transpired that nomadic Iraqi Bedouins, who traditionally migrate back and forth across the Saudi border, had been equipped with these shoulder-fired anti-aircraft missiles.

TRAINING INDIGENOUS TROOPS

The British SAS are reported to have trained escaped Kuwaiti soldiers at their base in the Oman. These soldiers were later used as guides on operations inside Kuwait. Whether any personnel from the 5th Special Forces Group were deployed in training Kurdish and Iraqi rebels, remains an open question. Their later deployment to northern Iraq to assist Kurdish refugees after the failure of the Kurds' rebellion, utilised the Green Berets' 'nation building' skills. However, 5th SFG personnel were attached to every coalition Arab battalion that went into combat during DESERT STORM. Living and training with these coalition units since the beginning of Operation DESERT SHIELD, Green Beret instruction emphasised individual and small-unit skills, such as land navigation, surveillance and reconnaissance, close-air-support operations and nuclear, biological and chemical protection. During combat, they provided assistance with communications; calling for air-strikes and coordinating combat support requirements. After the War, the Green Berets were responsible for training the reconstructed Kuwaiti armed forces.

COMBAT RESCUE

There were no aircraft from the US Air Force's Air Rescue Service in the Gulf. The rescue of downed aircrew was left to the 21st SOS, operating from bases in Turkey and covering western and northern Iraq, and the 20th SOS in Saudi Arabia, responsible for Kuwait and southern Iraq. Of the 38 Allied aircraft shot down, 14 were American. Twenty-one US aircrew were taken prisoner. Four pilots were rescued while evading capture. Lieutenant Devon Jones, a Navy F-14 pilot, was rescued by a 20th SOS MH-53J helicopter. Enemy soldiers were closing-in on his position, using DF-equipment to locate his SAR beacon. The helicopter destroyed two Iraqi trucks before lifting the pilot to

The American Special Operations Squadrons played a major role in the success of US special operations in the Gulf. The MH-53J Pave Low helicopters took part in the hunt for the Iraqi Scuds, in combat-rescue operations and raids on Iraqi radar installations. (*US DOD*)

safety. The F-14's other crew member landed elsewhere and was captured. The second successful operation resulted in the rescue of an F-16 pilot shot down in southern Iraq, just 40 miles from the Saudi border. The pilot's rescuers were part of the 3rd Battalion, 160th Special Operations Aviation Regiment, which normally supports a US Ranger battalion. The two other pilots are reputed to have been rescued from inside Kuwait, one by the Kuwaiti Resistance and the other by Special Operations Forces.

The 21st SOS experienced severe operating difficulties as all rescue missions had to obtain diplomatic clearance. Formalities took even longer if US aircraft needed to enter Syrian airspace. The two-man crew of an F-15E were shot down in western Iraq while hunting Scuds in the H-3 area. The rescue mission was delayed for 72hrs, while permission was obtained for a MC-130 to over-fly Syrian territory in order to re-fuel the rescue helicopters. Meanwhile,

SF-teams in the area conducted an unsuccessful search for the airmen, who were nearly 10 miles from their last reported position. By the time the Pave Low helicopters arrived, they had been taken prisoner.

RECONNAISSANCE AND SURVEILLANCE

The invasion of Kuwait proved to be an intelligence disaster for the CIA, which failed to predict Iraqi intentions. In order to gather the much-needed intelligence, America was forced to switch the attentions of its satellite fleet to the Middle East. Notable amongst these were the Lacrosse satellites, whose high resolution (1 metre) radar images were used to programme the American cruise missiles. However, the intelligence chiefs in Washington also required HUMINT, either from agents, ex-patriots or Special Forces teams. Intelligence-gathering became the primary task of Allied Special Forces in the Gulf and was probably crucial in informing General Schwarzkopf of Iraqi reactions to his deception plan and in locating key units and command and control centres.

SPECIAL WEAPONS: SCUD BUSTING

The biggest special forces story was the hunt for the Iraqi Scuds targeting Israel. Warning of Scud launches came from the infra-red cameras mounted on US-surveillance satellites. The information was passed to Alice Springs, Australia and then to the North American Space Command Centre in Colorado. From there it was passed to Washington and thence to Saudi Arabia and finally Israel. In an attempt to keep Israel out of the war, the Americans short-circuited the information through ground stations in Saudi Arabia, increasing the warning time for the Patriot missile batteries in Israel from two to seven minutes.

Meanwhile, the Special Forces hunted the launchers for Allied F-15E and A-10 aircraft in the H-3/H-2 area of western Iraq. Pave Low helicopters from the 20th SOS flew approximately 60 missions to insert and extract SF-parties. In all, the ground teams are credited with locating more than 40 mobile launchers that had evaded overhead reconnaissance. Others were found by 20th SOS aircrew. In the last hours of the war, Iraq prepared to saturate the Patriot batteries in Israel by firing 29 Scuds, but these were located by ground teams and destroyed by A-10 Warthogs in a furious fusillade of Maverick missiles and cannon-fire.

RAIDS AND SABOTAGE

Towards the end of the Gulf War, some of the Special Forces ground teams switched from intelligence-gathering to sabotage and 'direct action' missions.

SEAL teams stormed nine Iraqi-held oil platforms off Kuwait, while a combined attack with British SBS teams on Faylakah Island contributed to the deception that Allied forces would launch a sea-borne invasion around Kuwait City. However, it is obvious that many significant targets that might have affected the Iraqi war effort were not the sort that could traditionally be destroyed by a few pounds of plastic explosive or a sniper's bullet. Two particular pieces of technology magnified the effect of the ground teams by harnessing their efforts to Allied air power.

Some of the most impressive 'smart weapons' are the laser-guided munitions but these require the target to be illuminated throughout the projectile's flight by a laser designator on the aircraft, on an accompanying aircraft, or from a concealed ground position. Of these, the ground position provides the best opportunity to direct the bomb through a door or window close to the target's nerve centre (*eg*; a computer-room in a command and control centre). Special Forces teams carried ground laser designators, several times the size of a large camera and mounted on a sturdy tripod. Their operation required the ground teams to infiltrate to within at least 1,500m of the target and remain concealed until the air-strike materialised.

Another device reputedly carried by SF-ground teams is designed to jam the enemy's signals traffic. Small, battery-operated, disposable transmitters such as the *Racal RJS3140* have a life of around one to two hours and transmit a powerful signal that jams communications over a selected frequency bandwidth. The device can be programmed to switch on at a specified time to coincide with a friendly ground- or air-assault.

AIR-SUPPORT: SPECIAL OPERATIONS SQUADRONS

The 'air commando' units of the US Air Force played an important role in supporting conventional air and ground operations. The F-117 stealth fighters and scores of other aircraft, which started the air-war by attacking Baghdad in the early hours of the 17 January, passed undetected through a 'radar-black' air corridor in the Iraqi defences. The corridor was opened by a helicopter strike at early warning and ground control intercept radar sites in western Iraq. The strike force consisted of four Apache helicopters from the US Army's 101st Aviation Brigade, guided by two Pave Low helicopters from the 20th SOS. The Pave Low pilots used their experience of long-range covert missions and the aircraft's sophisticated inertial and Doppler radar systems and GPS navigation equipment to guide the Apaches to their targets. The radar sites were engaged at ranges of 3–6km by Hellfire missiles, Hydra-70 2.75in rockets and cannon fire.

MC-130E Combat Talons of the 8th SOS helped open the ground war on the night of 6 February, when they dropped two BLU-82 Daisey Cutter bombs to blast a corridor through the Iraqi minefields and defences for the

US Marines. The 15,000lb bombs are so powerful that every Iraqi soldier within three miles was killed. An SAS patrol 110 miles away, reported on the radio that they had seen Kuwait hit by a nuclear weapon. The advancing Marines found only dead enemy soldiers in the first two defence lines. The 8th SOS dropped 11 BLU-82 bombs during the fighting. The raids were followed up by dropping propaganda leaflets offering the Iraqis safe passage through the lines.

In a war in which surprisingly few SF-personnel were killed, the 16th SOS flying AC-130H Spectre gunships in the ground-support role suffered the greatest number of casualties in a single incident. A Spectre gunship, the *Spirit 03*, was supporting efforts to retake Khafji on 31 January, when it was shot down. Its five officers and nine enlisted crew members were all killed.

Acronyms

ACRU	Air Crew Rescue Unit. American Second World War escape and evasion field unit.
AFSATCOM	Air Force Communications Satellites.
AFSOC	US Air Force Special Operations Command.
AK	*Armia Krajowa* – Polish Home Army or 'Resistance'.
APC	Armoured Personnel Carrier.
ARVN	Army of [South] Vietnam.
BATS	Balkan Air Terminal Service. American Air Force unit that specialised in building airstrips, often behind-the-lines, and rescuing downed aircrew.
CIA	Central Intelligence Agency. America's foreign intelligence service.
CIC	American Counter-Intelligence Corps.
CIDG	Civilian Irregular Defence Group programme. CIA/Special Forces trained irregular militia in South East Asia.
COIN	COunter-INsurgency.
COMINT	Communications Intelligence. A major component of ELINT.
CQB	Close Quarter Battle.
CRW	Counter Revolutionary Warfare.
DEA	US Drug Enforcement Agency.
DF	Direction-Finding equipment/technology.
DIA	American Defence Intelligence Agency – responsible for collecting and processing military intelligence.
DI5	Defence Intelligence-5. The British Ministry of Defence's Defence Intelligence designation for the Security Service (formally Military Intelligence-5).

DI6	Defence Intelligence-6. Defence Intelligence designation for Britain's foreign intelligence service or Secret Intelligence Service (formally Military Intelligence-6).
DOSAFF	Soviet Union's All-Union Voluntary Society for Assistance to the Army, Air Force and Navy.
DZ	Dropping Zone. Area chosen to land parachutists.
ELINT	Electronic Intelligence. Gathered across the entire electromagnetic spectrum.
FAC	Forward Air Controller – ground observer or pilot acquiring targets for attack aircraft (see NGSFO).
FBI	Federal Bureau of Investigation.
FIBUA	Fighting in Built-Up Areas.
FINCO	Field Intelligence NCO (British Intelligence Corps).
FULRO	*Front Unifié de Libération des Races Opprimées* – the Front for the Liberation of the Oppressed Races. Montagnard political organisation.
GIGN	*Groupment D'Intervention de la Gendarmerie Nationale* – the French national HRU.
GPS	Global Positioning System – satellite navigation.
GRU	*Glavnoye Razvedyvatelnoye Upravleniye*. Main Intelligence Directorate of the Soviet General Staff or Soviet military intelligence.
GSG-9	*Grenzschutzgruppe*-9 – the German national HRU.
GTO	*Gotov k trude i oborony*. Soviet organisation that prepares recruits for military service.
HAHO	High Altitude High Opening – a variant of military parachuting.
HALO	High Altitude Low Opening – military free-fall parachuting.
HES	Hamlet Evaluation System – CIA estimate of number of Vietnamese villages held by the Communists.
HRU	Hostage Rescue Unit.
HUMINT	Human Intelligence. Intelligence obtained from a human source, usually an agent.
IMINT	Imagery Intelligence. Pictures or film, usually visible or infrared, obtained from a satellite or reconnaissance aircraft.
INSCOM	US Army Intelligence and Security Command.
ISA	Intelligence Support Activity. American commando unit which provides support for special operations.
ISLD	Inter-Services Liaison Department. The codename used by the British SIS in the Far East during World War Two.
IWESS	Infantry Weapons Effect Simulation System. Laser-based battle simulation training.
JSOC	US Joint Special Operations Command.
KGB	*Komitet Gosudarstvennoi Bezopasnosti*. The Soviet internal and foreign intelligence service or Committee for State Security.

KMT	*Kuomintang* (Chinese Nationalist Army).
KWPLD	Korean Worker's Party Liaison Department – North Korean foreign intelligence service.
LALO	Low Altitude Low Opening – low-level static-line parachuting.
LAPES	Low Altitude Parachute Extraction System.
LLDB	*Luc Luong Dac Biet*. South Vietnamese (ARVN) Special Forces.
LOC	Lines-of-Communication.
LRDG	Long-Range Desert Group. A Second World War, British commando unit.
LRRP	Long-Range Reconnaissance Patrol. A patrol that gathers intelligence from behind the enemy's lines.
LRS	Long-Range Surveillance. General term for units that maintain observation on enemy positions from static observation posts.
LRSC	Long-Range Surveillance Company – US Military Intelligence Brigades.
LRSD	Long-Range Surveillance Detachments – assigned to US armoured battalions.
LSV	Light Strike Vehicle.
LUP	Lying Up Position.
LZ	Helicopter or glider Landing Zone.
MACV	Military Assistance Command Vietnam.
MACVSOG	Military Assistance Command Vietnam Studies and Observations Group. American clandestine organisation responsible for special operations, predominantly in Cambodia, Laos and North Vietnam. See STDAT.
MIA	Personnel posted 'Missing in Action'.
MIKE	Multipurpose Reaction Forces or Mobile Strike Forces (Mike Forces). See MSFC.
MILES	Multiple Integrated Laser Engagement System. Laser-based battle simulation training.
MI6	See SIS and DI6.
MI9	Military Intelligence-9. Second World War British organisation responsible for escape and evasion.
ML	Mountain Leader – graduates of the Royal Marine's ML-1 and ML-2 courses.
MPABA	Malayan People's Anti-British Army.
MSFC	Mobile Strike Force Command (Vietnam).
MVD	*Ministerstvo Vnutrennikh Del*. Soviet Ministry of Internal Affairs.
NAVSOC	US Navy Special Warfare Command.
NEST	US Energy Department's Nuclear Emergency Search Team.
NGSFO	Naval Gunfire Support Forward Observers (see FACS).
NORFORCE	North West Mobile Force (Australian surveillance unit).

NSA	National Security Agency (US signals intelligence).
NVA	North Vietnamese Army.
NZSAS	New Zealand SAS.
OGPU	*Obyedinennoy Gosudarstvennoye Politicheskoye Upravleniye*. Russia's Unified State Political Directorate, a forerunner of the KGB.
OP	Observation Post. A concealed position used for covert observation of enemy forces or lines-of-communication.
OSS	Office of Strategic Services. America's first spy agency which combined paramilitary activities and intelligence gathering.
PFLP	Popular Front for the Liberation of Palestine.
PFLP-GC	Popular Front for the Liberation of Palestine – General Command.
PLO	Palestine Liberation Organisation.
PSB	Public Security Bureau – North Korean Security organisation.
PSYOPS	Psychological Operations.
REP	*Régiment Etranger de Parachutistes*. French Foreign Legion paratroops (2nd REP).
ROK	Republic of Korea.
RV	Rendezvous – pre-arranged meeting or way-point.
SAF	Special Action Forces (see SOF), also Sultan's Armed Forces (Oman).
SALUTE	Size, Activity, Location, Unit, Time and Equipment (intelligence indicators).
SAM	Surface-to-Air Missile.
SAR	Search And Rescue.
SAS	Special Air Service.
SASR	Australian SAS Regiment.
SATCOM	Satellite Communications.
SATNAV	Satellite Navigation.
SBS	Royal Marine's Special Boat Service (formally Squadron).
SD	Special Duties (usually airforce or intelligence support personnel [SD-Squadrons]).
SDECE	*Service de Documentation Extérieure et de Contre-Espionnage*. The French foreign intelligence service.
SEALs	Sea, Air, Land. US Navy's commandos.
SEP	Surrendered Enemy Personnel (used as counter-guerrillas).
SERE	Survival, Evasion, Resistance to interrogation and Escape.
SFAS	Special Forces Assessment and Selection – 'Green Beret' pre-selection course.
SIGINT	Signals Intelligence. A major component of ELINT.
SIS	British Secret Intelligence Service (see DI6).
SLAM	Search-Locate-Annihilate-Mission Companies – used by US Special Forces in Vietnam.
SLR	Self-Loading Rifle.

SOCOM	US Army's 1st Special Operations Command.
SOE	Special Operations Executive. A British organisation established during the Second World War to conduct paramilitary operations behind the lines [also Force 136 and Force 139].
SOF	Special Operations Forces.
SOG	See MACVSOG
SOLIC	Special Operations and Low Intensity Conflict.
SOS	US Special Operations Squadrons (see SD).
SSF	Canadian Special Service Force.
STABO	Stability Operations Extraction System [rig].
STAR	Surface-to-Air Recovery system.
STDAT	Strategic Technical Directorate Assistance Team. Activated in 1972 to replace MACVSOG.
SWAT	Special Weapons and Tactics units – American police HRUs.
SWCS	John F. Kennedy Special Warfare Center and School.
TES	Tactical Engagement Simulation. Laser-based battle simulation training.
USASOC	US Army Special Operations Command.
USSOCOM	United States Special Operations Command. Umbrella organisation for all US special warfare units
VC	Viet-Cong guerillas.
VLA	Very Light Aircraft.

Bibliography

Adams, James, *Secret Armies: The Full Story of SAS; Delta Force & Spetsnatz*, Century Hutchinson, London, 1987. ISBN 0–09–173452–5.

Adkin, Mark, *Urgent Fury: The Battle for Grenada*, Leo Cooper, London, 1989. ISBN 0–85052–0231.

American Department of Defence, *Soviet Military Power*, U.S. Government Printing Office, 1989.

Arnold, James R., *Rangers: The Illustrated History of the Vietnam War*, Bantam Books, New York & London, 1988. ISBN 0–553–34509–5.

Bermudez, Joseph S., Jr, *North Korean Special Forces*, Jane's Publishing Company, Coulsdon, Surrey, 1988. ISBN 0–7106–0528–5.

Bosiljevac, T.L., *SEALS: UDT/SEAL Operations in Vietnam*, Green Hill Books, Lionel Levanthal Ltd, United Kingdom, 1990. ISBN 1–85367–061–8.

Bradford R., and Dillon M., *Rogue Warrior of the SAS*, Arrow Books, London, 1989. ISBN 0–09–960450–7.

Bridson, Rory, *The Making of a Para*, Guild Publishing, Great Britain, 1989. ISBN 0–283–99918–7.

Brown, Ashley, *The Green Berets US Special Forces*, Orbis Publishing, London, 1986. ISBN 1–85155–006–2.

Burgess Maj. William H., (editor), *Inside Spetsnatz: Soviet Special Operations, A Critical Analysis*, Presidio Press, USA, 1990. ISBN 0–89141–339–1.

Burnett, F.R., Tovar, Hugh, B., and Shultz, Richard, H., *Special Operations in US Strategy*, National Defence University and National Strategy Information Center, Inc. Library of Congress catalog card no 84–601134.

Burrows, William E., *Deep Black*, Bantam Press, Great Britain, 1989. ISBN 0–593–01342–5.

Cawthorne, Nigel, *The Bamboo Cage*, Leo Cooper and Pen & Sword, London, 1991. ISBN 0–85052–148–3.

Clarke, Douglas L., *The Missing Man: Politics and the MIA*, National Defence University Press, 1979. US Government Printing Office, Washington DC. Stock No 008–020–00774–9.

Clutterbuck, Richard, *Terrorism & Guerilla Warfare*, Routledge, London & New York, 1990. ISBN 0–415–02440–4.

Colby, William with McCargar, James, *Lost Victory*, Contemporary Books, Chicago and New York, 1989. ISBN 0–8092–4509–4

Collins, John, M., *Green Berets, SEALS & Spetsnaz*, Pergamon-Brassey's, London & New York, 1987. ISBN 0–08–035747–4.

Cross, J.P., *Jungle Warfare: Experiences and Encounters*, Arms & Armour, Great Britain. ISBN 0–85368–913-X.

Cruickshank, Charles, *Special Operations Executive in the Far East*, Oxford University Press, UK, 1983. ISBN 0–19–285168–3

Cuneo, John R., *Robert Rogers of the Rangers*, Richardson & Steirman, New York, 1987. ISBN 0–931933–46–3.

Dear, Ian, *Ten Commando 1942–1945*, Grafton Books, London, 1989. ISBN 0–586–20432–6.

Dillon, Martin, *The Dirty War*, Hutchinson, London, 1988. ISBN 0–09–174308–7.

Dillon, Richard, *North American Indian Wars*, Arms and Armour Press, London, 1983. ISBN 0–85368–590–8.

England, James W., *Long-Range Patrol Operations: Reconnaissance, Combat and Special Operations*, Paladin Press, USA, 1987.

Eshel, Lt. Col. David, *Elite Fighting Units*, Arco Publishing Inc, New York, 1984. ISBN 0–668–06206–1.

Eshel, Lt. Col. David, *The US Rapid Deployment Forces*, Arco Publishing Inc, New York, 1985. ISBN 0–668–06211–8.

Farran, Roy, *Winged Dagger*, Grafton Books, London, 1988. ISBN 0–586–20085–1.

Fiennes, Ranulph, *Living Dangerously*, Macmillan, London, 1987. ISBN 0–333–44417–5.

Fishman, Jack, *And the Walls Came Tumbling Down*, Souvenir Press Ltd, London, 1982. ISBN 0–285–625195.

Foley, Charles, *Commando Extraordinary*, Grafton Books, London, 1987. ISBN 0–586–20261–7.

Follett, Ken, *On Wings of Eagles*, Corgi Books, London, 1984. ISBN 0–552–12610–1.

Foot, M.R.D., *SOE: The Special Operations Executive 1940–46*, British Broadcasting Corporation, London, 1984. ISBN 0–563–20193–2.

Foot, M.R.D., and Langley, J.M., *MI9: Escape and Evasion*, The Bodley Head, Great Britain, 1979.

Foster, Nigel, *The Making of a Royal Marine Commando*, Guild Publishing, London, 1988.

Garrett, David, *The Raiders*, David & Charles, Great Britain, 1980. ISBN 0–7153–9203–4.

Geraghty, Tony, *The Bullet Catchers*, Grafton Books, London, 1988. ISBN 0–58620622–1.

Geraghty, Tony, *Who Dares Wins: The Story of the SAS 1950–1982*, Fontana Paperbacks, London, 1980. ISBN 0–00–636678–3.

Gibson, Tom, *The Maori Wars*, Leo Cooper, London & Auckland, 1974.

Godson, Roy, *Intelligence Requirements for the 1980's: Covert Action*, National Strategy Information Center, USA, 1981. ISBN 0–87855–830–6.

Gudgeon, Thomas, *Reminiscences of the War in New Zealand*, Sampson Low, Marsten Searle & Rivington, London, 1879.

Harrison, Derrick, *These Men Are Dangerous*, Grafton Books, London, 1990. ISBN 0–586–207765–7.

Hanle, J. Donald, *Terrorism: The Newest Face of Warfare*, Pergamon-Brassey's, USA, 1989.

Hastings, Max, *Das Reich*, Michael Joseph Ltd, London, 1981.

Hersh, Seymour M., *Chemical and Biological Warfare: America's Hidden Arsenal*, Macgibbon & Kee, London, 1969.

Horner, D.M., *SAS Phantoms of the Jungle: A History of the Australian Special Air Service*, Allen & Unwin, Sydney & London, 1989. ISBN 0–04–520006.

Jungk, Robert, *Heller als Tausend Sonnen*, Bern, 1956.

Knobel, Kuno, *Victor Charlie: The Face of War in Vietnam*, Pall Mall Press, London, 1967.

Ladd, James A., *SBS: The Invisible Raiders*, Fontana Paperbacks, London, 1984. ISBN 0–00–636640–6.

Ladd, James A., *Commandos and Rangers of World War II*, David & Charles, Great Britain, 1989. ISBN 0–7153–9449–5.

Ladd, James A., and Melton, Keith, *Clandestine Warfare: Weapons and Equipment of the SOE and OSS*, Guild Publishing, London, 1988.

Livingstone, Neil C., *The Cult of Counterterrorism*, Lexington Books, Massachusetts, USA, 1990. ISBN 0–669–21407–8.

MacDonald, Peter, *Soldiers of Fortune: The 20th Century Mercenary*, Multimedia Publications Ltd, United Kingdom, 1986. ISBN 1–85171–036–1.

Mackness, Robin, *Oradour: Massacre & Aftermath*, Bloomsbury Publishing Ltd, London, 1988. ISBN 0–7475–0082–7.

Merrick, K.A., *Flights of the Forgotten: Special Duties Operations in World War Two*, Arms & Armour Press, London, 1989. ISBN 0–85409–029–1.

Morris, Eric and Hoe, Alan, *Terrorism: Threat and Response*, Macmillan Press, London, 1987. ISBN 0–333–39887–4.

Neave, Airey, *Saturday at MI9*, Grafton Books, London, 1989. ISBN 0–586–20341–9.

O'Brian, Terence, *Out of the Blue*, Arrow Books Ltd, London, 1988. ISBN 0–09–959210-X.

O'Brian, Terence, *The Moonlight War: The Story of Clandestine Operations in South-East Asia, 1944–5*, William Collins Sons & Co. London, 1987. ISBN 0–00–217803–6.

Office of Air Force History, *Search and Rescue in Southeast Asia*, Office of Air Force History, Washington DC, 1980.

Osborne, Milton, *Region of Revolt*, Pelican Books, 1971.

Otway, T.B.H., Lt. Col., DSO., *Airborne Forces*, Imperial War Museum, Department of Printed Books, London, 1990. ISBN 0–901627–57–7.

Owen, David Lloyd, *The Desert My Dwelling Place*, Arms & Armour Press, London, 1957. ISBN 0–85368–754–4.

Payne, Ronald, *Mossad: Israel's Most Secret Service*, Bantam Press, London, 1990.

Payne, Samuel, B., Jr, *The Conduct of War: An Introduction to Modern Warfare*, Basil Blackwell, Oxford, 1989. ISBN 0–631–15532–5.

Petersen, Barry with Cribbin, John, *Tiger Men: An Australian Soldier's Secret War in Vietnam*, Sidgwick & Jackson Ltd, Great Britain, 1988. ISBN 0–283–99816–4.

Ranelagh, John, *The Agency: The Rise and Decline of the CIA*, Weidenfeld & Nicolson Ltd, London, 1986. ISBN 0–340–41230–5.

'Remy', *The Gates Burst Open*, Arco Publishers Ltd, London, 1955.

Rezac, Tomas & Tsurkan, Valentin, *Wanted*, Progress Publishers, Moscow, 1988. ISBN 5–01–000471–2.

Rice, Edward, *Wars of the Third Kind*, University of California Press, USA, 1988. ISBN 0–520–06236–1.

Rickson, P.A., & Holliday, A., *Mission Accomplished*, William Kimber, London, 1974. ISBN 07183–01439–9.

Robbins, Christopher, *Air America*, Corgi Books, London, 1979. ISBN 0–552–12821-X.

Robbins, Christopher, *The Ravens: Pilots of the Secret War of Laos*, Corgi Books, London, 1987. ISBN 0–552–12823–6.

Sayer, Ian & Botting, Douglas, *America's Secret Army: The Untold Story of the Counter-Intelligence Corp*, Fontana, London, 1990. ISBN 0–00–636986–3.

Scott, Harriet Fast, & Scott, William, F., *The Armed Forces of the USSR*, Arms & Armour Press, 1984.

Shears, Richard, & Gidley, Isobelle, *The Rainbow Warrior Affair*, Unwin Paperbacks, London, Sydney, Boston, 1986. ISBN 0–04–900041–1.

Sheenan, Neil, *A Bright Shining Lie*, Pan Books, London, 1990. ISBN 0–224–02648–8.

Simpkin, Richard, *Race to the Swift*, Brassey's Defence Publishers, London, 1985. ISBN 0–08–031170–9.

Sterling, Claire, *The Terror Network: The Secret War of International Terrorism*, Weidenfeld & Nicolson, London, 1981.

Strawson, John, *A History of the SAS Regiment*, Grafton Books, London, 1986. ISBN 0–586–06715–9.

Thomas, Gordon, *Journey into Madness*, Corgi, London, 1989. ISBN 0–552–13007–9.

Thompson, Julian, *Ready for Anything: The Parachute Regiment at War 1940–1982*, Weidenfeld & Nicholson, Great Britain, 1989. ISBN 0–297–79620–8.

Volkman, E., & Baggett, B., *Secret Intelligence*, W.H. Allen & Co, London, 1989. ISBN 0–352–32528–3.

Warner, Philip, *Phantom*, William Kimber, London, 1982. ISBN 0–7183–0458–6.

Warner, Philip, *The SAS: The Official History*, Sphere Books Ltd, London, 1983. ISBN 0–7221–8910–9.

Welham, Michael, *Combat Frogman*, Patrick Stephens Ltd, London, 1989. ISBN 1–85260–217–1.

Williams, Wright, C., *The Marxists*, Pelican Books, London, 1962.

Woodward, Bob, *Veil: The Secret Wars of the CIA*, Headline Book Publishing PLC, Great Britain, 1988. ISBN 0–7472–31680.

Wright, Peter, *Spycatcher*, Heinemann, Australia, 1987.

FIELD MANUALS

AF Regulation 64–4 Volume 1 *Search and Rescue Survival Training*, Department of the Air Force.

FM 7–93, *Long Range Surveillance Unit Operations*, Department of the Army.

ST 31–91B, *US Army Special Forces Medical Handbook*, United States Army Institute for Military Assistance, Department of the Army.

FM 31–25, *Special Forces Waterborne Operations*, Department of the Army.

FM 31–20, *Special Forces Operational Techniques*, Department of the Army.

N 216, *Route Finding and Navigation for Scientific Expeditions*, Murdoch University, Western Australia.

Combat Survival: SAS Escape & Evasion Course Notes, Paladin Press Boulder, Colorado, USA.

JOURNALS

Adams, Tom, 'Special Operations Forces of the Soviet Union', *Military Intelligence*, Oct–Dec, 1982.

Arbuckle, Tammy & Fitzsimons, Bernard, 'Peru's Drug War', *International Defence Review*. April 1990.

Armstrong, Maj. Richard, 'Countering the Third Dimension', *Military Intelligence*, Jan-Mar, 1984.

Berkowitz, Marc, J., 'A Spetsnaz Threat to Rail M-X', *Armed Forces Journal International*, September 1989.

Burkhalter, Vice Admiral E.A., 'The Soviet Union's Subversive War Against America', *American Intelligence Journal*, September 1985.

Carnes, Commander Colland, F., 'Soviet Intelligence Support to International Terrorism', *American Intelligence Journal*, January 1986.

Derry, Archie, 'Emergency in Malaya: the Psychological Dimensions', *National Defence College*.

Donnelly, Chris, 'Operations in the Enemy Rear', *International Defence Review*, January 1980.

Dorr, Bob, 'Operation Just Cause', *Combat & Survival*, June 1990.

Edwards, Steven, 'The Last Detail', *Soldier of Fortune*, June 1990.

Eggers, Major General Thomas E., 'Today's Air Commandos: Air Force Special Operations Command', *Military Review*, June 1991.

Eshel, Tamir, 'SOF are Back in Action: Revitalization of US Special Operations', *Defence Update International*, January 1988.

Frost, Roger, 'Simulating Shoot-outs: the Growth of Tactical Engagement Simulation', *International Defence Review*, April 1989.

Housman, Damian, 'Special Operators Require Special Equipment', *Armed Forces Journal International*, July 1991.

Kutter, Col. Wolf D., 'Deep Behind Enemy Lines', *Military Review*, June 1990.

Livingstone, Neil & Halevy, David, 'Operation Betrayal: Delta/SEAL Rescue Force Poised to Snatch American Hostages in the Lebanon', *Soldier of Fortune*, October 1989.

Locher, James, R. III, Assistant Secretary of Defence for Special Operations and Low Intensity Conflict, 'Intelligence Support to Special Operations and Low Intensity Conflicts', *American Intelligence Journal*, Winter 1989–90.

Margelletti, Andrea, 'US Special Warfare Forces: Structure and Mission', *Military Technology*, No 10, Vol XIII, 1989.

Marks, Tom, 'Thailand's Terror Years', *Soldier of Fortune*, August 1990.

Metz, Steven, 'US Strategy and the Changing Low Intensity Conflict Threat', *Military Review*, June 1991.

Miller, Barry, 'GPS Proves its Worth in Operation Desert Storm', *Armed Forces Journal International*, April 1991.

Myagkov, Aleksei, 'The Soviet Union's Special Forces', *Soviet Analyst*, Jan 1980.

Parker, Geoffrey, 'A Surgeon in Guerilla Warfare', *Journal of the Royal Army Medical Corps*, September 1946.

Royal United Services Institute for Defence Studies, 'The Long Road to the Rapid Reaction Corps', *RUSI Newsbrief*, June 1991.

Schoen, Glenn & Derleth, William, 'The KGB Fields New Hostage Rescue Unit', *Armed Forces Journal International*, October 1989.

Schemmer, Benjamin, F., 'USAF MH-53J Pave Lows Led Army Apaches Knocking Out Iraqi Radars to Open Air War', *Armed Forces Journal International*, July 1991.

Schemmer, Benjamin, F., 'Special Ops Teams Found 29 Scuds Ready to Barrage Israel 24 hours before Ceasefire', *Armed Forces Journal International*, July 1991.

Schemmer, Benjamin, F., '8th Special Ops Squadron Nicknamed 8th bomb Squadron after BLU-82 missions', *Armed Forces Journal International*, July 1991.

Schemmer, Benjamin, F., 'No USAF Combat Rescue Aircraft in Gulf; it took 72 hours to Launch One Rescue', *Armed Forces Journal International*, July 1991.

Schemmer, Benjamin, F., 'Alleged US-UK Special Ops Heist of Iraqi Missiles before Desert Storm "Didn't Happen"', *Armed Forces Journal International*, July 1991.

Starr, Barbara, Boatman, John, Wilson, J.R., Bodansky, Yossef, Jackson, Heitz James, 'Low Intensity Conflict: Planning for a New Kind of War', *Jane's Defence Weekly*, May 1990.

Steadman, Nick, 'Teaching marksmanship: not just a hit or miss affair', *International Defence Review*, April 1989.

Stiner, General Carl W., 'The Strategic Employment of Special Operations Command', *Military Review*, June 1991.

Suvorov, Viktor, '*Spetsnaz:* the Soviet Union's Special Forces', *International Defence Review*, September 1983.

Willis, Guy, 'Low-level Parachutes', *International Defence Review*, April 1989.

TELEVISION DOCUMENTARIES

'Behind the Lines: The Royal Marine's Mountain and Arctic Warfare Cadre', BBC.
'America's Secret War', Panorama, BBC.
'Great Journeys: The Ho Chi Minh Trail', BBC.
'The Battle for the Golden Road', Guy Baskin, Cromwell Royce, Perth, Australia.

Index

ACE (Allied Command Europe) Mobile
    Force 260
Achille Lauro hijacking 239
Achnacarry Commando Training School 20
Acquadetto Pugliese raid (1941) 203
ACRU (Air Crew Rescue Units) (US) 175
Aden 129, 226
Adwan, Kemal 246
Afghanistan 13–14, 106, 216–17, 224
AFSATCOM satellite 49
AFSOC (Air Force Special Operations
    Command) 11
aid 145, 164, 204
Air America, Inc 97–8, 144, 146, 188, 228
Air Asia Co 97
173rd Airborne Brigade (US) 140, 155
82nd Airborne Division (US) *ill* 253, 15, 34, 254,
    256, 259–60
101st Airborne Division (US) 155
1st Air Cavalry (US) 140
24th Airmobile Brigade (UK) 261
Air Rescue Service (USAF) 188, 264
Air Reserve (US) 99
AJUF (Anti-Japanese Union and Forces) 116
AK (*Armia Krajowa*) (Poland) 112, 227
Alamo Scouts (US) 6, 182–13
Albania 112–13, 118
Alexandria 211
Algeria 248
Alison, J 120
Alten Fjord (Norway) 212
Aman (Israeli Intelligence) 7, 209–10, 239,
    245–7
Amiens prison, raid on *ill* 180, 178–9
Amin, Hafizullah 216–17
Amin, Idi 192–3

Amundsen, Dr Kirsten *quoted* 93, 213–14
Andropov, Yuri 228
Angola 106, 252
An Hoi, death of 124
Annamite Mountains 133
Anti-Fascist Organisation (Burma) 114
Apache Force (Vietnam War) 140
Ap Loy (Vietnam) 186
Arab Revolt (WW I) 4
ARC-LIGHT strikes 162, 164, 166
Arctic warfare *ill* 75, *ill* 261
    training *ill* 26, *ill* 77, 75–7
Ardennes offensive 217–18
Argentina 48
Argentina *see* Falklands War
Army Air Corps (UK) 125
14th Army (UK) 114
Arnhem 182
ARVN (Army of the Republic of Vietnam) 143,
    187, 189
    see also LLDB
Ascension Island 202, 251
assassination 3, 12, 15, 120, 143, 210, 214,
    217–18, 223, 228, 230–1, 246
assault commandos *ill* 6, 1–2
281st Assault Helicopter Company 158
Aung San 114
Australia *ill* 169, 6, 48, 107, 133, 149
    Army School of Health 30
    Commandos *ill* 6, *ill* 257
    RSUs (Regional Surveillance Units) 168–9
    see also SAS Regiment (Australia)
Austria 5
Austria-Hungary 211
160th Aviation Battalion (US) 98
101st Aviation Brigade (US Army) 267

Aviation Tech Services   98
AWADS (Adverse Weather Aerial Delivery
   System)   99
Ayn al-Sabah (Syria)   86

'Baader Meinhof' group   192–3
BAAG (British Army Air Group)   177
Baghdad   264, 267
Bagnold, Major Ralph   70
Bagram (Afghanistan)   216
Bahnar tribesmen   138, 143
Bakau (Gambia)   195
Balashika, Colonel   217
Balingcari   182
Banjul (Gambia)   194–5
Bank, Colonel Aaron   9
Ban Karai Pass (Vietnam)   166
Ban Me Thuot (Vietnam)   *map* 132, 138, 141,
   143–4, 158
Bao Dai, Emperor of Vietnam   145
Bari   112, 203
'Barrel Roll' strikes   146
Barrionuevo, Osman Morote   245
Baskin, Guy   29
Basmachi rebels   12
BATS (Balkan Air Terminal Service)   *ill* 176,
   175–6
Battambang (Thailand)   149
The Battle for the Golden Road (film)   29
BCRA (*Bureau central de Renseignements et de
   l'Action*)   109
Beckwith, Colonel C   190–1, 235
Bedouins   264
BEF (British Expeditionary Force)   173–5
Beirut   240, 245
Bekaa Valley (Lebanon)   242
Belgium   5, 109, 173, 206, 226, 250–1, 252, 261
   see also Para-Commando Regiment
Ben Nevis   25
Berkowitz, Marc   *quoted* 211
Berling, General   112
Biafra   226
Biological weapons   209
Bir el Aabed (Lebanon)   240
Blackburn, General Donald D   184
'Black September'   246
Blandon, J   243
Bloch, Mrs Dora   193
Bolivia   11, 243
Bolzano (Italy)   212
Border Scouts (Borneo)   127
Borneo   46, 78–9, 121
   Borneo Chinese   125
   Indonesian war   *ill* 126, *ill* 229, 42–3, 64, 107,
      124–8, 125, 133, 149, 155, 223–4, 228
Bougainville   217
Bradley, General   *quoted* 218
'Brandenburg' Special Unit   214–15
Brauman (Gestapo officer)   179
Brazil   212

Brenner, SS Brigadefuhrer   227
'Briggs Plan'   121–2
'Bright Light' combat rescue missions   144, 155,
   160
Brindisi   203
Britain   *see* Royal Navy; RAF; SAS (UK); UK; and
   individual units
Britel (Lebanon)   240
Brittany   199
Brunei   125
Bruneval (France), raid on   *ill* 205, 179, 204
Buckley, William   240
Bulgaria   113, 228
Burma   9, 80, 97, 113–14, 114, 118–19, 147,
   228
Bush and Forest Rangers (New Zealand)   5
Business Security International (US)   242

Cabanatuan (Philippines)   182–3
CAG (Civil Affairs Group) (US)   101
Calvert, 'Mad Mike'   121–2
Cambodia   *map* 132, 106, 133, 141, 158
   native forces   107, 145, 149
   and Vietnam War   148–9, 157, 159–60, 163
Cameron (RN)   212
Canada   58, 224, 262
canoeing   *ill* 90, 26–7, 89
Carli cartel   243
Carter, President   98
Casey, William Joseph   9
Castro, Fidel   228, 243
CAT (Chinese Air Transport)   97
8th Cavalry (US)   156
Cawthorne, Nigel   *quoted* 165
'Cedar Walk' programme   149
Central America   14
Central and South America   107
Central Intelligence Agency   *see* CIA
Ceylon   94, 116
Chalaux   199
Chamonix   76
Champas (Vietnam)   138
Cham tribesmen   159
Chao Fah   148
Chau Dara   143
Chenowth Fast Attack Vehicle (US)   263
Chen Ping   *see* Man Wa
Chiang Kai-shek   97, 118
Chile   202
China   107, 118, 147, 150–1
   Nationalists (KMT)   97, 118–19, 144, 147
   and Vietnam War   133, 144, 164–5
   in World War II   95, 117
   see also Borneo Chinese; Malayan Chinese;
      Nung tribesmen
Chinese Air Transport   *see* CAT
Ching Hee Park, President   224
Chin Peng   119
Chin tribesmen   114

Choctaw Indians 4
Choi Un Hui 225
Christian, Ian 120
Chun Doo-Hwan, President 225
Churchill, Winston 116, 182, 211
CIA (Central Intelligence Agency) 7–9, 99
  Covert Action Branch 99, 136, 223
  Provincial Reconnaissance Teams 247
  in Burma 97
  in China 118–19
  in Eastern Europe 118
  and Gulf War 265
  in Iran 190
  in Japan 229–30
  and Kennedy assassination 228
  in Laos 98, 145–8, 223
  in Lebanon 240, 245–6
  in Panama 260
  in Tibet 97–8
  and Vietnam War 98, 133–6, 138, 143–4,
    165–6, 184
  and drugs 243
  see also Air America, Inc
CIC (Counter-Intelligence Corps) (US) 178
CIDG (Civilian Irregular Defence Group
  Programme) *see under* Vietnam War
CINCLANT (Commander-in-Chief
  Atlantic) 256
Civil Air Transport company 97
Clairvaux prison (1978) 238
Clandestine Communist Organisation 125
Claret patrols 125
Claymore mines 67, 154, 156
climbing training *ill* 237, 25–6, 32, 34, 76
Clineball, Sergeant N 184
CNN (Cable News Network) 259
CNR (*Conseil National de la Résistance*) 110
'Coastwatchers' (Australia) 7
Cochababma (Bolivia) 11
Colby, William *quoted* 135, *quoted* 222–3, 9,
  136, 138, 196, 248
Collins, J *quoted* 105–6, *quoted* 223
5th Colonial Infantry Regiment (France) 117
Columbia 243, 245
Combined Operations Assault Pilotage Parties
  (UK) 6
COMINT (communications intelligence) 8
Comintern agents 107
10 Inter-Allied Commando 217
2 (Army) Commando (UK) 203
communications 4–9, 94
  see also ELINT; radio; satellites; SIGINT
Congo 9, 98, 250–1, 252
Contras 228
Coral Sea, USS 191
CORDS (Civil Operations and Revolutionary
  Development Support) (US) 136, 247
Corsica 252
counter-insurgency (COIN) 4–5, 107, 128, 135,
  151, 223

counter-terrorism 7, 35, 191–3, 232–4, 232–49,
  239–40, 242, 245–7
  counter-terrorist training 235
  maritime 27
covert action *see* deniable operations
CPT (Communist Party in Thailand) 150
Creek Indians 4
Crete 217
crime, organised 228–9, 242–5
Crockatt, Brigadier NR 173
Crooke, Major Ian 195
Cross, John *quoted* 61, *quoted* 67
Cuba 9, 107, 228, 243, 252
Cubans 256
Cyprus 228, 239, 246
Czechoslovakia 118, 217
  invasion of (1968) 13, 215–16

Dahlonega (USA) 33
Da Nang *map* 132, 144, 164
Dan Hoi prison 186
'Dark Ocean' society 230
Darlac Province (Vietnam) 138
Dartmoor 22, 27
Darulaman (Afghanistan) 216–17
DEA (Drug Enforcement Agency) (US) 243
dedicated aircraft 94, 163–4, 165
de Jongh, Andrée 174
Delta Force (US) *ill* 241, 98, 158, 190, 235,
  239–41, 258, 260, 263
Denchey, Lance-Corporal Paul 80
deniable operations 160, 222–31
Denmark 111
'Desert One' airfield 190–1
desert warfare 50, 68–74, 87
Devon Regiment 121
DF (direction finding) technology 48
Dhofar (Oman) 128–30
DIA (Defence Intelligence Agency) (US) 99, 144,
  170, 184, 186, 240
Diem, President 133–4, 138
Dignity battalions (Panama) 260
Dillon, Martin *quoted* 248
DI6 *see* MI6
DI5 (UK) 241
divers 26–7, 35, 90–1
25th Division (US) 155
Djibouti (1976) 238
Dodds-Parker, Sir Douglas 55
Dolomites 76
Dominican Republic 9
Don Diem (Vietnam) 158
Donovan, David *quoted* 248
Donovan, Major-general 'Wild Bill' 11
DOSAFF (Voluntary Service for Co-Operation
  with the Army, Navy and Air Force)
  (Russia) *ill* 37, 36, 170
drivers 30, 32, 36, 69–70
drugs 58, 119, 228, 242–5, 248–9, 260

Druze militia   245
Dry, Lt Spence   187–8
Duke, Sergeant   *quoted* 143
Dulles, Alan Welsh   9, 58
Dunkirk evacuation   174
Dyak tribesmen   121, 127–8
Dzerzhinsky Division   13

EAM (Greece)   113
EDES (Greece)   113
Egypt   204, 209, 226, 239
Eisenhower, President DD   145, 218
ELAS (Greece)   113
'Elephant' mission   114
Elgin (USA)   33
ELINT (electro-magnetic intelligence)   8, 46
El Salvador   98, 238
EMFFI (*Etat-Major des Forces françaises de l'Intérieur*)   110
England, James   *quoted* 155
ENIGMA   118
Entebbe hostage rescue   191–3
EPL (People's Liberation Army) (Columbia)   243
Erulin, Lt-Col   252
escapes   34, 54, 60–1, 161, 173–8, 175, 182–9
Eskimo Scouts   168
Estonia   118
Ethnic Liberation Organisation of Laos   148
Eureka radio beacons   206–7
Eversole, USS   188
Exercise Golden Pheasant   260
Exercise Long Look   71
extraction   66–7, 87, 94–5, 165

Fadlallah, Sheikh   245–6
Falklands War   24, 48, 201–2, 202
Fan Fawr   22
FANK (*Forces armées nationales khmères*)   148–9
FARC (*Fuerzas Armadas Revolucionarias Columbianes*)   243
51 Far North Queensland Regiment (Australia)   168
Faylakah Island   266
FBI (Federal Bureau of Investigation)   241
Fearless, HMS   255
'Ferret Force'   121–2
Fertig, Colonel Wendell   9
FIBUA (Fighting in Built-Up Areas)   *ill* 233, 232
Fiennes, Sir Ranulph   59–60
Fijians   124
FINCOs (Field Intelligence NCOs)   101
Finland   110–11
firgats   130
419 Flight (RAF)   95
FNLC (Congolese National Liberation Front)   252–3
Foley, Charles (author)   181
food   55–7, 61, 65–6, 67, 76
   water   69–70, 76–7, 79
Foot, Professor MRD   *quoted* 108

Force 136   117
Force 136 (SOE)   114, 116, 121, 177
Foreign Internal Defence   106–7
foreign-weapons training   39–40
Fort Benning   32–3, 156
Fort Bragg   9, 11, 29, 33, 52–3, 184, 235, 259–60
Fort Eustis   98
Fort Gulick (Panama)   9–11
Fort Sam Houston   52
Foster, Nigel   *quoted* 24
France   5, 84, 110, 117, 145, 184, 194, 209–10, 226, 228, 234, 236, 238, 252–3
   and *Rainbow Warrior*   223
   and Vietnam   138, 143, 164
   in World War II   *ill* 111, 131, 173, 199, 206
Free French   131
French Resistance   *ill* 4, *ill* 176, 3, 54, 95, 109–10, 179, 197–8, 198–9, 206
Frank, Lt-Col Brian   54
FTP (*Francs-Tireurs et Partisans*)   110
FULRO (*Front Unifié de Libération des Races Opprimés*)   141, 143, 159
Fulton, Robert E Jr   87

Gabon   226
Gaddaffi, Colonel   226
Gambia   194–5
Garrow, Capt Ian   174
Gaulle, General de   110, 117
Gaviria, Pablo Escobar   243, 245
Gbenye, Christopher   251
Geneva Accords (1954)   131, 145, 147
Geneva Agreements (1962)   147
Geraghty, Tony   *quoted* 40–1
Germany
   East Germany   171, 214–15, 226, 228
   West Germany   84, 86, 235, 247, 261
      GSG-9 (*Grenzschutzgruppe 9*)   236, 241–2
      and hostage rescue   234
      Mountain and Winter Warfare School   76
      Special Forces training in   167, 190
   in World War II   5, 12–13, 107, 109, 111–13, 118, 175, 179–80, 182, 196–9, 201, 203–6, 205, 207–9, 212–15, 227
Giancana, Sam   228
Giap, General   248
Gibraltar   211
GIGN (*Groupement d'Intervention de la Gendarmerie*)   236–8, 241
Ginestra river (Italy)   203–4
Giomfjord (Norway)   203
Gleiwitz (Poland)   214
gliding   36, 86, 206–7
Golan Heights   7
Golani Infantry Brigade (Israel)   193
Golden Triangle   119
Gorgopotamos bridge   113
Gorizia   212

GPS (Global Positioning Systems) *see* satellites
Grana Bridge (Norway) 197
Gran Paradiso (Italy) 76
Gran Sasso (Italy) 181
Grayback, USS 187–8
Greece 5, 113
'Greek Letter' projects 157–9
   see also Delta Force (US)
Green Berets (US Army Special Forces)
   see Special forces *under* US Army, and individual
     units
Grenada, invasion of (1983) 101, 256–8
'Group 565' 161
GRU (Soviet Military Intelligence) 7, 12–14, 36,
   86, 170–1, 210–11, 214
   2nd Directorate 102, 171, 215
   5th Directorate 213
GSFG (Group of Soviet Forces Germany) 215
GTO (Gotov k trude i oborony) (Russia) 36–7
103rd Guards Airborne Division (Russia) 216
Guatemala 9, 106
Gudgeon, Thomas 5
guerrillas 3–5, 7–8, 116, 121, 151
   see also partisans and individual groups
Guerrilla Strike Force (Vietnam War) 139
Gulf War (1990–1) 49, 71–2, 101, 263–8
Gurkhas *ill* 163, 121, 127

Hadad, Dr Wadi 192
Haifa raid 86
Hambleton, Lt-Col Iceal 188–9
'Happy Hundred' 122
'Happy Wanderer' exercises 30
Harold E Holt, USS 188
Harvey, Pharis *quoted* 230
'Hatchet Force' 159
   SLAM companies 160
Haukelid, Knut 207
'hearts and minds'
   in Borneo 125–6
   in Malaya 122–4, 128
   in Oman *ill* 129, 130
   in Vietnam 133–6
Heisenberg, Werner 208
Helberg, Claus 207
helicopters *ill* 97, 87, 245–6, 261
Helicopter Task Force 160 (US) 235
Helms, Richard 9
HES (Hanlet Evaluation System) (Vietnam) 247
Heydrich, Reinhard 217
Hezbollah 86, 240, 242, 245
'Hilton Assignment' 226
Hislop, Captain John 38
Hitler, A 180, 204, 207–9, 214, 217
Hmong tribesmen 98, 145, 147, 223
Ho Chi Minh 107, 117
Ho Chi Minh Trail *map* 132, 98, 133, 147, 149,
   158, 160–7, 197
   see also Vietnam
Holland 5, 116–17, 125, 167, 261

Marines 167
Honduras 260
Hormuz, Straits of 128
Horner, Lt-Col *quoted* 126
hostages
   hostage rescue *ill* 233, *ill* 237, 7, 27, 35,
     190–1, 199, 234–5, 250–1
   Hostage Response Team 241
   HRUs (Hostage Rescue Units) 232–4
   by police 236–8
'Houndsworth' force 199
Hoxha, Enver 113
Hre tribesmen 138
Huallaga Valley (Peru) 243, 245
Hue *map* 132, 144
human torpedoes 211–12
HUMINT 8, 99, 170–1, 190, 206, 210–11, 242,
   246–7, 265
   'Monarch Eagle' 99
Hungary 112, 118, 176–7
   1956 uprising 13, 106
Hussein, King 210

Iban tribesmen (Malaya) *ill* 120, *ill* 229, 121–2
Exercise Ice Flip 25–6
'Igloo White' project 164
Iles, Colonel George J 184
IMINT (imagery intelligence) 8
Independent Companies (Australia) 6
India 118
Indonesia *ill* 249, 9, 98, 116–17, 124–5, 125,
   127
   Indonesian Border Terrorists 125
   Indonesian Communist Party 128
   Special Forces 125
196th Infantry Brigade (US) 158
9th Infantry Division (US) 155
75th Infantry Regiment (US) 156
27th Infantry (US) 158
infiltration, covert
   training 167
Inniskilling Dragoons 121
INSCOM (Intelligence and Security Command)
   (US) 240, 242
insertion 96, 161, 214
   by air *ill* 88, 81–7, 252–3, 254
   by sea *ill* 90, 87–9, 87–93, 118, 254–6
   stay-behind 114–16, 168
insurgency 106–7, 223
intelligence *ill* 100, 2–3, 5, 8, 12, 94, 99–100,
   127– 8, 143, 152, 170, 205, 222–3, 224, 266
   photographic 8
   recovery of agents 172–3
   in Vietnam War 135, 143–4, 144, 149, 166
Intelligence Corps (UK) 241
interrogation 55, 57–60
Intrepid, HMS 255
IRA 248
Iran 9, 86, 187, 226, 240

Iranian Embassy, London 234
US Embassy hostages 190–1, 235
Iraq 71–2, 106, 209–10, 254, 261, 263–4,
    266–7
Ireland 107
    Northern Ireland 234, 248
Irrawaddy river 114
Irving, David *quoted* 205
ISA (Intelligence Support Activity) (US) 239–40
Ishmiyarov, Colonel R 238
Israel 86, 192–3, 204, 235, 238, 246
    and Gulf War 266
    intelligence *see Aman*
    Navy 246
    35 Parachute Brigade 193
    Unit 101, 235
    see also Mossad
Italy 239, 261
    intelligence service 226
    in World War I 211
    in World War II 112, 179–81, 211–12
IWESS (Infantry Weapons Effect Simulation
    System) 44

Jackson, President Andrew 4
Japan 212, 229–31
    Japanese Red Army 228
    in World War II 80, 113–14, 116–17, 131,
        168, 177–8, 182–3, 212, 217
Jarai tribesmen (Vietnam) 136, 140, 143
Jars, Plain of (Laos) 98, 145
Jawara, Sir Dawda 194
Jedburgh teams 109, 114, 117, 198
Jewish Underground 176–7
John F Kennedy Special Warfare Centre *see* Fort
    Bragg
John Paul II, Pope 218, 228
Johnson, President Lyndon *quoted* 135
Joint Deployment Agency (US) 256
Joint Special Operations Command *see* JSOC
Jones, Lt Devon 264
Jones Professor RV *quoted* 205
Jordan 210, 235
JRTC (Joint Readiness Training Centre)
    (US) 235
JSOC (Joint Special Operations Command)
    (US) 11, 235
Jungk, Robert *quoted* 208–9
jungle warfare *ill* 79, *ill* 244, 40–1, 50, 77–80,
    87, 135
Jungle Warfare School (UK) 61, 67

Kaa Fjord (Norway) 212
Kabul 216
Kachin tribesmen 114, 119
KAL 858 225–6
Kalashnikov rifles 39–40
Kandahar (Afghanistan) 216
Kang Min-Chui, Captain 225
Kao Neua Pass (Vietnam) 166
Karen Hills 114

Karen tribesmen 114
Karlskrona (Sweden) 212
Katanga 251
Kathov, Arkady 245
Katyn 112
KCIA (South Korean Intelligence Service) 229–30
Keegan, Major-General 166
Kennedy, President John F 133
    assassination of 228
Kenya 192, 228
Kenyatta, President 192
KGB 12–14, 36, 224, 245
    organisation 102, 223
    and assassination 3, 14–15, 214, 228
    and hostage rescue 234, 238
    and Spetsnaz 7, 102, 215–16
Khafij 268
Khamba tribesmen (Tibet) 98, 118
Khe San *map* 132, 144
Khmer Kampuchea Krom 145
Khmer Krom tribesmen 145
Khmer Rouge 133, 143, 148
Khmer Serei 145, 149
Khmer Special Forces 149
kidnapping 15, 208, 225, 245
Kim Chi-O, Captain 225
Kim Chung Tae, Lt-Gen 224
Kim Dae Jung 229–30
'Kipling' force 199
Kiryat Shomona, raid on 86
Kissinger, Dr Henry 184
Klinghoffer, Leon 239
Knobel, Kuno *quoted* 143, 164–5
Kolwezi (Zaire) 252
Komsomol training (Russia) 36
Kontum *map* 132, 144
Korea
    Korean War 58, 118, 147
    North Korea 118, 224–6, 228
        KWPLD (Korean Workers' Party Liaison
            Department) 224–5
        North Korean Army 224
        Workers' Peasant Red Guard 224
    South Korea 107, 224, 229–30
        Capital 'Tiger' Division 155
        South Korean CIA 230
        South Korean Rangers
            and SERE 57
        and Vietnam War 133
Kor tribesmen 138
Kota Tinggyi (Malaya) 94
Kuomintang 118–19
Kurds 106, 261, 264
Kutter, General Wolf D *quoted* 200
Kuwait 263–5, 267
KWPLD *see under* Korea
Ky, General 142

Lake District
    training in 25–6

LALO (Low Altitude Low Opening) *see under*
  parachuting
La Maddalina 180
Lands End 25
languages 25, 46, 125, 264
Laos *map* 132, 98, 107, 133, 144, 145–8,
  149–51, 157, 160, 163–6, 188, 223, 228
  Free Lao movement 145
  intelligence operations in 144
  US forces instruction *ill* 146
  in World War II 117
Lao Theung tribesmen 147
Lao United Front 148
Larnaca (Cyprus) 246
lasers 43–4, 267
Latvia 118
Laurent, Colonel 251
Lawrence, Col TE *ill* 108, 4
Laycock, Brigadier Robert 217
'Layforce' 201
Lebanon 86, 245–6, 246
  and drugs 242–3
  hostages in 240
  Lebanese Intelligence 246
Lenin, VI 107
Les Kosem 143
Les Ormes (France) 199
Libya 86, 107, 192, 226
Lidice (Czechoslovakia) 217
Lie Ton Ten (Malaya) 121
7th Light Infantry (US) 260
Light Strike Vehicle *see* LSV
Li Hak Chi 124
Lindell, Mary 174
Lindsay, General James *quoted* 86
Lithuania 118
Little Rock, Arkansas 235
Livingstone, Neil C *quoted* 239
LLDB (*Luc Luong Dac Biet*) (Vietnam) 141,
  143–4, 155, 158, 287
Lloyd Owen, Major General David *quoted* 19
Lockheed 229
Long Jawi (Borneo) 127
Longline Ltd 73
Long Range Desert Group *see* LRDG
Long Range Patrol and Surveillance
  Companies 99
Long Range Reconnaissance Patrols *see* LRRPs
Lon Nol, General 148–9
Lopburi (Thai Army Special Warfare
  Centre) 149
RAF Lossiemouth 59
LRDG (Long Range Desert Group) *ill* 68, 5, 7,
  19, 69– 71, 73, 203, 264
LRPs (Long Range Patrols) *see* LRRPs
LRRPs (Long Range Reconnaissance Patrols)
  in Vietnam *ill* 157, *ill* 159, 139, 152–67,
    187
  and drugs 245
  Weingarten school 167

LRSC (Long-Range Surveillance Companies)
  (US) 167
LRSUs (Long Range Surveillance Units) 7
LSVs (Light Strike Vehicles) *ill* 74, 73–4, 263
7th Luiycka Naval Assault Division 214
Luttensee Mountain and Winter Warfare School
  (Bavaria) 76
Luttwak, Dr Edward N *quoted* 186
Luzon 182–3
Lympstone Commando Training Centre 20

Ma'alot School (Israel) 235
MacArthur, General Douglas 118, 230–1
MACV (Military Assistance Command,
  Vietnam) 136, 138, 149, 157
MACVSOG (Studies and Observation
  Group) 138, 144–5, 149, 157, 159–60,
  162, 187, 189, 226
mafia 228
Magellan NAV 1000M *ill* 72
Malaya 40, 64, 79, 88–9, 94, 119–24, 125, 128,
  133, 155
  Malayan Chinese 119–21, 124, 128, 177
  Malay Races Liberation Army 121, 124, 150
  Malay Scouts (SAS) 40, 121–2
  paramilitaries 228
  and PSYOPS 100–1, 107
  in World War II 114–16, 116, 139
Mandalay 114
Man Wa 116
Manzariyeh (Iran) 191
maquis *ill* 110, 51–2, 109–10, 198–9
Marsh, John 11
Masirah 191
McClure, Brigadier-General Robert 9
McCoy, Alfred *quoted* 228
M 19 (Columbia) 243
Medellin cartel 243, 245
medical services 51–4, 76, 79–80, 146, 154–5,
  175
  aid to civilians *ill* 53, 123, 126–7, 135, 140
Mekong Delta *map* 132, 144–5
mercenaries 3, 137–8, 226–7, 250–1
MI6 3, 116, 118, 128, 223–4
MI9 109, 173, 175, 178, 199
Mihailovic, Colonel Draze 113, 175
Mike Forces (Multipurpose Reaction
  Forces) 139–40, 143, 158
Military Advisory and Assistance Group, Laos
  (US) 147
Military Intelligence Brigades (US) 167
Milorg (Norwegian resistance) 111, 207
Min Yuen (Malaya) 121
MIS-X (US Military Intelligence Escape and
  Evasion Service) 175
MK-ULTRA project 58
M'nong tribesmen 141
Mobile Command (Canada) 262
Mobile Guerrilla Force 158
Mobile Launch Teams (US) 144

Mobility Troops 71–3
Mobutu, President 252
Mogadishu hostage rescue 236
Montagnards (Vietnam) *ill* 142, 136–8, 139–1,
    142–3, 228
Mont Blanc 76
Montgomery, Field-Marshal BL 24
Morocco 52
Morse Code 30, 49–50
Mossad (Israel) 7, 192, 209–10, 235, 246–7
Mountain and Arctic Warfare Cadre (UK) *ill* 26,
    25, 254, 256
mountain warfare 50–1, 87, 254
    see also above
Moussey (France) 54
MPABA (Malaysian People's Anti-British
    Army) 120–1
M Special Unit (Australia) 6
Mucci, Colonel 182–3
Mu Gia Pass (Vietnam) 166
Muir, Flt-Lt JA 94
Munich Olympics (1972) 232, 246
Muntinglupa prison 178, 182
Muong tribesmen 144
Musandam Peninsula (Oman) 128
Musko (Sweden) 93, 212
Mussolini, Benito 179–81, 193, 211
Mustapha, Major Abdul-Rahim 247
MVD (Ministry of Internal Affairs) *see under*
    Soviet Union
My Tach (Vietnam) 140

Nahal 204
Nairobi 192
Nakhon Phanom (Thailand) 98, 164
Nam Yu (Laos) 147
narco-terrorism *ill* 244, 242–5, 243, 245
National Democratic Front (Burma) 119
National Guard (US) 99, 168
National Liberation Front (Vietnam) 138
National Park Police (US) 242
National Security Agency *see* NSA
National Security Council (US) 146
NATO 76, 167, 170, 211, 260–1, 262
Natour, Mohammed 247
navigation
    for dedicated submarines 92
    in desert patrols 70
    satellite 71
NAVSOC (Navy Special Warfare Command) 11
Nepal 118
Netanyahu, Lt-Col Yonatan 192–3
New Zealand 5, 107, 124, 133
Nguyen Van Kiet 189
Nha Trang (Vietnam) *map* 132, 143
    Recondo school 154–5
Nicaragua 98, 106–7, 228
Nicholls, Major 'Fighting' 4
Nigeria 226
Nimitz, USS 191

ninja 230–1
Nixon, President Richard 98
NKVD 112, 118
Noone, Dick 124, 139
Noone, Pat 139
Norfolk, Virginia 235
'Norforce' (Australia) 168–70
Noriega, President Manuel 243, 258–60
Normandy landings 5, 24, 197–8, 199, 217
Norris, Lt Thomas 189
North, Colonel Oliver 239
2nd/1st North Australia Observer Unit 168
Northern Ireland *see under* Ireland
North Korea *see under* Korea
Northland Railway (Norway) 196–7
North Vietnam *see under* Vietnam
Norway 25, 75, 206–7, 212
    in World War II 111, 196–7, 203
NSA (National Security Agency) (US) 98, 144
nuclear weapons
    nuclear protection 241
    German in WW II 206–8
    in Gulf War 267
    Iraqi 209–10
    Israeli 209
    US 210–11
Nung tribesmen 137–8, 144, 158–9, 166, 226
NVA (North Vietnamese Army) *see under*
    Vietnam
NZSAS (New Zealand SAS) 64, 123–4, 127,
    149, 155

O'Brian, Terence 94
Ochoa, Fabio 245
OCO (Office of Civil Operations) 136
OFCO (Offensive Counter-Intelligence
    Operations) (US) 242
Office of Strategic Services *see* OSS
OGPU *see* KGB
'Oktobrists' 36
O'Leary, Pat 174
1988 Olympics 228
Oman *ill* 129, 73, 101, 107, 128–30, 226, 228,
    264
    Sultan's Armed Forces (SAF) 130
OPEL Reconnaissance Team 156
Operational Detachment Delta (US) 35
Operation ARCHERY 203
Operation ATTLEBORO 158
Operation BARBAROSSA 214–15
Operation BITING 204
Operation BLACK DRAGON 252
Operation BLACKJACK 158
Operation BRIGHT LIGHT 187
Operation CARTOON 203
Operation CHARACTER 114
Operation CHARIOT 203
Operation CHINAT 'LI MI' 118
Operation COLOSSUS 203–4
Operation DANIEL BOONE 144

Operation DESERT SHIELD 254
Operation EAGLE CLAW 190–1
Operation FIRST CULVERIN 116–17
Operation FREEDOM RUNNER 149
Operation FRESHMAN 206–7
Operation GREEN DRAGON 252
Operation GREIF 218
Operation GUNNERSIDE 207
Operation GUSTARVUS 16
Operation IVORY COAST 183–6
Operation JERICHO 178–9
Operation JUST CAUSE 258
Operation KITCAT 144
Operation LEAPING LENA 157
Operation LEOPARD 252–3
Operation LOYTON 54, 57
Operation MUSKETOON 203
Operation NATION 114
Operation PRAIRIE FIRE 144
Operation QUEEN HUNTER 98
Operation RED DRAGON 250–2
Operation SHINING BRASS 144
Operation SNOWCAP 243
Operation SWITCHBACK 138
Operation TARBRUSH 217
Operation THUNDERBOLT 193
Operation THUNDERHEAD 187–8
Operation URGENT FURY 256–8
Operation WHITE DRAGON 252
Ordzhonikidze (Russia) 238
orlyonok camps (Russia) 36
Ortega, Daniel 228
Osirak 209–10
'Oslo Report' 205
OSS (Office of Strategic Services) (US) 3, 97,
    107–9, 109, 114, 117, 175, 209
  in Burma 118
  in Indo-China 131, 143
  in Italy 112
  in Malaya and Thailand 116
  in Norway 111, 196–7
  and recruitment to CIA 9
  in Romania 177
  in Thailand 116
  in Yugoslavia 113
Oswald, Lt-Cdr Hugh 91
OUN (Organisation of Ukrainian
    Nationalists) 227
Ovechkin family 238
Overhead Reconnaissance Office (US) 240

Pakistan 14, 224
Palestine 86
  see also PFLP; PLF; PLO
Pamirez Sanchez, Ilich 192
Panama 10–11
  and drugs 243
  US invasion of (1989) 258–60
Paolucci (human torpedo) 211
Parachute Regiment (UK) 127, 182, 203–4

selection and training *ill* 21, 20–4
  see also Pathfinders
parachutes 83–4, 86, 252–3, 256
parachuting *ill* 65, *ill* 111, 2, 12–13, 27, 32, 54,
    84, 89, 95–6, 112, 118, 139, 256
  HAHO (High Altitude High Opening) 85–6,
    96, 236, 263
  HALO (High Altitude Low Opening) *ill* 85,
    84–6, 96, 161, 236, 254, 263
  LALO (Low Altitude Low Opening) 83–4
  LAPES (Low-Altitude Parachute Extraction
    System) 256
  static-line *ill* 82, 256
  training *ill* 37, 27, 30, 36, 81, 83, 85
Para-Commando Regiment (Belgium) 167, 199,
    250–1
paramilitary forces *ill* 8, 227–31
Park, President 229
Parker, Geoffrey *quoted* 51–2
partisans *ill* 176, 67, 95, 107–8, 199, 227
  see also guerillas; French Resistance *under*
    France; maquis; and individual groups
Pathet Lao 98, 133, 145, 147, 150, 164
Pathfinders (Parachute Regiment) *ill* 255, 254–6,
    256–7
  training 27, 254–5
Patrice Lumumba Friendship University
    (Moscow) 15
patrolling 34, 63–4, 64–5, 125–7, 164
Patton, General GS 54
PDF (Panama Defence Forces) 259
Pebble Island (Falklands) *ill* 201, 201–2
Peenemunde raid 205–6
Pegu Yomas mountains 114
Peled, Benny 192
Pen-Y-Fan 22
PEO (Programme Evaluation Office) 146–7
Perak (Malaya) 120
Perrot, H Ross 187
Perry, Commodore 230
Perth (Western Australia) 29
Peru 202, 243, 248–9
Peterhead Jail 234
Petersen, Barry *quoted* 58
Petersen, Barry (author) 130
PFLP (Popular Front for the Liberation of
    Palestine) 86, 192, 235, 246
'Phantom' (GHQ Liaison Regiment) 5, 38
Philippines 178
  escapes in World War II 182
Phnom Penh *map* 132, 143, 149
Phoenix programme *see under* Vietnam
photography 27
Phu Bia massif 148
Pickard, Group Captain 179
Piedra island 243
Pilabra Regiment (Australia) 168
'Pink Panthers' (Mk IX Land Rovers) *ill* 73, 73
Pinsk prison 112, 177
'Pioneers' (Russia) 36

Piranha submarine   91
Place (RN) Rear Admiral Godfrey, VC   212
Plateros   183
Plei Me (Vietnam)   143
PLF (Palestine Liberation Front)   239
PLO (Palestine Liberation Organisation)   107,
   239, 246–7
Poland   109, 111–12, 206, 214, 218, 227
   resistance   96, 111–12, 177
police   241, 243, 245, 247
   and hostage rescue   234, 236–8
Pollard, Jonathan Jay   246–7
'Ponury' (SOE agent)   112
Ponza (Italy)   180
Portugal   116
Prague   215–16
prisoner rescue   158, 173
   inside jobs   177–8
   in World War II   199
Project Copper   149
Project Gamma   158–9
Project Omega   158
Project Raven   48
proxy forces   228–9
PSYOPS (psychological operations)   58–9,
   99–101, 130
   4th Psyops Group (US)   100–1
   see also 'hearts and minds'
Punan tribesmen (Borneo)   125

Qaboos bin Sa'id, Sultan of Oman   130
Queen Elizabeth, HMS   211

radar   *ill* 205, 89, 204, 267
radio   *ill* 47, *ill* 50, 64–5, 69–70, 78, 112,
   144, 207, 254
RAF   *ill* 180, 125, 179–80, 198, 203, 206,
   263
   Bomber Command   204–5
   Brize Norton   25
   in Malayan Emergency   122
   160 Special Duties Squadron   94–5
   357 Special Duties Squadron   94–5
   358 Special Duties Squadron   94–5
   Special Duties Squadrons   177
   47 Squadron   96
   70 Squadron   96
   138 Squadron   95
   161 Squadron   95
   624 Squadron   96
'Raiding Forces Middle East'   203
Rainbow Warrior sinking   223
Rangers (US)   2, 6, 156–7, 167, 190–1,
   256–9, 263–4
   functions   32
   6th Ranger Battalion (US)   182–3
   75th Ranger Regiment   11, 32, 157, 258
   Ranger School   *see* Fort Benning
   selection and training   *ill* 31, 32–3
   see also Rogers' Rangers

Rangoon   114, 225
rapid reaction forces   242, 253–4, 260–2
   NATO   261
Ras Gharib   204
Ras Zaafrana   204
'Ravens' (pilots)   98, 147
Rayhan (Syria)   86
Reagan, President Ronald   11
Recondo Schools   87, 149, 154–5
reconnaissance   *ill* 2, 1, 5–7, 33, 67, 166
   and combat swimming   91
   in Gulf War   265–6
   indigenous units   168–70
Reconnaissance Commando School   *see* Recondo
   School
'Red Army Faction' (Germany)   247
'Red Cell' (US)   242
REP (*Régiment Etranger des Parachutistes*)   238,
   252–3
rescue   *ill* 174, *ill* 184, *ill* 189, 98, 172–95, 256–8,
   262
   Entebbe   191–4
   in Gambia   194–5
   in Gulf War   264
   in Iran   190–1
   recovery of the sick   87
   SAR beacons   64, 67, 154, 264
   in Vietnam   183–9
   in World War II   177–83, 178–83
Rezac, Tomas *quoted*   227
Rhade tribesmen (Vietnam)   *ill* 159, 136, 138,
   140–1, 143
Rhodesia   122, 124
   Rhodesian Air Services   226
Rio Gallegos airfield (Argentina)   202
Rjukan (Norway)   25
Roadrunner teams (Green Berets)   38, 158
Roadwatch teams   7, 165–6
'Robin Sage'   34
Rogers, Major Robert   63–6
Rogers' Rangers   5, 63–4
Romania   118, 175–7
Rommel, Field-Marshal Erwin   199, 217
Rosselli, John   228
Rossetti (human torpedo)   211
1st Rotary Wing Test Activity   98
Royal Australian Navy   7
Royal Marines (UK)   4, 24–5, 55, 71, 203
   Comacchio Group   241
   3 Commando Brigade   25
   Mountain and Arctic Warfare Cadre   *ill* 26, 25,
      75–6, 254, 256
   SBS (Special Boat Service)   6, 96, 201–2, 241,
      254–5, 263, 266
      training and selection   26–7
   training and selection   *ill* 23, 20, 22–5
Royal Military Police (UK)   241
Royal Navy   125, 211
RSUs (Regional Surveillance Units)
   (Australia)   168

Sabah (Borneo) 66, 80, 124–5
sabotage 15, 91, 111, 196–14
  railway sabotage *ill* 200, 111–13, 199
Sa'id bin Taimur, Sultan of Oman 128–9
Saigon *map* 132, 138, 141, 144, 160
Sakakida, Richard 178
Salalah (Oman) 128
Salang Highway (Afghanistan) 216
Salines airfield (Grenada) 256–8
Saratoga, USS 239
Sarawak 124–5, 127
Sarawak Rangers 122, 127
Sardinia 180
SAS (Belgium) 109, 199
SAS (France) 109
SAS Regiment (Australia) 34, 67, 71, 80, 127,
  139, 155
  in Borneo 126
  patrol procedures 66
  selection for 29–31
  and SERE 56–7
SAS (Rhodesia) 53–4
SAS *see* NZSAS (New Zealand); SAS
  (Rhodesia); SAS (U); SAS Regiment
  (Australia)
SAS (UK) *ill* 41, 7, 28–9, 63, 66, 73, 96, 109,
  112, 155, 167, 182, 194, 198–9, 201–2,
  203, 223, 226, 241, 264, 267
  in Borneo 128
  functions 1
  and intelligence 101
  and languages 125
  Mobility Troop 74
  in Oman 128–30
  patrol procedures 65
  1 Regiment 198–9
  2 Regiment 54, 198–9
  21 Regiment (TA) 122, 263
  22 Regiment 39, 122, 127, 195, 201–2, 234,
    240–1, 245, 263
    Counter-Revolutionary Warfare Wing 234
    and drugs 245
    Mountain Troop 75, 202
  23 Regiment (TA) 178, 263
  Sabre Squadrons 234
  '11 SAS Battalion' 203
  selection and training *ill* 28, 35
  24 Signals Squadron 234
  in World War II 217
satellites 49, 71–3, 86, 234, 240, 243, 263, 265
Saudi Arabia 71, 254, 261, 263–4
Savak 190
Sayaret Matkal (Israel) 192–3, 204, 235, 246
SBS (Special Boat Service) *see under* Royal Marines
Schwarzkopf, General Norman 263, 266
Scoon, Sir Paul 258
Scud missiles 72, 265–6
SDECE (*Service de Documentation Extérieure et
  de Contre-Espionage*) 7, 143
Seaforth Highlanders 121

SEAL Teams *ill* 92, 11, 93, 187–8, 235, 239–40,
  242, 254, 256–7, 259, 263, 266
  Cambodian 149
  selection and training 35
Sea Reconnaissance Unit (US) 6
'Seaspray' 98
Secret Service Executive Protection Division
  (US) 242
Security and Co-Ordination Team (US) 242
Sedang tribesmen 138
selection 19–38
  principles of 19–20, 38
  for Parachute Regiment *ill* 21, 20–2
  for Royal Marines *ill* 23, 22–7
  for SAS *ill* 28, 28–31
  for Spetsnaz *ill* 37, 35–8
  for US Army Special Forces *ill* 35, 33–5
  for US Rangers *ill* 31, 32–3
Senegal 194–5
Senoi Praak (Malaya) *ill* 123, 124
Seoul 224
SERE (Survival, Evasion, Resistance to
  Interrogation, and Escape) 34, 54–62
  training 175
*Service de Documentation Extérieure et de
  Contre-Espionnage see* SDECE
Seymour, Colonel Ray 44
Shackely, Theodore G *quoted* 222–3
Shal-Dag (Israel) 235
Shan tribesmen (Burma) 119
Sheik Abdalah Barracks (Lebanon) 240
Shenandoah Airlease company 98
Shi'ites 86
Shindand (Afghanistan) 216
'Shining Path' (Peru) 243, 245, 249
Shin San Ok 225
Shomton, Brigadier-General Dan 193
Sicily 5
SIGINT (signals intelligence) 8, 46, 166, 239,
  267
  see also ENIGMA
'Sigma' project 158
152 Signals Squadron (Australia) 30
Sihanouk, Prince 143, 148
Sihanoukville (Cambodia) *map* 132, 148
Sikakida, Richard 182
Simba rebels 250–1
Simhoni, Major-General 239
Simons, Colonel Arthur 'Bull' 184, 186–7
Simpkin, Brigadier Richard *quoted* 15, 1
Singapore 124, 177
SIS (Secret Intelligence Service) (UK) 205, 226–7
Sittang river 114
Six-Day War (1967) 235
Skardon, Lt 66
ski-ing 76–7
Skorzeny, Otto *ill* 194, 180–1, 193, 217
Skyhook 87
SLAM (Search-Locate-Annihilate-Mission)
  teams 38, 160

Slim, General William   114
SLR rifle   64
'Snake-Eaters'   *see* Green Berets
SOCOM (Special Operations Command)   *see under* US Army
SOE (Special Operations Executive)   3, 107–9, 109, 111–14, 116–18, 121, 175, 177, 197–8, 203, 207, 217, 226
  AMF section   109
  DF section   109
  EU/P section   109
  Force 136   114
  F section   109
  weapons training   *ill* 42, 42
Son Tay (Vietnam)   184, 186
Soroy Sound (Norway)   212
Soui Da (Vietnam)   158
Souphanouvong, Prince   145
South Korea   *see under* Korea
South Vietnam   *see under* Vietnam
Soviet Union   7, 12–13, 60, 101–2, 102, 107–8, 110, 148, 165, 204, 212–14, 224, 226–8, 245
  in Afghanistan   13–14, 216–17, 224
  Airborne Divisions   15
  Baltic Fleet Intelligence Service   213
  and coups d'état   215
  and hostage rescue   234, 238
  Ministry of Internal Affairs (MVD)   13–14, 238
  Special Forces   *ill* 14, *ill* 37, 3, 12–15
    see also Spetsnaz
  and Vietnam War   14, 133
  in World War II   12–13, 111–12, 113, 175
Sowan, Ismael   247
Spain   3, 12, 113, 175, 261
Special Air Services   *see* SAS (UK)
Special Boat Service   *see under* Royal Marines
Special Forces
  definition   1–3
  command and control   7
  rôles   3–7
  training   62
  see also individual countries and units
Special Operational Volunteers (Malaya)   122
Special Operations Aviation Brigade (US)   98
160th Special Operations Aviation Regiment   264
Special Operations Executive   *see* SOE
Special Operations Teams (UK)
  in Borneo   128
Special Service Force (Canada)   *ill* 261
101 Special Training School, Singapore   *ill* 115, 114–15
Spencer, Chapman   116
Special Operations Panel (US)   105
Spetsnaz (Soviet Union)   *ill* 37, 1–2, 7, 12–13, 36–7, 86, 170–1, 214
  and Afghanistan   216–17, 224
  and coups d'état   213–17
  incursions in Alaska   168
  Naval Spetsnaz   212–14
  organisation   13, 170

selection and training   35–8, 46
  and Sweden   93, 213–14
  and US nuclear weapons   210–11
spies   *see* HUMINT
Spike reconnaissance teams   159
SSF (Special Service Force) (Canada)   262
2nd SS Panzer Division   197–8
STABO (Stability Operations Extraction System) Rig   87, 154
Stanleyville   251
Stanner, Prof WEH   168
STAR (Fulton Surface To Air Recovery System)   87
STDAT (Strategic Directorate Assistance Team)   188–9
'Steve Canyon Programme'   98
Stirling, David   71, 201
St Nazaire   203
submarines   *ill* 213, 88–93, 116–17
  bottom-crawling   93, 212–14
  midget   93, 211–12
  Piranha   91
  Russian incursions by   93
  Seeteufel   212–13
  Subskimmer–80   91–3
  X-craft   212
Suharto, President   128
Sukarno, President   124–5, 128
Sultan Yaakub (Lebanon)   86
Sumatra   117
supply   *ill* 96, 94–8, 109
survival   *ill* 56, *ill* 59, *ill* 75, 33–4, 54–7, 63–80, 154
Sweden   93, 116, 175, 196, 206, 212, 214
swimming   26–7, 30, 33, 91, 236
Switzerland   175
Sykes, Christopher   *quoted* 54
Syria   7, 86, 107, 265
Szenes, Hanna   172, 177

Tadzhikistan   14
Taiwan   118–19
Tampa   98
Tangen Bridge (Norway)   197
Taranto   203
Task Force 160   98
TAT (Technical Analysis Team)   242
Tay Ninh   144
Technical Surveillance Countermeasures Team (US)   242
Templer, General Sir Gerald   122
Tempsford (Beds)   95
terrorism   15
  protection of terrorist targets   240–2
  see also counter-terrorism, narco-terrorism
TES (Tactical Engagement Simulation)   43
Tet Offensive (Jan 1968)   143
Thailand   *map* 132, 107, 116, 119, 124, 133, 139, 145, 147, 149–51, 151, 164, 186, 228
'Unity' infantry   147

Thakin Party (urma) 114
Tibet 9, 97–8, 107, 118, 228
Tinnsjo, Lake (Norway) 207
Tirpitz 203, 212
Tito, Marshal 113, 175–6
Togo 226
Tokyo 229
Tong Gon AeGuk Ho (freighter) 225
Tonkin, Gulf of 186–7
torture 58
Townshend, Col Roger *ill* 153
Trafficante, Santos 228
training 39–80, 154
  of allies 105–30, 241, 243
  communications training 46–51
  escape and evasion training 60–2
  interrogation resistance 57–60
  jungle training 40, 77–80
  language training 46
  medical training 51–4
  static-line parachuting 81, 83
  survival training 54–7, 63–8
    desert warfare 68–74
    mountain and arctic 75–7
  weapons training 39–46
599th Transportation Group (North
  Vietnam) 133
38 Transport Group (RAF) 95
Trinquier, Colonel Roger 145
Tripoli 226
Truong Son Brigades (Viet-Cong) 160, 167
Tsurkan, Valentin *quoted* 227
Tukhachevsky, Marshal M 12
Tunisia 239, 246–7
Tupas, Ernest 178
Turkey 261, 264

Udorn (Thailand) *map* 132, 184–5
UDT 13 187
Uganda 191–3, 193
UIA (Ukrainian Insurgent Army) 227–8
UITG (United Individual Training Group) 149
UK 3–5, 133, 261
  14th Army 114
  Special Forces *see* Royal Marines: Parachute
    Regiment; SAS (UK) and individual units
Ukraine 118, 228
  in World War II 227
Ulpio Traiano (Italy) 211
UMO (Ukrainian Military Organisation) 227
United Nations 125, 249, 251
USA 3–5, 99–100, 115–17, 131, 148–9, 194,
  217, 228–9, 240, 251, 261
  Agency for International Development 136
  Information Agency 136
  National Security Act (1947) 8–9
  POWs 164–5, 175, 182–3, 184
  Special Forces *see under* US Army and
    individual units
  see also USAAF; USAF; US Army; US Navy

USAAF 97, 177, 207
USAF 95, 145–6, 148, 161–2, 165–6, 235, 256,
  259, 264, 267–8
  15th Air Force 175
  Air Rescue Service 264
  23rd Air Force 98–9
  112th Field Activities Group 184
  AFSOC (Special Operations Command) 11
  1st Special Operations Group 11
  SOS (Special Operations Squadrons) *ill* 265,
    98–9, 99, 144, 259, 263–5, 266–8
  training 33, 46
US Army
  6th Army 183
  Special Forces *ill* 10, *ills* 137, 1, 3–5, 7–11, 32,
    57, 98–1, 141–2, 142–3, 147–8, 167, 184,
    223–6, 243, 246–8, 264
  USASOC (US Army Special Operations
    Command) 11
  II Corps 159
  III Corps 158–9
  IV Corps 158–9
  Detachment B–51 143
  Detachment A 159
  Detachment B–50 158–9
  Detachment B–52 158
  Detachment B–56 158
  Detachment B–57 159
  Special Forces Groups
    1st 9, 138, 144, 149
    3rd 9
    5th 9, 87, 138–9, 139–40, 144, 154–5,
      157–9, 160, 263
    7th 9, 138, 144
    10th 167, 190
    11th 9
    12th 9
    19th 9
    20th 9
  training *ill* 35, 33–5, 38–40, 61
    and language training 46
    medical training 52–3
    SFAS (Special Forces Assessment and
      Selection) (US) 33–5
  see also Rangers and individual units
USARV (US Army in Vietnam) 149
U Saw (Prime Minister of Burma) *quoted*
  113
US Marine Corps 33, 35, 149, 245, 256, 259, 267
  Lebanese barracks bombing 240
  Marine Raiders 6
US Marshal's Service (US) 242
US Navy 242, 246–7, 261
  Sea Reconnaissance Unit 6
US Rapid Deployment Force 33
USSOCOM (US Special Operations
  Command) 11, 33, 86, 93, 98, 157, 186
USSR *see* Soviet Union
Ustashe (Yugoslavia) 113
Uwharrie National Forest (USA) 34

Vaagso (Norway) 203
Valiant, HMS 211
Vang Pao, General 98, 145–7, 148
Venezuela 202, 243
Vermork (Norway), raid on 111, 206–7
Very Light Aircraft *see* VLA
Vienna 227
Vientiane *map* 132, 145, 148
Viet-Cong 61, 133, 136, 139–1, 143, 159,
    161–2, 165, 167, 247–8
  medical treatment 54
  96th Division 158
Viet Minh 131, 138, 143, 145
Vietnam 117
  North Vietnam *map* 132, 131, 133, 144, 147,
    157, 184, 186, 223
  North Vietnamese Army *ill* 150, 98, 140,
    147–9, 148, 150–1, 153, 156, 161, 165,
    189
  Russian advisers in 14
  South Vietnam 9, 133, 135, 140, 142–3, 147,
    184, 248
    Vietnamese Air Force 158
    see also ARVN
  Vietnam War *ill* 134, *ill* 137, 14, 38, 60, 79,
    101, 131–45, 153–67, 226, 248 *see also* Ho
    Chi Minh Trail
    CIDG (Civilian Irregular Defence Group
      Programme) 9, 107, 138, 140, 143–4
    escape and evasion in 61, 67, 183–9
    hearts and minds in 133–6
    insertion and extraction 87, 161
    paramilitaries in 228
    Phoenix counter-terror programme in 136,
      247–8
    US POWs in 58, 164–5, 184
    see also CIA, Ho Chi Minh Trail, LRRPs
Viminale (Italy) 211
VIP protection 234
Viribus Unitis, sinking of 211
'virtual reality' training systems 44, 46
VLA (Very Light Aircraft) 86

V (Military Assistance Command, Vietnam)
  MACVSOG (Studies and Observation
    Group) 166
Vo Bam, General 160
Vockmann, Colonel Ross 9
'V' weapons 209

Walker, Arthur 120
Waltzmann Mountain 76
Warsaw Rising 96, 112
'Waterpump' programme 147
weapons training 39–44, 46
'White Star' Mobile Training Teams (US) 147
Willis, Guy *quoted* 43
women 46, 169
  in spetsnaz 36
Woodhouse, Col John 66
Woodward, Bob 245
World War I 4–5, 211
World War II 3–8, 12–13, 47–8, 51–2, 54–5, 64,
    80, 87–8, 94–5, 112–13, 196, 201, 204–5,
    214, 217, 230, 254
  escapes 60–1, 173–5, 177–8
  insurgency support during 107–17
  rescues in 172–83
  and sabotage 3, 196–209, 211–12

yakuza 229–30
Yalu River 118
Yamam (Israel) 235
Yamamoto, General Isoroku 217
'Yankee Team' missions 146
Yau tribesmen 147
Y-Bham Enuol 141
'Yellow Fruit' (US) 242
Yellow Sea 225
Yemen 107, 129–30, 130, 226
Youssef, Abu 246
Yugoslavia 113, 175
  in World War II *ill* 176, 208, 113, 176

Zaire *see* Congo
Zin Mo, Major 225